WJEC/EDUQAS
Religious Studies for AS & A Level
Christianity

Revised Edition

Peter Cole
Series editor: Richard Gray

WJEC Eduqas bears no responsibility for the sample answer provided, any commentary or marks awarded.

The teaching content of this resource is endorsed by WJEC Eduqas to support AS and A Level Religious Studies.

This resource has been reviewed against WJEC Eduqas' endorsement criteria. As this resource belongs to a third party, there may be occasions where a specification may be updated and that update will not be reflected in the third party resource. Users should always refer to WJEC Eduqas' specification and Sample Assessment Materials to ensure that learners are studying the most up to date course.

It is recommended that teachers use a range of resources to fully prepare their learners for the exam and not rely solely on one textbook or digital resource.

WJEC, nor anyone employed by WJEC has been paid for the endorsement of this resource, nor does WJEC receive any royalties from its sale.

Although every effort has been made to ensure that website addresses are correct at time of going to press, Hachette Learning cannot be held responsible for the content of any website mentioned in this book. It is sometimes possible to find a relocated web page by typing in the address of the home page for a website in the URL window of your browser.

Hachette UK's policy is to use papers that are natural, renewable and recyclable products and made from wood grown in well-managed forests and other controlled sources. The logging and manufacturing processes are expected to conform to the environmental regulations of the country of origin.

To order, please visit www.HachetteLearning.com or contact Customer Service at education@hachette.co.uk / +44 (0)1235 827827.

ISBN: 978 1 0360 0491 0

© Peter Cole and Richard Gray 2025

First published in 2020

This edition published in 2025 by

Hachette Learning,

An Hachette UK Company

Carmelite House

50 Victoria Embankment

London EC4Y 0DZ

www.HachetteLearning.com

The authorised representative in the EEA is Hachette Ireland, 8 Castlecourt Centre, Castleknock Road, Castleknock, Dublin 15, D15 YF6A, Ireland

Impression number   5 4 3 2 1

Year   2029 2028 2027 2026 2025

All rights reserved. Apart from any use permitted under UK copyright law, no part of this publication may be reproduced or transmitted in any form or by any means, electronic or mechanical, including photocopying and recording, or held within any information storage and retrieval system, without permission in writing from the publisher or under licence from the Copyright Licensing Agency Limited. Further details of such licences (for reprographic reproduction) may be obtained from the Copyright Licensing Agency Limited, www.cla.co.uk

Cover photo © Joel Behr – stock.adobe.com

Illustrations by Integra Software Services Pvt. Ltd

Typeset by Integra Software Services Pvt. Ltd., Pondicherry, India

Printed in the UK by Bell and Bain Ltd, Glasgow

A catalogue record for this title is available from the British Library.

Contents

About this book 4

Theme 1: Religious figures and sacred texts 8
A: Jesus: his birth   8
B: Jesus: his resurrection   17
C: The Bible as a source of wisdom and authority in daily life   27

Theme 1: Religious figures and sacred texts 36
D: The Bible as a source of wisdom and authority   36
E: The early Church (in Acts of the Apostles)   47
F: Two views of Jesus   57

Theme 2: Religious concepts 66
A: The nature of God   66
B: The Trinity   73
C: The Atonement   81

Theme 2: Religious life 88
D: Faith and works   88
E: The community of believers   95
F: Key moral principles   103

Theme 3: Significant social developments in religious thought 110
A: Attitudes towards wealth   110
B: Migration and Christianity in the UK   120
C: Feminist theology and the changing role of men and women   128

Theme 3: Significant historical developments in religious thought ... 140
D: Challenges from secularisation   140
E: Challenges from science   152
F: Challenges from pluralism and diversity within a tradition   163

Theme 4: Religious practices that shape religious identity (1) 176
A: Religious identity through diversity in baptism   176
B: Religious identity through diversity in Eucharist   184
C: Religious identity through diversity in festivals   191

Theme 4: Religious practices that shape religious identity (2) 201
D: Religious identity through unification   201
E: Religious identity through religious experience   213
F: Religious identity through responses to poverty and injustice   228

Glossary 240
Index 242
Photo credits 246

About this book

With the A Level in Religious Studies, there is a lot to cover in preparation for the examinations at the end of the course. The aim of these books is to provide enough support for you to achieve success at A Level, whether as a teacher or a learner.

This series of books is skills-based in its approach to learning, which means it aims to combine covering the content of the specification with examination preparation from the start. In other words, it aims to help you get through the course while at the same time developing some important skills needed for the examinations.

To help you study, there are clearly defined sections for each of the AO1 and AO2 areas of the specification. These are arranged according to the specification themes and use, as far as is possible, specification headings to help you see that the content has been covered.

The AO1 content is detailed but precise, with the benefit of providing you with references to both religious/philosophical works and to the views of scholars. The AO2 responds to the issues raised in the specification and provides you with ideas for further debate, to help you develop your own evaluation skills.

Ways to use this book

In considering the different ways in which you may teach or learn, it was decided that the books needed to have an inbuilt flexibility to adapt. As a result, they can be used for classroom learning, for independent work by individuals, as homework, and, they are even suitable for the purposes of 'flip learning' if your school or college does this.

You may be well aware that learning time is valuable at A Level and so we have also taken this into consideration by creating flexible features and activities, again to save you the time of painstaking research and preparation, either as teacher or learner.

Features of the books

The books all contain the following features that appear in the margins, or are highlighted in the main body of the text, in order to support teaching and learning.

Key terms of technical, religious and philosophical words or phrases.

Key term

Holy Spirit: God as he is active in the world

Key quotes either from religious and philosophical works and/or the works of scholars.

> **Key quote**
>
> I ... decided, after investigating everything carefully from the very first, to write an orderly account.
>
> (Luke 1:3)

Key person boxes summarise essential figures.

AO1 activities that serve the purpose of focusing on identification, presentation and explanation, and developing the skills of knowledge and understanding required for the examination.

> ### AO1 Activity
> Prepare a 30-second news flash on how Jesus' birth is presented in Matthew and a 30-second news flash on how Jesus' birth is presented in Luke.
>
> This practises the AO1 skill of selecting and presenting the key relevant information.

AO2 activities that serve the purpose of focusing on conclusions, as a basis for thinking about the issues, developing critical analysis and the evaluation skills required for the examination.

> ### AO2 Activity *Possible lines of argument*
> Listed below are some conclusions that could be drawn from the AO2 reasoning in the Accompanying text

Specification content boxes highlight exactly what is being covered in each section and how it connects to the specification.

Glossary of all the key terms for quick reference.

AO2 skills: critical analysis and evaluation

A good way to prepare yourself for an AO2 part (b) evaluation answer is to consider the different ways to approach this. Sometimes writing frames or anacronyms may be suggested. Whilst these are useful, they are meant as 'scaffolding' or support for an answer, but the danger is that they end up restricting more natural and personal evaluation.

One useful approach is to think about some different styles of writing and relate these to 'characters' that are easily remembered.

Strong evaluative characters

We can look at what are considered **strong evaluative character styles** that display all the qualities that avoid the pitfalls above. By this we mean different aspects, elements or ingredients of an effective critical analysis and evaluation.

If we look at the table below, we can see 7 characters, each of which has a specific strength and quality that display skills of critical analysis and/ or evaluation. The strength of each character forms a **part** of a strong evaluation. In a full AO2 answer it may be useful to vary the characters in terms of depth and breadth.

The characters can be used as a checklist not a structured plan or rigid writing frame. The best way to use them is to consider the different styles and skills **before** writing an answer and then measure your answer by checking that the critical analysis and evaluation elements are there.

Examples of this can be seen in the sample answer we provide. In these sample answers you may notice that not all the character styles have been used in the same order, detail or combination; however, generally, most are often covered.

> ### ⦿ Key person
> **Rudolf Bultmann (1884–1976):** a German theologian who called for the 'demythologisation' of the New Testament

> ### Specification content
> The extent to which the birth narratives provide insight into the doctrine of incarnation.

In the table below, we have attempted to demonstrate how each character may fulfil the criteria for a band 5 evaluation using the descriptors it presents. These are highlighted in bold in the third column.

Character	Strength	Application and AO2 Band descriptor link
Tennis player	<ul><li>The tennis player deals with specific lines of arguments (often from either named scholars or schools of thought) and returns counter arguments.</li><li>The tennis player manages arguments and counter arguments, making sure there is consideration of several lines of argument in response to the statement in the question.</li><li>This is sometimes understood as 'for' or in support of an argument and 'against'; however, this does not necessarily always have to be done in an even or balanced way since some answers may wish to argue effectively towards a conclusion that is supported by several lines of reasoning, evidence and argument that support each other.</li></ul>	<ul><li>The tennis player ensures that **thorough, sustained and clear views are given** in an answer.</li><li>The tennis player also ensures that the **views of scholars/schools of thought are used extensively**.</li></ul>
Detective	<ul><li>The detective has a forensic ability to examine, collate and clarify evidence and provide examples. The detective makes sure that the argument presented is substantial in that it is based in evidence and examples to support the reasoning presented.</li><li>The detective selects details that are accurate and relevant in a thorough way. They make sure that there is correct reference to specialist language in the correct context.</li></ul>	<ul><li>The **views of scholars/ schools of thought are used appropriately and in context**.</li><li>There is a **thorough and accurate use of specialist language and vocabulary in context**.</li></ul>
Philosopher	<ul><li>The philosopher likes to raise and ask interesting and relevant questions.</li><li>The philosopher often indicates that there may be problems or challenges to a specific approach and likes to suggest a solution.</li><li>When an argument or analysis is in 'full flow' we may think of questions that we would like to raise in response to views analysed. The philosopher loves to do this.</li></ul>	<ul><li>The philosopher character is typical of **perceptive evaluation**.</li><li>The philosopher successfully **identifies the issues raised by the question set**.</li></ul>
News reporter	<ul><li>The news reporter provides perspective, clarity, an overview of the debate. Commentary is vital in an AO2 answer as it demonstrates that the student is engaging with the debate that the statement presents. It is an easy way to demonstrate that you are thinking about the issues.</li><li>The best way to provide yourself with an opportunity to develop a more personalised approach is to practice pausing and reflecting upon points made, developing them with evidence and examples and commenting on the qualities a line of argument possesses.</li></ul>	<ul><li>Using a news reporter style ensures that a response **thoroughly addresses the issues raised by the question set**.</li></ul>

Explorer	• The explorer likes to suggest some alternative ways of answering a question. Sometimes it feels as though a debate needs a different angle, approach or perspective. The explorer often suggests new ways of attempting to arrive at a solution to the debate. • This can often be your own response in considering a given statement including a new suggestion or perhaps a question you would like to raise. • You can even try to bring in other strands and evidence beyond the immediate topic from other areas of the course.	• This ensures that there is **confident and perceptive analysis of the nature of connections between the various elements of the approaches studied**.
Critical thinker	• The critical thinker points out more technical aspects of an argument. The critical thinker is often concerned with how an argument 'works' and 'flows'. • The critical thinker sometimes challenges more forensic aspects of an argument. • The critical thinker checks for coherence and consistency. Does the evidence support the conclusion? Is there a counter argument?	• The critical thinker ensures that there is **extensive, detailed reasoning** in an answer.
Judge	Makes an overall ruling and concludes matters. The judge in some ways is the most vital character. They cannot stand alone and rely upon others and their contributions to make a final decision. This can be in favour or against the statement, or, it may be that the statement itself is questionable. Often an overall judgement ends an answer; however, sometimes an overall conclusion may start the answer and then discuss, analyse and reason why this may be the case. Strong evaluative answers often have several judgments or mini-conclusions throughout the answer.	• The judge is the final voice of an answer. They may appear anywhere in an answer but usually summarises at the end. The judge should be clear evidence of **confident critical analysis**.

Summary of a strong evaluative answer

- Offers clear, sustained and varied lines of argument (view) like the exchanges of a tennis player.
- The varied evidence of scholarly views and schools of thought are precisely examined and coherently presented like the report of a detective.
- Issues are identified to focus on, and questions may be raised like a philosopher.
- Engages with a debate by offering commentary and reflection upon the points presented like a news reporter.
- May explore some new ways of answering the question and possibly refer to other elements of the course like an explorer.
- Contains reasoning that is detailed, ordered, coherent and effective like a critical thinker.
- Ensures there is an overall judgment made that clearly links to the reasoning and evidence contained in the answer like a judge.

Religious figures and sacred texts

This section covers AO1 content and skills

Specification content
Consistency and credibility of the birth narratives; harmonisation and redaction

 **Key terms**

Gospels: The record of Jesus' life and teaching in the first four books of the New Testament

Magi: Latin for 'wise men', originally the word meant 'an oriental priest, learned in astrology' and probably from Persia (Iran)

A: Jesus: his birth

Make sure you have read and understood the set texts:
Matthew 1:18–2:23; Luke 1:26–2:40.

The birth narratives in Matthew and Luke

Although there are four **Gospels** (Matthew, Mark, Luke and John) in the New Testament that recount the life of Jesus, only Matthew and Luke contain accounts of Jesus' birth.

Matthew's version

Matthew focuses on Joseph and links the events to Old Testament prophecies. This version records how Joseph intends to marry Mary. However, finding out that she is pregnant, knowing he is not the father, he intends to divorce her quietly rather than expose her to public disgrace. Then an angel appears to him in a dream telling him that Mary conceived through the Holy Spirit and he is to marry Mary and call the child Jesus.

Matthew then records that the **Magi**, or Wise Men, who have followed a star 'from the East' visit Jesus and give him gifts of gold, frankincense and myrrh. Because the Wise Men fail to report back to Herod about the child, Herod orders all boys under two years old to be killed. Joseph is warned in a dream to flee to Egypt to escape Herod and, following another dream, only returns to Nazareth after Herod dies.

Luke's version

Luke focuses on Mary, and the account is interwoven with the account of John the Baptist's birth. The angel Gabriel tells Mary of her pregnancy. When she questions how that is possible given she is a virgin, Gabriel tells her that it is by means of the Holy Spirit. Mary, on a visit to her pregnant cousin Elizabeth, expresses her joy in a song of praise (1:46–55). Elizabeth gives birth to John the Baptist, and her husband, Zechariah, subsequently gives a prophecy about John the Baptist's future work (1:68–79).

Luke then records how Joseph and Mary have to travel to Bethlehem to be registered for the census Caesar Augustus has called. Because there is no room for them at the inn, the baby Jesus is born in a manger (probably in a stable or outhouse). Meanwhile, some shepherds are informed by angels of Jesus' birth and go immediately to Bethlehem to visit him.

> **Key quote**
>
> The fact is that we have in Matthew and Luke two independent accounts of the birth of Jesus.
>
> (M Roberts)

On the eighth day, Jesus is circumcised and named Jesus. Then, a month later, Mary and Joseph take Jesus to the Temple in Jerusalem to offer a sacrifice of thanksgiving. Moved by the Spirit, Simeon recognises Jesus and refers to him as 'a light for revelation to the Gentiles'. Then Mary, Joseph and Jesus return to their home in Nazareth.

Differences in the accounts

- Matthew writes from Joseph's perspective, Luke from Mary's.
- Only Matthew records the appearance of the star, the visit of the Wise Men, the slaughter of the boys and the flight to Egypt.
- Matthew has extensive quotations from the Old Testament. Luke does not, but has three songs of Mary, Zechariah and Simeon.
- Luke mentions that Jesus is born 'in a manger'. Matthew speaks of 'a house'.
- Only Luke records Mary's visit to Elizabeth, the birth of John the Baptist, the census of Caesar Augustus, the visit of the shepherds, the circumcision and presentation of Jesus in the Temple.

The historicity of the accounts

Certainly, the **birth narratives** do contain references to historical figures such as Herod (Matthew's Gospel), Caesar Augustus and Quirinius (Luke's Gospel). However, they raise difficulties. Herod's massacre of the boys is not recorded anywhere else, but it is consistent with Herod's character. He murdered three of his own sons.

Luke (1:3) implies he is writing an accurate historical account, and it is true that Quirinius was governor of Syria. However, many scholars place the date of Quirinius' governorship some eight years after Herod's death, and so later than Jesus' birth. Josephus, the first century Jewish historian, refers to a census by Caesar Augustus but dates it at 6 CE. In addition, it was not the Roman practice to require people to return to their ancestral home for registration.

> **Key quote**
>
> I … decided, after investigating everything carefully from the very first, to write an orderly account.
>
> (Luke 1:3)

Some scholars claim that Luke misleads his readers with the three songs that he includes in his narrative. They argue that the early Christian community was already singing these songs before Luke attributed them to various characters in his Gospel.

Supernatural events in the accounts

Perhaps the biggest cause of doubt about the **historicity** of the accounts of Jesus' birth are the references to supernatural events accompanying the birth.

- **Angels:** In both Matthew and Luke, angels appear, giving messages. In Matthew, an angel appears to Joseph on three occasions and an angel appears to the Wise Men. In Luke, an angel appears to Mary, and a choir of angels visits the shepherds.
- **Supernatural knowledge:** Both Simeon and Anna in the Temple recognise Jesus as the Messiah.

 Key term

birth narratives: the accounts of Jesus' birth in the Gospels of Matthew and Luke

A stained glass depiction of Herod's massacre of the boys

 Key term

historicity: historical accuracy

T1 Religious figures and sacred texts

- **The star:** The Wise Men are guided miraculously to Jesus by a star.

  The identity of this celestial phenomenon has most often been explained as a planetary conjunction (apparent close approaches of two or more planets to each other). However, it led them south, whereas celestial bodies normally move from east to west. Also, it led them directly to the place where Joseph and Mary were staying, which stellar phenomenon cannot do.

- **The virgin birth:** Both Matthew and Luke claim that Jesus was miraculously conceived of the Holy Spirit and born of a virgin. For many, this is probably the most difficult challenge to belief. The narratives imply that Jesus was human by virtue of his mother and divine by virtue of being conceived by God. Jesus appears to be both human and divine.

> **Key quote**
>
> Look, the young woman [the Greek version uses the word '*virgin*'] is with child and shall bear a son, and shall name him Immanuel.
> (Isaiah 7:14)

Harmonising the accounts

Another reason some people have for doubting the two accounts is the apparent differences between them. If the accounts are true, then shouldn't they be similar and consistent?

However, as the accounts do not blatantly contradict one another, there is no reason both accounts cannot be true. Why couldn't Jesus have been visited by both Wise Men and shepherds? It may be possible to explain other apparent differences. For instance, both Matthew and Luke may have selected or have had access to accounts of only some of the events. Matthew may have had access to information that was not available to Luke, and vice versa.

The time sequence may also account for apparent differences. For instance, while Luke writes about Jesus being born in a *manger*, Matthew refers to a *house*. This may be explained by the crowd for the census having left by the time the Wise Men visited, and so the family could have been able to move lodgings to a house. Similarly, Mary, Joseph and Jesus may have fled to Egypt sometime after Jesus was presented in the Temple.

There are also many similarities between the two gospel accounts. Both Matthew and Luke agree that Jesus was born in Bethlehem when Herod was King of Judea. They also agree that the name of the mother was Mary, that she was betrothed to Joseph, that she was a virgin and that Jesus was conceived by the Holy Spirit. And they agree that people travelled to visit the newborn baby and that Jesus came to save not only the Jewish people, but all people, just as the prophecies had foretold.

The approach of redaction criticism

One explanation for the differences in the birth narratives may be that the author had a particular theological perspective that he wanted to convey to his readers. For instance, Matthew's Gospel is seen as having been written for Jewish readers and so tells the story of Jesus' birth from Joseph's viewpoint. He wants to show that Jesus was connected, through Joseph, with Israel's legendary King David and that he is the fulfilment of Old Testament revelation of God. Hence, his account has six Old Testament quotations.

This approach to understanding how the account was compiled is known as **redaction criticism**. It assumes that the original traditions about Jesus circulated as independent units in the early Church. Each Gospel writer chose the material that he wanted and arranged it to suit his own theological interests, making significant additions and omissions and changing the wording to make a theological point.

> ## Key quote
>
> Redaction criticism ... looks at the Gospels as complete documents, and sees the evangelists as individual theologians (even 'authors') in their own right.
>
> (S Smalley)

In contrast to Matthew, Luke seems to be writing to non-Jewish people (*Gentiles*). He tells the story from Mary's point of view. When he does appeal to Old Testament prophecy, he doesn't quote from the Hebrew version, but the Greek version, the **Septuagint**. The emphasis in Luke's Gospel is that Jesus brought salvation to poor and needy people, and that God is concerned with those who are underprivileged and downtrodden. This may account for why Luke includes the story of the shepherds, rather than the wealthy Wise Men bearing expensive gifts.

The story of the presentation of Jesus in the Temple also makes clear that Joseph and Mary were poor people. The sacrifice they make is the sacrifice of the poor ('a pair of turtle-doves or two young pigeons'). On such occasions, wealthy people were expected to sacrifice a lamb. This story, together with the prominence given to the birth of John the Baptist, emphasises the connection between Jesus and the Jewish religion so that, despite the Greek flavour of his Gospel, Luke, like Matthew, is convinced that Jesus is the fulfilment of the Old Testament revelation of God. John the Baptist represents the last of the Old Testament prophets and foretold the appearance of John the Baptist, the forerunner to the Messiah, Jesus.

The doctrine of the incarnation

The English word **incarnation** comes from the Latin, which is made up of two basic elements, *in* + *carnis* ('flesh'). *Incarnation*, therefore, means 'becoming flesh'.

The doctrine of the incarnation expresses the belief that Jesus Christ was God in human form. According to this belief, Jesus' life on Earth was only a short period in the story of one who had always been and will always be. His birth at Bethlehem was not the beginning of the story, nor was his death on the cross the end. The belief asserts that while Jesus lived on Earth, people found themselves in the presence of God in the flesh. As John's Gospel puts it (1:14), 'the Word became flesh and dwelt among us, full of grace and truth; we have beheld his glory, glory as of the only Son from the Father'.

The most widely accepted definitions of the incarnation and the nature of Jesus were made by the First Council of Nicea in 325 CE, the Council of Ephesus in 431 CE and the Council of Chalcedon in 451 CE.

> ## Key quote
>
> We believe ... in one Lord Jesus Christ, the Son of God, begotten of the Father ... being of one substance with the Father ... for our salvation came down from heaven and was incarnate and was made man.
>
> (First Council of Nicea, 325 CE)

 Key term

redaction criticism: a theory that regards the author of a text as editor of source material that they adapted to suit their own theological interests

 Key term

Septuagint: the Greek translation of the Hebrew Bible in the third to second centuries BCE; also referred to as the *LXX* in reference to a legend of 70 Jewish scholars translating the Torah

Specification content

Interpretation and application of the birth narratives to the doctrine of the incarnation (substantial presence and the kenotic model)

 Key term

incarnation: God in human form in the person of Jesus

T1 Religious figures and sacred texts

What they assert is that Jesus Christ was both fully God: begotten from, but not created by the Father; and fully man: taking his flesh and human nature from the Virgin Mary.

The two natures

These two natures, human and divine, were united in the one person of Jesus. This is known as the *hypostatic union*.

It is important to understand that the doctrine of the incarnation does not see Jesus as half human, half God. It states that Jesus is fully God and fully human.

- He is fully God because he is believed to have existed from the beginning with God, and was God. His appearance here on Earth was only a brief period in this existence. After his resurrection, he is believed to have returned to his Father with whom he now reigns for evermore.
- He is fully human because he was a man of flesh and blood, born as any other person is born; he was a helpless baby; he had to learn to walk and talk like every child; he ate and slept and drank; he experienced hunger, weakness, temptation and disappointment; he died.

> **Key quote**
>
> We ... confess one and the same Son, our Lord Jesus Christ, the same perfect in Godhead and also in manhood ... to be acknowledged in two natures ...
>
> **(Council of Chalcedon, 451 CE)**

The person of Jesus, therefore, combines two natures – a divine nature and human nature. Not surprisingly, this doctrine has been challenged. For example: how could an omniscient God become a baby, and how could Jesus, if he was God, be tempted (Mark 1:13) or not know when the world was to end (Mark 13:32)?

Through the history of Christianity, there have been attempts to emphasise one nature in Jesus' person at the expense of the other, and such attempts are seen as heresy. However, the doctrine of the incarnation gives equal validity to both.

Incarnation as kenosis

The term *kenosis* comes from Greek and means 'to make empty'. The word appears in Paul's letter to the Philippians (2:7), where Paul says that Jesus, 'who, being in very nature God, did not consider equality with God something to be used to his own advantage; rather, he made himself nothing by taking the very nature of a servant, being made in human likeness'.

'Made himself nothing' is sometimes translated as 'emptied himself' (*kenosis*).

Kenotic theology attempts to understand the incarnation in this light. Its main concern is to solve some of the difficulties arising from Jesus having both a divine and a human nature.

The question is: what does Paul mean when he says that Christ 'made himself nothing'? It cannot be that Jesus emptied himself of his divinity and stopped being God. If he was truly God, he must have continued to be God during his earthly ministry, maintaining the substantial presence of God, although his divine attributes were hidden.

Instead, the 'emptying' consists of:
- a preincarnate self-limitation by Jesus, agreeing to take 'the very nature of a servant, being made in human likeness', therefore fully human while maintaining substantial presence as fully divine.
- the self-emptying of his own will as a human being and becoming a servant, and submitting entirely to the will of God.

> **Summary**
> - Only Matthew's and Luke's Gospels give accounts of the birth of Jesus.
> - The supernatural elements in the accounts and the differences between the accounts cast doubt on their historical reliability.
> - Others note that there is no actual contradiction between the accounts, and the Gospel writers just focus on different parts of the event.
> - Redaction criticism argues that the Gospel writers selected material to suit their theological interests.
> - Christian doctrine teaches that Jesus was both fully human and fully divine.

> **AO1 Activity**
>
> a Explain examples from the birth narratives that support the view that:
>   i   Matthew's Gospel focuses on Joseph.
>   ii Luke's Gospel focuses on Mary.
>
>   This helps consolidate your learning, by developing the skill of selecting relevant examples and explaining how they illustrate the focus of the question.
>
> b Draw a diagram to illustrate the similarities between the two accounts of the birth narrative.
>
>   This helps develop your organisation skills, by selecting and ordering evidence and examples.

This section covers AO2 content and skills

Specification content

The extent to which the birth narratives provide insight into the doctrine of the incarnation

Issues for analysis and evaluation

The extent to which the birth narratives provide insight into the doctrine of the incarnation

Possible line of argument	Critical analysis and evaluation
The birth narratives in the Gospels give an account of Jesus being born of a virgin.	The accounts of the virgin birth are based on ancient myths that ascribed supernatural births to a figure to turn them into a hero and are not to be understood literally.
Although there are ancient myths involving virgin births, the birth narratives in the Gospels are reliable historical accounts. Many scholars see Luke as someone who was historically accurate in his writings.	There are too many doubts about the reliability of the birth narratives. Many argue that they were written long after the events and were made up by the early Church, based on Old Testament prophecies. The epistles of Paul, which are earlier than the Gospels, do not mention the virgin birth. The incarnation is clearly an incoherent idea – it is not possible to be fully God and fully human.
It is unscientific to dismiss the supernatural in the New Testament accounts of the birth narratives.	Bultmann argues that the birth narratives need to be 'demythologised' to understand them in the modern world.
If the accounts are reliable, they provide insight into the doctrine of Jesus being both fully God and fully human.	The word *virgin* is a mistranslation and means 'a young woman of marriageable age'. It has nothing to do with God becoming flesh. To claim that Jesus was born of a virgin is not the same as claiming that Jesus was fully God and fully human.
It is too narrow to consider only the birth narratives.	We need to consider the whole of Jesus' life, including his death and resurrection, to gain insight into the incarnation. But again, it is necessary to decide how reliable the accounts are.

AO2 Activity

a Analyse three possible conclusions that could be drawn from the critical analysis and evaluation of the extent to which the birth narratives provide insight into the doctrine of the incarnation. What are their strengths and weaknesses? Which conclusion is the strongest?

b Using the strongest conclusion, select three lines of argument that you might use to support this conclusion. Explain why you have selected these.

Exam practice

Sample question
Evaluate the relative importance of redaction criticism for understanding the biblical birth narrative.

Sample answer

Redaction theory is the theory that New Testament writers altered existing material about Jesus to suit their own agenda. It assumes that the original stories about Jesus circulated as independent units in the early Church. Each Gospel writer selected the material that they wanted and arranged it to shape their theological message, making significant additions and omissions and changing the wording to make a theological point.

If this theory is correct, then it would mean that the Gospel writers were individual authors, each with a particular agenda, who shaped the material they received. They were not primarily concerned with writing a chronological account, and so the Gospels should be read as theology rather than history.

For instance, Matthew's Gospel seems aimed at a Jewish readership. He refers to Jesus much more in terms of a Jewish messianic context. In the birth narratives, Matthew is seen as redacting his material to include the title 'Son of David' and presents Jesus as the 'New Moses'. In particular, the birth narratives repeatedly quote from the Old Testament and show Jesus as the fulfiller of these prophecies and therefore the true Messiah.

In contrast, Luke seems to be shaping his material for a Gentile readership. He includes in his birth narrative a census that involves the entire Roman world. There are no stories about the Magi and their gifts, but instead it is lowly shepherds who first visit the baby Jesus.

This critical approach clearly raises questions about the historical reliability of the birth narratives, including the very nature of Jesus and his incarnation. It makes us interpret the birth narratives in a very different way from that of reading them as historical accounts of what actually happened. Many would argue that understanding that the authors of Matthew and Luke were influenced by pagan mythology, with heroes born of a virgin and mysterious stars in the sky appearing at their birth, makes much more sense of the birth stories. The writers were making a theological point, not a historical chronological account.

However, redaction criticism is not without its own critics. It seems questionable to assume that Matthew and Luke were not interested in recording accurate historical information but felt free to create their own material. Luke's preface explicitly states a historical interest and is consistent with historical information found in other documents of the time.

This section covers AO2 content and skills

Specification content
The relative importance of redaction criticism for understanding the biblical birth narrative

News reporter
A clear explanation of redaction criticism; a good introduction to the debate of whether redaction criticism helps understanding of the birth narratives.

News reporter
The answer immediately addresses how redaction criticism can be seen to help understanding. The focus is on reading the accounts not as historical writing but more as theological works. A good overview of how the evaluation may go.

Detective
Some good examples are given to illustrate the insight that redaction criticism provides to the birth narratives.

Detective
Having looked at Matthew's account, the answer now considers Luke's account. This provides an excellent contrast, drawing out clearly the differences in the theology between the accounts. These examples from the birth narratives make clear how redaction criticism provides this understanding of why the narratives differ.

Critical thinker
Some good reflective questioning about the consequences of this approach of redaction criticism to the biblical texts.

Tennis player

Detective

The answer now develops a critical approach to the findings of redaction criticism. It gives evidence supporting alternative understandings of the birth narratives.

T1 Religious figures and sacred texts

The answer raises some good cautionary comments about redaction criticism and concludes that history and theology are not mutually exclusive. The argument has been consistent throughout and has been well evidenced.

It is a good answer that has a clear line of argument. Perhaps the conclusion regarding theology and history not being mutually exclusive could be developed further.

Redaction criticism is a useful reminder that the Gospel writers were writing theology rather than history, and that they had a variety of potential audiences. However, we should treat redaction criticism with caution as its methodology is questionable.

Why could the gospel writers not have been both theologians and historians? The two positions are not mutually exclusive.

The Christian faith has always believed that it had a historical foundation and that theology was an interpretation of history. The early Church actually appealed to historical events to demonstrate the truth of its beliefs.

Over to you

For this first task, try using the framework/writing frame provided to help you practise the AO2 skills to answer the question below.

As the units in each section of the book develop, the amount of support will reduce gradually to encourage you to be independent and to perfect your AO2 skills.

Question

Evaluate the view that it makes no sense to claim that Jesus was both God and man.

Writing frame

The issue for debate here is the reasonableness or otherwise of the doctrine of the incarnation, which asserts that …

Jewish people and Muslims, and some Christian denominations such as Unitarians, would accept the contention on the grounds that …

Most mainstream Christian traditions would, however, reject it on the grounds that …

It is my view that … and I base this argument on the following reasons:

B: Jesus: his resurrection

Make sure you have read and understood the set texts: Matthew 10:28; John 20–21; 1 Corinthians 15; Philippians 1:21–24.

The word *resurrection* means 'to bring back into existence'. Christians believe that, following his death on the cross and his burial, Jesus rose again from the dead. For 40 days he appeared to many of his followers. Matthew, Mark and Luke's Gospels record that Jesus warned his disciples that he would be killed but rise again on the third day. At the time, the disciples did not understand and, when Jesus was arrested, they were thrown into utter confusion and fled. Yet, within a short time of his crucifixion, they had become convinced that he was alive. They began to preach that God had raised Jesus from the dead and that he was the **Messiah**, the saviour promised in the Old Testament.

The resurrection in John 20–21

John 20

a) John and Peter enter the empty tomb (1–9)

When John entered the tomb (20:2), 'he saw the strips of linen lying there, as well as the cloth that had been wrapped around Jesus' head. The cloth was still lying in its place, separate from the linen' (20:7) and 'he saw and believed' (20:8). Peter also entered the tomb soon afterwards, but neither understood from scripture that Jesus had to rise from the dead (20:9).

b) Jesus appears to Mary Magdalene (10–18)

Jesus appeared to Mary Magdalene in the garden, but she didn't recognise him at first and assumed he must be the gardener. This suggests that there had been some change in his resurrection body or that she was just not expecting to see Jesus, since she assumed he was dead. Jesus sends Mary with a message for the disciples: 'I am ascending to my Father and your Father, to my God and your God' (20:17).

c) Jesus appears to the disciples (19–23)

On the evening of the day of the resurrection, Jesus appears to the group of disciples (20:19–23). It appears that his body has undergone some change, as he is able to move through locked doors and he shows them the wounds in his hands and his side. Jesus then instructs the disciples, 'As the Father has sent me, I am sending you' (20:20). Then Jesus breathes on them and says 'Receive the Holy Spirit'. The verb *breathe* is the same as the one used in Genesis 2:7 to describe God's action when he created man from the dust of the ground and 'breathed into his nostrils the breath of life'. It implies that this marks the beginning of a new creation: the Christian Church.

The giving of the Spirit in 20:22 raises the question of whether John is describing the same event as Luke describes in Acts 2:1–13 when the Holy Spirit descends on the apostles at Pentecost. However, at Pentecost, the result was that the disciples immediately began preaching fearlessly about Jesus. Here they remained fearful since, a week later, they are in a room hiding behind locked doors (20:26). Also, Jesus' promise was that the Spirit would be given only after he had returned to the Father (John 16:7), and that had not yet happened. Therefore, the giving of the Spirit in John seems to mark the inauguration of the Church's mission. The mission does not actually begin until the outpouring of the Spirit on Pentecost.

This section covers AO1 content and skills

Specification content

Interpretation and application to the understanding of death, the soul, the resurrected body and the afterlife, with reference to Matthew 10:28; John 20–21; 1 Corinthians 15; Philippians 1:21–24

Key term

Messiah (literally 'anointed one'): a figure who is expected to unite Jewish people and save them from their oppressors, ushering in an era of peace

---

T1 Religious figures and sacred texts

d) Jesus appears to Thomas (24–29)

John records that Thomas was not present when Jesus first appeared to the disciples. He does not believe them, claiming that he will only believe when he sees the wounds and puts his finger where the nails were (20:25). A week later, again in a locked room, Jesus appears and, seemingly aware of Thomas' demands for proof, invites Thomas to feel his wounds. Thomas' confession 'My Lord and My God' (20:28) is a climax to the chapter.

> **Key quote**
>
> But he said to them, 'Unless I see the nail marks in his hands and put my fingers where the nails were, and put my hand into his side, I will not believe.'
>
> (John 20:25)

The Incredulity of Saint Thomas by Caravaggio

e) The purpose of John's Gospel (30–31)

The chapter ends with John's statement that his purpose in writing his Gospel is to enable people to believe without having seen, and that by believing they may have life in Jesus' name (20:31).

John 21

a) Jesus appears to the disciples by the Sea of Galilee (1–14)

The disciples have been fishing all night and caught nothing. Jesus then appears on the shore and shows them where to fish. Immediately, they are unable to haul the net because of the large number of fish. The boat almost sinks with the huge catch of fish that they net. Then John says to Peter 'It is the Lord' (21:7) and they all eat breakfast of bread and fish with Jesus.

b) Jesus commissions Peter to shepherd his people (15–23)

After breakfast, Jesus asks Peter (calling him Simon, son of John) whether he loves him more than the other disciples. When he replies that he does, Jesus commands him to 'feed my lambs'. Jesus then asks him twice again. After Peter professes his love, Jesus spells out the cost of that love and announces the kind of death by which Peter would glorify God (18–19).

c) John's testimony confirmed (24–25)

John 21:24 identifies the author of the Gospel as John, the disciple who Jesus loved. His Gospel claims to be an eyewitness account, and that his disciples know that John's testimony is true. The Gospel ends with one last testimony to the greatness of Jesus.

> **Key quote**
>
> This is the disciple who is testifying to these things and has written them, and we know that his testimony is true
>
> (John 21:24)

Paul's understanding of the resurrection: in 1 Corinthians 15

Paul accepts without question that the resurrection of Jesus was a historic event. He reminds the Corinthians (v5–8) that there were many witnesses; Jesus had appeared to Peter, to the Twelve and to more than 500, most of whom were still living. Then he appeared to James and to all the apostles, and last of all to Paul himself.

Paul argues against those who claimed that there is no resurrection of the dead. Christian believers are also resurrected since Jesus was resurrected. If there is no resurrection, then Jesus himself was not resurrected. If Jesus was not resurrected, then the Christian faith is futile (15:14). It would mean that those who died had perished, their sins unforgiven and the Christian faith founded on a lie. But he asserts that Jesus had been raised from the dead.

> **Key quote**
>
> And if Christ has not been raised, our preaching is useless and so is your faith.
>
> (1 Corinthians 15:14)

In v21, Paul declares again that, just as death came to all people through the disobedience and resulting broken relationship with God of one man – Adam – so resurrection and restored relationship will come to all in Christ through the perfect man, Jesus, when he returns to judge the world.

> **Key quote**
>
> The last enemy to be destroyed is death. For he has put everything under his feet.
>
> (1 Corinthians 15:26–27)

With what kind of body are the dead raised?

In v35–50, Paul discusses the kind of body the dead are raised with. He uses the analogy of seed planting. The body that is planted in the earth is perishable, dishonourable, weak, physical. The body that is raised is imperishable, glorious, strong, spiritual. The resurrection body excels over the earthly body like a fully grown plant excels over its seed. Paul asserts that 'just as we have borne the image of the earthly man, so shall we bear the image of the heavenly man' (15:49). He concludes that death has been swallowed up in victory and lost its sting, so that the Corinthians can be assured that their labour for the Lord is never in vain.

> **Key quote**
>
> But God gives it a body as he has determined, and to each kind of seed he gives its own body. Not all flesh is the same: people have one kind of flesh, animals have another, birds another and fish another. There are also heavenly bodies and there are earthly bodies …
>
> (1 Corinthians 15:38–40)

Paul makes clear that it is a bodily resurrection rather than the Greek idea of just the soul being immortal.

Resurrection, therefore, is not the same as resuscitation. Those resuscitated return from the dead the same as when they were alive (for example Lazarus) and would die again. But when Jesus was resurrected, his body appeared in a different form. He could walk through locked doors (John 20:19) and vanish from sight (Luke 24:31). Yet he could also walk, talk and eat.

Jesus' risen body is a new mode of existence, and the resurrected body of Christians will be in this image.

Modern interpretation

Rudolf Bultmann

Rudolf Bultmann

Specification content

The views of Rudolf Bultmann and NT. Wright on the relation of the resurrection event to history

 Key person

Rudolf Bultmann (1884–1976): a German theologian who called for the 'demythologisation' of the New Testament

 Key terms

demythologise: reinterpreting what are considered to be mythological elements of the Bible

myths: a story containing divine beings or supernatural themes to explain natural events or social and political concerns

Rudolf Bultmann was a German theologian who argued that all that is necessary for Christian belief is that Jesus lived, preached and died by crucifixion. He was convinced that the supernatural elements in the accounts, such as the virgin birth and the resurrection, were attempts to explain the divine in human terms. Such events were impossible to believe for the modern reader without discarding all modern intellect and knowledge. Bultmann classified such stories as '**myths**', and so attempts to interpret the New Testament in a way that changes its 'mythological' flavour but retains its meaning. He referred to this reinterpretation as a need to **demythologise**.

> **Key quote**
>
> We cannot use electric lights and radios and in the event of illness avail ourselves of modern medical and clinical means and at the same time believe in the spirit and wonder world of the New Testament.
>
> (Rudolf Bultmann)

The resurrection, Bultmann argues, was not a historical event. It is a myth, a story designed to sustain faith. It is mythological terminology of the time. No scientifically minded modern reader can believe in the resurrection of a corpse.

Bultmann writes, 'If the resurrection were an historical fact, faith would become superfluous. What is decisive is not that Jesus came to life again, but that he is, for you, the Risen One. The one who was crucified is alive again if you see him as such with eyes of faith'.

The resurrection, in its demythologised form, is seen as the realisation that the cross of Christ was not a defeat but a victory. The disciples suddenly realised that when he suffered death, Jesus was already the Son of God. Therefore, his death by itself was a victory over the power of death. The Lord of Life had given himself over to death and had thereby conquered it.

" Key quote "

If the resurrection were a historical fact, faith would become superfluous. (Rudolf Bultmann)

Thus, the crucifixion of Jesus contained the resurrection within it. There was no second historical event. Faith in the resurrection is really the same thing as faith in the cross being able to save people from their sins. Easter is thus about the arising, not of Jesus, but of the faith of the early Church. The resurrection takes place within individuals as they hear the word of God preached, and experience the rise of faith.

Nicholas T Wright

In his book *The Resurrection of the Son of God* (2003), the English theologian **Nicholas T Wright** argues that Jesus' resurrection marks the beginning of restoring creation that he will complete when he returns.

Wright considers the Jewish belief in resurrection:

- In the Old Testament, the belief in resurrection is 'vague and unfocused'.
- The Hebrew Sheol is the place of the dead where people are asleep.
- Some Psalms (Psalm 73:23–26) express a hope for life after death, based on God's love in the present that will continue into the future.
- In Isaiah 26, Ezekiel 37 and Daniel 12, resurrection is part of the hope for the whole nation, and they refer to bodily resurrection.
- In post-biblical Judaism, it was thought that people do not pass directly from death to resurrection, but go through an interim period, after which the death of the body will be reversed. Thus, resurrection refers to the undoing of death.
- The spectrum of Jewish beliefs about life after death runs from the Sadducees, who deny the idea of resurrection, to the Pharisees, who insist upon it.
- There was also a belief that a Messiah would come who would defeat God's enemies and establish God's rule.

It was from this background that the early Christians emerged. They believed:

- in the resurrection of the body
- that resurrection is an act of new creation; not simply a return to the same sort of body as before, but involves the gift of a new body with different properties
- that they would be bodily resurrected when Jesus, the Messiah, returned to judge the world

Key person

Nicholas T Wright (b. 1948): a leading English New Testament scholar and former Bishop of Durham

Nicholas T Wright

T1 Religious figures and sacred texts

- that while Jewish people who believed in resurrection spoke about the interim state of those who had died, early Christians spoke of people being 'asleep in Christ' (for example 1 Corinthians 15:18)
- that because of the resurrection, Jesus was the Son of God; he was the personal embodiment and revelation of the one true God.

The connection between Jesus' resurrection and Messiah

Although Jesus had not done what the Jewish people hoped and believed that the Messiah would do – defeat God's enemies, restore the Temple, establish God's reign on Earth – early Christians understood that Jesus' resurrection showed that Jesus was Israel's Messiah. In him, 'the creator's covenant plan, to deal with the sin and death that had infected the world, had reached its long-awaited and decisive fulfilment' (N.T. Wright).

Early Christians emphasised that Jesus was raised from the dead by God. Jesus had been executed as a messianic pretender, but God had vindicated him. 'It was a sign that this living God had acted at last in accordance with his ancient promise, and shown himself to be God, the unique creator and sovereign of the world. Jesus as the agent of the creator God is accomplishing the task of ridding the world of evil and ultimately death itself' (NT Wright).

Key quote

The best *historical* explanation is the one which inevitably raises all kinds of *theological* questions; the tomb was indeed empty, and Jesus was indeed seen alive, because he was truly raised from the dead.

(NT Wright)

Such an interpretation of the resurrection set the early Christians on a collision path with other Jewish groups of their day. However, Jesus' followers believed that his 'resurrection, marking him out as Messiah, was a call to Israel to find a new identity in following him and establishing his Kingdom' (NT Wright).

Key quote

Proposing that Jesus of Nazareth was raised from the dead was just as controversial 1900 years ago as it is today.

(NT Wright)

'The soul' and its connection with beliefs about life after death

The Greek philosopher Plato thought an afterlife for the soul was possible, but not bodily resurrection. The poet Homer saw the abode of the dead as a place of shadows. By the time of Jesus, parts of Judaism had become influenced by this Hellenistic thinking. While Sadducees denied a future life beyond death, there were other Jewish people who rejected a belief in resurrection but argued for a future blissful life for the righteous in which disembodied souls would enjoy a perfect life forever. However, Pharisees did believe in resurrection, but argued that the dead were in an intermediate state, like an angel or a spirit, and only in the future would they be embodied.

In Matthew 10:28, Jesus made a distinction between body and soul. Some, influenced by Hellenistic thinking, interpret this to mean that human beings have an immortal soul that survives death. Others argue that it refers to the Hebrew idea of nephesh – 'the whole human being seen from the point of view of one's inner life, that mixture of feeling, understanding, imagination, thought and emotion …' (NT Wright).

In 1 Corinthians 15:35–41, Paul discusses the resurrection body. He uses the seed/plant analogy, but does not suppose that resurrection bodies grow from corpses; neither, in his earthly body/heavenly body distinctions, is he suggesting that resurrection means becoming a star or moon. He explains in verses 42–49 that the non-corruptible resurrection body is where the animating principle of the body corrupted by sin (the 'soul') has been replaced by the life indwelt by the Spirit of God.

Summary

- Christians believe that, following the death on the cross and his burial, Jesus rose again from the dead in a bodily form.
- John gives an account of Jesus' resurrection appearances in his Gospel.
- Resurrection is not the same as resuscitation since Jesus' body appeared in a different form.
- Paul the apostle teaches about the resurrected body in his letter to the Corinthians.
- Rudolf Bultmann reinterpreted the resurrection by demythologising the accounts.
- NT Wright argues that the resurrection of Jesus shows that Jesus is the Messiah.

AO1 Activity

a Outline Paul's understanding of Jesus' resurrection.

This helps your ability to select and present the key, relevant features of 1 Corinthians.

b On small revision cards, summarise the key features of Rudolf Bultmann's understanding of the resurrection. Support the summary with extracts from quotations.

This helps you prioritise and select a core set of points to develop an answer and ensure that you are making accurate use of specialist language and vocabulary in context.

T1 Religious figures and sacred texts

> **This section covers AO2 content and skills**

> **Specification content**
> The historical reliability of the resurrection

Issues for analysis and evaluation

The historical reliability of the resurrection

Possible line of argument	Critical analysis and evaluation
The Gospel accounts accurately recount an actual historical event.	There are discrepancies between the accounts. For instance, in John, Jesus appears to Mary Magdalene after she tells the disciples, but in Matthew, he appears to the women before they tell the disciples. Even though there is much in the accounts that agree, the discrepancies cast doubt on its historical reliability.
The Gospels are the word of God and so are trustworthy.	The discrepancies demonstrate that the Gospels are not trustworthy. Many scholars would disagree with the view of the Gospels being 'God breathed'. They are writings by human beings. However, Paul does seem to attempt to prove the resurrection in 1 Corinthians 15, and the early Church did seem to believe the resurrection as a literal physical event.
Discrepancies are not evidence of an unreliable testimony.	Discrepancies are better accounted for by form and redaction criticism. These suggest that the Gospels were not written by eyewitnesses but were composed a long time after Jesus' life. They are theological writings rather than historical writings.
There are better ways to explain the rise in the belief of the physical resurrection of Jesus.	For example, the body was stolen or he did not actually die on the cross. These are more likely than a corpse coming back to life.
The resurrection should be classed as a myth.	It is unreasonable to expect modern reporters to believe in the resurrection of a corpse. Rather, it is a story designed to sustain faith. It is a story, according to Bultmann, that reflects the realisation that the cross of Christ was not a defeat but a victory. Faith in the resurrection is faith in the saving efficacy of the cross.
To take the resurrection as literal is contrary to faith.	Though many Christians appeal to the resurrection for believing in the Christian faith, Bultmann argued that if the resurrection were historical fact, then faith would become superfluous; neither does the resurrection in itself give meaning to the event of the crucifixion.
	The resurrection takes place within individuals as they hear the word of preaching and experience that rise of faith.

AO2 Activity

a Analyse three possible conclusions that could be drawn from the critical analysis and evaluation of the historical reliability of the resurrection. Select evidence and examples to support each of the three conclusions. Select one conclusion that you think is the most convincing and explain why it is so.

b Now contrast this with the weakest conclusion of the three. Justify your argument with clear reasoning and evidence.

This section covers AO2 content and skills

Exam practice

Sample question
Evaluate the nature of the resurrected body.

Specification content
The nature of the resurrected body

Sample answer
On reading the Gospel accounts of Jesus' resurrected body, it is clear that it differs significantly from his earthly body. When Jesus appears to Mary Magdalene, she does not recognise him at first and supposes him to be the gardener. Likewise, the disciples fail to recognise Jesus when he appears by the Sea of Galilee. This implies that there has been some change to his resurrection body. John's account records how Jesus was able to appear and vanish at will and to pass through locked doors, and yet he is no ghostly apparition because the disciples can see and touch his wounds; he takes food and cooks breakfast.

A good introduction referring to John's Gospel account of Jesus' resurrected body, and how it was different from his earthly body.

In 1 Corinthians 15, Paul makes clear that because Christ was raised from the dead, Christians can be certain that they will also be raised from the dead, and he addresses the nature of that resurrection body. It will be imperishable, glorious, strong, which is different from the earthly body, which is perishable, dishonourable, weak and subject to death. The resurrection body will be spiritual, in the sense that it will not be subject to death.

The answer then moves on to Paul's statements linking Christ's resurrected body to the believer's resurrection body. Again, the answer shows good knowledge of the relevant biblical text.

Paul contrasts 'spiritual' body with 'natural' body. He is not referring to the substance of the resurrection body, but rather the source of the physical resurrection body. In other words, the glorified resurrection body will be a spirit-dominated body, driven by the Holy Spirit, and not our flesh or fallen human desires. We can think of spiritual as non-physical, and some commentators refer back to Jesus' resurrection body where he appeared and then disappeared. However, Jesus' body did not dematerialise and vanish into thin air only to appear materialised again somewhere else. Rather the Greek has the sense of moving to a place where he could be seen (or not seen). Therefore it is not a true disappearance.

There is further development of Paul's statements about the spiritual nature of the resurrection body, followed by a discussion about interpreting 'non-physical' and that Jesus appeared and disappeared.

Paul argues that, just as we cannot predict what will grow from some unfamiliar seed, so in the same way we cannot predict exactly what the resurrection body will be like. However, what comes from the seed is much more glorious than the seed itself. There will be continuity as well as change. The earthly body will not be totally abandoned, nor will it be totally kept. This reflects Jesus' body at his resurrection, and Paul comments that we shall bear the likeness of the man from heaven.

Further exploration and discussion of Paul's statements about the resurrected body, showing good knowledge of the set text.

T1 Religious figures and sacred texts

Tennis player

Philosopher

This understanding of the resurrection body all rests on the reliability of the Gospels and of Paul's letter to the Corinthians. The New Testament does consistently refer to the resurrection body being the same physical body but transformed.

The answer starts to raise questions about the source of the information on the resurrected body.

Maybe we should accept that the 'mystery' of the resurrection extends beyond the act itself to that of questions about the nature of the resurrection body.

Judge

A good answer that reflects a thorough knowledge of the set text.

Over to you

For this task, select six key points from the ten listed, which are relevant to the evaluation question below. Put your selection into the order that you would use to address the question. When explaining why you have chosen these six to answer the question, you will find that you are developing a process of reasoning.

This helps you to develop an argument to decide whether or not the gospel accounts of the resurrection of Jesus are historically true.

Question

Assess the view that the Gospel accounts of the resurrection of Jesus are historically true.

Evaluation

1. Early Christians believed that Jesus was the Messiah.
2. They believed this despite him not achieving what the Messiah was supposed to achieve.
3. They believed it because they believed that Jesus had risen from the dead.
4. Other Jewish leaders had promised that they would be resurrected, but nobody believed that they had been, for the obvious reason that they had not.
5. The Gospel accounts of the resurrection are not simply a way of talking about him 'going to heaven when he died'. It was 40 days after the resurrection that he was exalted to heaven.
6. The risen Jesus invites the disciples to touch him to make sure he is a real human being. At the same time, he appears and disappears, sometimes through locked doors. The evangelists are telling, with bewilderment, stories about how Jesus' body was now different.
7. However, some people would say that Jesus somehow survived the crucifixion.
8. Others might argue that the tomb was empty, but there had been no resurrection.
9. Yet others might think that the disciples simply had visions of Jesus.
10. If so, would the disciples have spent the rest of their lives preaching what they knew to be a lie?

C: The Bible as a source of wisdom and authority in daily life

Make sure you have read and understood the set texts: Ecclesiastes 12:13–14; Luke 6:36–37; Psalm 119:9–16; Psalm 119:105–112; Genesis 1:26–28; Ecclesiastes 9:5–9; Psalm 46:1–3; Matthew 6:25.

What is the Christian Bible?

The English word *bible* comes from the Greek meaning 'the books'. The Christian Bible is a collection of sacred books bound together in two volumes known as the *Old Testament* (39 books) and the *New Testament* (27 books). In addition, there is another collection of books, referred to as the **Apocrypha**. **Protestants** do not accept the Apocrypha as part of the accepted sacred scriptures (the canon), but the Catholic and Orthodox Churches do include them.

The Old Testament was written originally in Hebrew. It is the scriptures of Judaism as well as being sacred to Christians. Written and edited by many authors over a period of many centuries, it tells the story of God's revelation of himself to the people of Israel from the earliest times until their return from exile in Babylon in 538 BCE. Being Jewish, Jesus would have read the books of the Old Testament.

> **This section covers AO1 content and skills**
>
> **Specification content**
>
> The ways in which the Bible is considered authoritative: as a source of moral advice (Ecclesiastes 12:13–14; Luke 6:36–37); as a guide to living (Psalm 119:9–16; Psalm 119:105–112); as teaching on the meaning and purpose of life (Genesis 1:26–28; Ecclesiastes 9:5–9); and as a source of comfort and encouragement (Psalm 46:1–3; Matthew 6:25)
>
> **Key terms**
>
> **Apocrypha:** a set of books usually placed between the Old Testament and the New Testament when they appear in the Bible. Recognised as canonical by the Roman Catholic Church but not by Protestants
>
> **Protestant:** a member of the parts of the Christian Church that separated from the Roman Catholic Church during the sixteenth century

The Old Testament was written originally in Hebrew

The New Testament was written originally in Greek and focuses on the life of Jesus and early Christians. There are:

- four Gospels (Matthew, Mark, Luke and John), which tell the story of Jesus' life and ministry
- the Book of Acts of the Apostles, which records the founding of the early Church
- a collection of 21 letters (Epistles) to various churches, 14 of which it is thought Paul wrote
- the Book of Revelation, which contains visions and images about Jesus' return as judge and King, and the promise of the creation of a new heaven and a new earth.

T1 Religious figures and sacred texts

The Bible reveals God and his plan to enable human beings to have eternal life

Christians believe that the Bible reveals God's plan to save human beings from the consequences of sin (disobedience to God) – the consequences being separation from God for eternity. In the Old Testament, there are hints and insights as to how this salvation (rescue) will be accomplished. But it is in the New Testament that it is revealed fully – that through Jesus' death on the cross, human beings can be forgiven and can enjoy God's company in this life and the other side of death.

> **Key quote**
>
> The New Testament lies hidden in the Old, and the Old Testament is unveiled in the New.
>
> (Augustine)

Most Christians read the Bible as a continuous salvation history that begins in the Old Testament. The Bible records the activity of God within human history, beginning with the Fall and God's promise to Abraham, which is fulfilled in Jesus and the possibility of eternal life with God for all people.

Events of the Old Testament

- The Bible begins with an account of how God created the universe and our world. In creating human beings, Genesis 1:27–28 states 'So God created humankind in his own image ... and blessed them and said to them; "Be fruitful and increase in number; fill the earth and subdue it."' Human beings were in a unique relationship with God and were to be maintainers of the created order.
- Everything was good, until Adam and Eve, the first man and woman, disobeyed God and brought sin and death to the world. Their disobedience is known as *the Fall*. Their sin is known as 'original sin' and is the tendency to evil, supposedly innate in all human beings. It is held to be inherited from Adam as a consequence of the Fall.
- God makes a covenant with Abraham that he will have countless descendants who will inherit a Promised Land.
- Israelites become slaves in Egypt but God calls Moses to liberate them. Their escape and the subsequent 40 years they spend in the wilderness is known as the *Exodus*. During this time, Moses receives the Ten Commandments, which Israelites must obey.
- Israelites conquer and enter the Promised Land. The land is divided between the Twelve Tribes, but the people are unfaithful to God. They cry to God for help. But after each time God responds, they soon fall back to unfaithfulness.
- In about 1000 BCE, Saul is made King and then his son-in-law, David, succeeds him. Under David and his son Solomon, Israel becomes a mighty empire with Jerusalem as its capital, and a Temple is built in Jerusalem. David became regarded as the ideal King and seen as the forefather of the Hebrew Messiah in Jewish prophetic literature. Many Psalms are attributed to him.
- At the death of Solomon, the Kingdom splits into two kingdoms: Israel and Judah. However, most of the kings were unfaithful to God. So God calls prophets such as Amos, Hosea and Isaiah to summon the people to faithfulness.

- As the people are still disobedient, God lets Assyria conquer Israel in 721 BCE and Babylon conquer Judah in 587 BCE. The people of Judah, now known as *Judeans* or *Jews*, spend 50 years in captivity in Babylon, a period known as the *Exile*. They return to Judah to rebuild Jerusalem.
- The last book in the Old Testament is Malachi. Its final chapter refers to the coming judgement of God on evildoers – a day to come when God promises to remove evil, 'But for you who revere my name ... you will go out and frolic like well-fed calves. Then you will trample on the wicked' (Malachi 4:2–3). In the final verses, God announces that he will send the prophet Elijah to his people before that great and dreadful day of the Lord (Malachi 4:5).
- The Old Testament story ends here with the promise of the return of Elijah and the people waiting for God's Saviour, the Messiah, a new David, to save them from their enemies and restore the Kingdom.

Events of the New Testament

The New Testament takes up the story some 400 years later, when Israel is under Roman control. God sends his son, Jesus Christ, into the world as Saviour and Messiah – the person Jewish people had long been waiting for. In Matthew 17:10–13, it is clear that Jewish people believed that Elijah must appear before the Messiah came. When Jesus says that Elijah has already come, the disciples realise that Jesus is referring to John the Baptist.

Through Jesus' miracles and teaching, his disciples realise that he is the Messiah, but when he is crucified by his enemies, they think that all is lost. After three days, however, God raises Jesus from the dead, thus affirming that he is the Son of God. New Testament writers realise that sin and death are now conquered forever, because those who believe in Jesus will share his resurrection. God's original plan for his creation is thus brought full circle and will be completed at Jesus' second coming when he will judge the world and create a new heaven and a new earth.

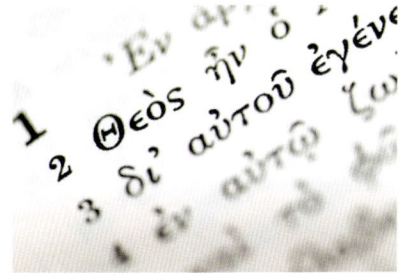

The New Testament was written originally in Greek

It is interesting to note that when Jesus is asked a question by Sadducees, who did not believe in resurrection, about resurrection (Mark 12:18–27), he points them back to Moses and the burning bush (Exodus 3:1–17). He argues that God is not God of the dead, but of the living.

The final part of the New Testament, after the four Gospels, records what happens after the Holy Spirit descends on the disciples at Pentecost. It gives them courage to preach about Jesus, first to Jewish people and then, led by Paul, to Gentiles (non-Jews) as well. Many Christian communities are set up. In a short space of time, Christianity spreads throughout the Roman Empire.

The Bible's teaching on the meaning and purpose of life

Meaning refers to how we make sense of life and why we are here. Believers may say they find no meaning in life apart from God because God is life. Every person has been created in the image of God and created for eternity. Therefore the Bible provides meaning to the origins of life by way of the creation narratives, and it has a hope for a future existence through resurrection of the dead.

> **Key quote**
>
> Within the covers of the Bible are the answers to all the problems men face.
> (Former American President Ronald Regan)

T1 Religious figures and sacred texts

Above all, the meaning of life can be found in Jesus, the Son of God, who said of himself, 'I am the way and the truth and the life' (John 14:6). According to John (17:3), Jesus also said, 'Now this is eternal life: that they know you, the only true God, and Jesus Christ, whom you have sent'. God created people to worship him and to enjoy a relationship with him forever. In John 10:10, Jesus says, 'I have come that they have life, and have it to the full'.

Purpose refers to the aspirations that motivate our activities. In other words, purpose is about what we live for and how we should live. For Christians, the Bible teaches people that there is more to life than food and clothing (Matthew 6:25). Jesus' greatest commandments were to 'love God' and demonstrate 'love for neighbour'. The story of the Good Samaritan (Luke 10:25–37) is an example of love in action.

> ## Key quote
> Therefore I tell you, do not worry about your life, what you will eat or drink; or about your body, what you will wear. Is not life more than food, and the body more than clothes?
> **(Matthew 6:25)**

The Book of Ecclesiastes begins by arguing that everything is meaningless, but concludes in the last two verses as follows: 'Now all has been heard; here is the conclusion of the matter; Fear God and keep his commandments, for this is the duty of all humankind. For God will bring every deed into judgement, including every hidden thing, whether it is good or evil' (Ecclesiastes 12:13–14).

Therefore, the purpose of human life is to find God, to know him, to do his will, to serve him, to obey him and to show him to the world. It is to worship God and to give him the glory that is due to him. Christians believe that those who believe and follow Jesus will share his resurrection and have eternal life.

The Bible as a guide to everyday living

The Bible provides a guide to everyday living. Psalm 119:105 states 'Your word is a lamp for my feet, a light on my path'. Christians believe that the Bible does this by pointing people to Jesus. People are not saved through their behaviour, but through faith in Jesus. True faith, however, will result in a special kind of behaviour inspired not by the fear of punishment but by love for God. If human beings love God, Jesus will live in them by means of the Holy Spirit, and lead them to obedience. When they fail, they can repent and seek forgiveness. The Holy Spirit possesses the Christian to gradually change them into the sort of person that God created them to be.

> ## Key quote
> How can a young person stay on the path of purity? By living according to your word.
> **(Psalm 119:9)**

Jesus did not issue his followers a set of detailed regulations for daily living, but he set an example. The Christian life is therefore about following Jesus in his obedience; his rejection of selfish desire; his prayerful humility; his concern for poor, vulnerable and marginalised people; and his service to others. The Christian does as Jesus did.

What then about the Old Testament Law? Are Christians bound by the Law of Moses? Once again, the key is to follow Jesus.

In the Sermon on the Mount (Matthew 5:17–19), Jesus says that he has come not to abolish the Law of Moses or the Prophets but to fulfil them. The phrase 'the Law and the Prophets' is a way of referring to the whole of the Old Testament. Christians believe that the whole of the Old Testament is a unity that prophetically anticipated Jesus and the Kingdom. So, the long-awaited age, which the Old Testament looked to, had arrived in Jesus. For instance, the commands associated with the Temple find their fulfilment in Jesus (Matthew 12:6), as do the ritual Laws.

But what about the ethical demands such as 'do not murder'? Jesus identifies a deeper level of obedience. Unlike the scribes and Pharisees who externally managed expectations, Jesus demands a heart-level transformation – they are to renounce hatred (Matthew 5:26–30). The command against adultery is fulfilled when people renounce even lustful thoughts (Matthew 5:26–30). In the Kingdom of God, it is the inner person that needs transforming. Jesus demands from his followers a higher degree of holiness. They must obey not the letter but the spirit of the Law. It is not only their actions that need to be right, but their motives as well.

As to the Jewish Law about dietary regulations, the Council of Jerusalem (Acts 15) decided that Gentile Christians did not have to submit to all the rigours of the Law of Moses. Christians are called to be free. Perfect freedom, however, comes only through obedience to God's will.

The Bible as a source of comfort and encouragement

Paul, in his letter to the Romans, writes that the scriptures were written 'to teach us, so that through the endurance taught in the scriptures and the encouragement they provide we might have hope' (Romans 15:4).

The Bible is a source of comfort and encouragement because it portrays a god who is in control of all things, who keeps his promises and whose love for human beings does not change.

Psalm 46 reminds Christians that 'God is our refuge and strength, an ever-present help in trouble. Therefore, we will not fear' (verses 1–2).

The Bible recounts stories of how God has worked in the lives of men and women with whose hopes and failures Christians in all ages can identify. The human condition is fundamentally the same today as it was in biblical times. People still struggle with the same difficulties as previous generations – temptation, sin, bereavement, poverty, suffering, the fear of death. The Bible has something to say on all these things:

- On temptation and sin, it teaches that even the most revered people, such as King David, may fail from time to time. But if there is repentance, God will forgive.
- On bereavement, it teaches that death is not the end. In John 11:11, Jesus tells the disciples that his departed friend, Lazarus, 'has fallen asleep, but I am going there to wake him up'. Jesus then raises Lazarus to life. The majority of Christians believe that there is resurrection and life after death for all believers.
- On poverty, it teaches that Jesus understood the reality of poverty and stressed the need to give to disadvantaged people, provide for them and treat them fairly. He identified with poor people and taught that it was difficult for a rich person to inherit the Kingdom of God.

Rembrandt: *The Raising of Lazarus*

T1 Religious figures and sacred texts

> ## Key quote
>
> The Bible is the Magna Carta of the poor and oppressed. The human race is not in a position to dispense with it.
> (T Huxley)

- On suffering, it teaches that in the life to come 'there will be no more death or mourning or crying or pain' (Revelation 21:4). God is the Father of compassion and the God of all comfort 'who comforts us in all our troubles, so that we can comfort those in any trouble with the comfort we ourselves receive from God' (2 Corinthians 1:4).
- On the fear of death, it teaches that Jesus has conquered death, so that human beings who believe in him should not fear death, as they will share in his resurrection.

> ## Key quote
>
> If Christ has not been raised, your faith is futile.
> (1 Corinthians 15:17)

Summary

★ The Christian Bible consists of the Old Testament (39 books) and the New Testament (27 books).

★ The Old Testament books were written in Hebrew and the New Testament books were written in Greek.

★ Most Christians believe that the Bible reveals God's plan to save human beings from the consequences of sin by means of Jesus' death.

★ It is a progressive revelation about salvation.

★ The Bible is a source of comfort and encouragement, and a guide to everyday living.

AO1 Activity

a Read Psalm 119:9–16 and Psalm 119:105–112. Identify three ways from each passage that would guide and instruct Christians in how to live.

This helps you develop the ability to select and present excellent evidence and examples from a set Bible passage.

b Draw a line down the middle of a sheet of paper. In the left-hand column, list and explain four Old Testament events that show an aspect of God's salvation plan for humanity. In the right-hand column, list and explain four New Testament events that show an aspect of God's salvation plan for humanity.

This helps you develop the ability to select and prioritise appropriate material.

Issues for analysis and evaluation

The relative value of the Bible as teaching on the meaning and purpose of life

> **This section covers AO2 content and skills**

> **Specification content**
> The relative value of the Bible as teaching on the meaning and purpose of life

Possible line of argument	Critical analysis and evaluation
The Bible is God's spoken word and reveals the meaning and purpose of life in terms of the grand narrative of the origin and sustaining of life, God's control over events and the salvation of human beings through the death and resurrection of Jesus.	Many regard these narratives as myth rather than history. Evolution explains creation without need of a god. History appears to be written by those who 'win' and Jesus is just an outstanding human being, not God incarnate.
The huge popularity of the Bible reflects its importance to human beings in terms of providing answers about the meaning and purpose of life.	Many Bibles have been given away by various missionary and evangelistic groups, rather than sold. The high sales of a book are not necessarily connected to the value of the book. The Bible may be the bestselling book in the world – yet it may also be the least read bestselling book.
It is the moral advice contained in the Bible that provides teaching on the meaning and purpose of life. Psalm 119 refers to God's word as 'a lamp for my feet, a light on my path'.	Certainly there are commandments and principles in the Bible, but there are many ethical systems that offer equally good guidance on the meaning and purpose of life, without any reference to God.
God is the only one who is fully and truly good, and therefore the Bible, as God's revelation, is of value in teaching the meaning and purpose of life.	Many atheists are morally good. The Bible depicts a god who many find both good and evil.
The Bible has influenced our culture in terms of understanding the meaning and purpose of life. Not only Sundays, but our calendar in general reflects biblical events. Our rites of passage reflect biblical teaching, as do our laws.	We live in a multicultural society, not a Christian society. Many secular rituals are replacing religious rituals. The Bible is an ancient book that reflects ancient beliefs. It does not address many current legal issues.

> **AO2 Activity**
> a   Analyse three possible conclusions that could be drawn from the critical analysis and evaluation of the relative value of the Bible as teaching on the meaning and purpose of life. What are their strengths? Which conclusion do you think is the weakest?
> b   Evaluate three lines of argument to show that this is the weakest argument. Explain why you have chosen these.

This section covers AO2 content and skills

Specification content
The extent to which the Psalms studied offer a guide to living for Christians

The answer immediately makes the case for why the Psalms are not a guide to living today for Christians. There are clear arguments put forward to support this view.

Argument with some supporting evidence for the alternative view.

The answer engages in a brief 'for' and 'against' structure, giving support for the varying views.

The argument then turns to more detailed reasoning in support of Psalms being a guide.

The conclusion is consistent with the rest of the answer and raises challenges as to why, overall, the Psalms are not a full guide, but just a partial guide to living.

A good answer covering a number of arguments both for and against. Perhaps the conclusion needs developing.

Exam practice

Sample question
Evaluate the extent to which the Psalms studied offer a guide to living for Christians.

Sample answer

Many of the Psalms were originally written for use in the Temple in Jerusalem – an institution that no longer exists – and so it is not surprising that many people find them irrelevant. They reflect the Old Testament, which many Christians believe has been fulfilled by the life, death and resurrection of Jesus. Written some 3000 years ago, they depict a different, pre-scientific worldview in terms of cosmology or how to treat your enemies. Therefore, it is not surprising that many Christians do not consider them as a guide for living as a Christian today.

However, many Christians regard the Bible as 'God's word' relevant for all peoples at all time. They argue that the Psalms offer fundamental truths about God aimed at bringing a change in the reporter's life. Jesus quoted the Psalms, and many Christians believe that the Psalms refer to Jesus and view the Bible as one unfolding story of salvation.

Scholars argue that the purpose of the Psalms was later reinterpreted to suit the needs of Judaism, which again implies they have very little to offer Christians as a guide to living as Christians. Indeed, some of the Psalms seem not to accord with Jesus' teaching – for instance, Jesus' teaching to love everyone, including your enemies – yet some of the Psalms Jesus himself used, which suggests that they are still relevant to Christians.

The Psalms are personal and offer encouragement, solace, meaning and purpose to life, sharing with the reporter many of life's greatest questions: Why am I here? Why does evil prosper over good? What is God like? In that sense, they speak to every faith and to every age.

Indeed, the Psalms are used in many church services as a source of prayer, reflection and devotion. They offer instruction to the believer to follow God's word. God's word is, according to Psalm 119, 'a lamp for my feet, a light on my path'. They offer comfort to those who are worried about sin, suffering and death. They can often stir our emotions and are the basis of many hymns.

However, how clear and precise is the advice in the Psalms, in terms of a guide to living for Christians? Many might argue that they are rather vague and limited. They fail to discuss many twenty-first-century issues, such as end of life. It does suggest that the Psalms should be seen alongside other biblical texts, rather than as a full practical guide for Christian living.

Over to you

For this task, develop each of the key points below by adding evidence and examples to evaluate fully the argument presented in the evaluation statement.

This helps you to answer examination questions for AO2 by ensuring that 'sustained and clear views are given, supported by extensive, detailed reasoning and/or evidence' (Level 5 AO2 band descriptor).

Evaluation

The evaluation statement is about the Bible as the word of God and how it provides complete guidance for Christians. A key point that could be used is that 'some argue that the Bible is the inspired word of God'. This first point has been developed for you. Now consider the other examples of possible key points and develop each of those by adding evidence and examples.

1. Some argue that the Bible is the inspired word of God. Development: The Bible's 66 books, written by many different authors over many centuries, have a common theme – the redemption of God's people. It claims itself that it is the word of God for 'teaching, rebuking, correcting and training in righteousness' (2 Timothy 3:16). Like God himself, it is without error and authoritative. Its message is eternal for all peoples of all times.
2. Christian theology teaches that Jesus, not the Bible, is the word of God.
3. The Bible does not deal with modern issues directly. Therefore, it is not complete in detail, even if it is complete in guidance.
4. Different scholars interpret the Bible differently. Therefore, it cannot give complete guidance.
5. The Bible deals with religion and morality and is therefore a complete guide for life today.
6. The historical context of the Bible limits its relevance today because society today is very different from society during Old and New Testament times.

Religious figures and sacred texts

This section covers AO1 content and skills

Specification content
How the Christian biblical canon was established

D: The Bible as a source of wisdom and authority

The Hebrew Bible (*Tanakh*) and the Old Testament

Different faiths and traditions have different sacred texts. Judaism has the Tanakh (also called the *Hebrew Bible*). The name *Tanakh* comes from its division into three parts:

- **Torah:** the Law
- **Nevi'im:** the Prophets
- **Kethuvim:** the Writings.

Therefore, many Jewish people refer to the Hebrew Bible by the acronym 'TNK' (pronounced *Tanakh*), derived from the initial letters of the three divisions (Torah, Nevi'im, Kethuvim). Many Jewish people see it as God's revelation to Israel. Judaism agrees on the books that form the Hebrew Bible.

Christianity sees itself as the fulfilment of Judaism, in that it claims that Jesus is the long-awaited figure that Jewish people believe God had promised. However, Judaism does not believe Jesus fulfilled messianic prophecies. Neither does it accept Jesus as a divine being; an intermediary between human beings and God. Jewish people believe the Messiah is yet to come.

Like Jewish people, Christians also regard the Hebrew Bible as sacred texts, but refer to it as the *Old Testament*. The word *testament* means a 'covenant' or 'contract'. The Hebrew Bible records a number of covenants that God made with people, such as Abraham, Moses and David.

In the Book of Jeremiah, God promised a new covenant, or a new contract, with the people of God: 'The days are coming, declares the LORD, when I will make a new covenant ... It will not be like the covenant I made with their ancestors ... This is the covenant I will make with the people of Israel after that time ... I will put my law in their minds and write it on their hearts. I will be their God, and they will be my people. I will forgive their wickedness, and will remember their sins no more' (Jeremiah 31:31–34).

Christians believe that Jesus established this new covenant when he suffered and died on the cross, and that he referred to at the Last Supper, on the night he was betrayed (Matthew 26:26–28; 1 Corinthians 11:25; Hebrews 8:13).

Therefore, Christians regard the accounts of Jesus' life and death, the life of the early Church and various letters by Paul and others as sacred texts. They are collected together in the New Testament (since they are about this new covenant that Jeremiah referred to).

The Christian biblical canon

The Old Testament

Judaism collected together an agreed and authoritative list of books that were regarded as sacred texts, called the Tanakh (or the Hebrew Bible). An official, authoritative list is called the *canon*. The word comes from Greek and means 'measuring rod'; it refers to a standardised closed list of scripture,

Reading the Torah

WJEC/Eduqas Religious Studies for AS & A Level Christianity

containing the authoritative rule of faith and practice, the standard of doctrine and duty. Hence, the Jewish canon is the Tanakh.

> **Key quote**
>
> … a canonical book is one that the Church acknowledges as belonging to its list of sacred books, as inspired by God, and as having a regulating (rule) of value for faith and morals.
>
> **(RF Collins)**

In Christianity, the canon consists of the Old and the New Testament.

The canon of the Protestant Old Testament Bible is the same content as the Tanakh, though in a different order. However, the list of books in the Catholic Old Testament is slightly different. This is because:

- the Jewish canon was not closed at the time of the New Testament and some books added to the Hebrew Bible but later removed remained included in the Catholic Old Testament
- the New Testament writers used the Greek version of the Hebrew Bible (the Septuagint – see page 11), which included Jewish writings written only in Greek and which were later excluded from the Jewish canon; these books were Tobit, Judith, 1 and 2 Maccabees, Wisdom, Sirach, Baruch, as well as additions to Daniel and Esther.

The Catholic Church believes that all books of the Bible are fully and equally inspired.

Protestants rejected the extra books found in the Catholic Old Testament and referred to them as the *Apocrypha* since they were of unknown origin and questionable value. Therefore, the Protestant Old Testament contains the same books as those in the Hebrew Bible (but in a different order) and some books, such as the Book of Kings in the Hebrew Bible have been divided into two books, such as 1 and 2 Kings.

> **Key quote**
>
> The books commonly called the *Apocrypha*, not being of divine inspiration, are not part of the canon of scripture …
>
> **(The Westminster Confession of Faith)**

The different order may be explained either because:

- the Old Testament follows the order of the Greek version of the Hebrew Bible, which placed the Minor Prophets at the end rather than Ezra, Nehemiah and Chronicles, or
- the Old Testament replaced the ending of the Hebrew Bible (which places the focus on the Jewish people having returned from Exile and rebuilt their nation) with the Minor Prophets that, in part, looked ahead to the return of Elijah, which the New Testament interprets as John the Baptist.

The New Testament

There is no disagreement about the number (27) or order of New Testament books among the Christian Churches (that is, the canon).

The Gospels, which recount the life, death and resurrection of Jesus, are placed first. They are followed by the narrative of the birth of the Church (Acts of the Apostles), and the letters attributed to Paul; first those to the churches (generally, the longest letters are first) and those to individuals (the Pastoral Epistles). These are followed by letters not attributed to Paul (again with the longest ones first). The New Testament ends with the only piece of apocalyptic literature in the New Testament: the Book of Revelation.

> **Key quote**
>
> Gospels understood as testimony are the entirely appropriate means of access to the historical reality of Jesus.
>
> (R Bauckham)

How the Christian biblical canon was established

The Old Testament

At the time of Jesus, the only sacred text was the Hebrew Bible (the *Tanakh*), which Christians adopted and later named the *Old Testament*. We do not know the exact date when Jewish believers considered canonical any of those books.

Many scholars believe that the three parts represent three successive stages in forming the canon, with the Torah as the earliest part to be recognised. It was shared orally for perhaps centuries and then written down (though conservative Jewish people and Christians would put the date much earlier). The writings of the prophets came next, with the collection of Writings (*Kethuvim*) possibly not recognised as authoritative by Jewish people until the first centuries CE. In fact, Luke 24:44 implies a time when the canon was not completed. Jesus refers to the scriptures as 'the Law of Moses, the Prophets and the Psalms'. In other words, the only one of the Writings referred to as scripture is the Psalms.

The first-century Jewish historian Josephus mentions the Law, the Prophets and 'four books', which he describes as 'hymns to God and precepts for the conduct of human life'. These four books are thought to have been the Psalms, Song of Solomon, Proverbs and Ecclesiastes. This suggests the final part of the Hebrew Bible canon was in process, although not yet fixed.

The condition for books to be incorporated into the canon were that:

- the books had to survive; there are references in the Hebrew Bible to books that we have no knowledge of today (for example The Book of Jashar that Joshua 10:13 refers to)
- the books must be seen as supporting the central ideas and themes of the Torah
- the books were recognised by a wide variety of Jewish people in diverse locations as supporting their faith and practice.

The New Testament

In the very early years of Christianity, Christian teaching was conveyed orally by the Apostles, and by the sayings of Jesus. The next phase in the development of the Christian canon came with Paul's letters to various churches, beginning in about 53 CE. These letters were prized by the churches that received them; they were eventually copied and circulated. They were soon followed by the writing of the Gospels, as well as other letters and the Book of Revelation. The traditional date for the Book of Revelation is about 95 CE.

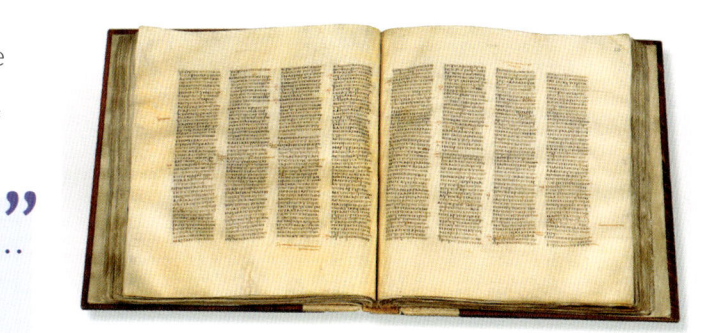

> **Key quote**
>
> The Bible is the cradle wherein Christ is laid.
> (M Luther)

A page of Luke's Gospel from a fourth-century copy of the New Testament

In the second century, there were many collections of Christian writings; most of these contained the four Gospels as well as many letters of Paul. There was a growing recognition that these writings were *scriptures*, just as important as the Hebrew Bible (2 Peter 3:15–16). Many churches in Syria and elsewhere used a harmony of all four Gospels that was created in the second century and used for several centuries. This was called the *Diatessaron* (meaning 'made of four').

The Muratorian Canon is perhaps the oldest known list of books in the New Testament, with some scholars dating this at about 170 CE. It contains 22 of the 27 books in today's New Testament. It also mentions some books that were forgeries, and warned against using them. This supports the view that the early Christians were careful about the selection process.

How were the books selected?

Like the Hebrew Bible, there are no written criteria to guide the selection of books to the canon. However, there are three factors that clearly guided the early Christian Church:

- Books considered 'scripture' had to have a connection to the Apostles, either being written by them or by someone in direct contact with them.
- The writings had to have a connection with churches recognised as supporting faith and practice by Christians in diverse places.
- The books had to conform to the faith of Christianity. Christianity has always been clear that the coming of Jesus, his life, death and resurrection are of the utmost importance for the relationship between humanity and God.

There were few disagreements. Perhaps one of the best known was a church leader called Marcion who, in about 140 CE, created a Bible that rejected the Hebrew Bible and contained a Gospel of Luke (without the birth narratives) and the letters of Paul. However, this was soon rejected, since early Christians believed strongly that the Christian Bible should contain the Old Testament as well as Christian writings, on the basis that the same God who was at work in Israel was also active in the life of Jesus.

> **Key quote**
>
> There is current also [an epistle] to the Laodiceans, [and] another to the Alexandrians, [both] forged in Paul's name to [further] the heresy of Marcion.
> **(The Muratorian Canon)**

The consensus among scholars is that the same 27 books constituting the canon today were the 27 books generally recognised in the first century, and written before 120 CE. The 27 books were canonised at the Council of

T1 Religious figures and sacred texts

Hippo in 393 CE and later affirmed at the Council of Carthage in 397 CE and 419 CE. One of the oldest bibles in existence, the *Codex Vaticanus*, was written around 350 CE and has the 27 books of the New Testament that all Christian denominations accept today.

Diverse views on the Bible as the word of God

> **Specification content**
> Diverse views on the Bible as the word of God

Most Christians believe that the Bible is *inspired*. The word *inspire* comes from a Greek verb meaning 'to breathe on or in'. In 2 Timothy 3:16, Paul writes 'All scripture is God-breathed …'. In 2 Peter 1:21, Peter writes 'For prophecy never had its origin in the human will, but prophets, though human, spoke from God as they were carried along by the Holy Spirit'. So Christians are united in believing that the Bible is the 'word of God' because they see that, in some sense, God is the author of the Bible.

> **" Key quotes "**
>
> It is wicked to doubt that they [the writings of the Apostles and prophets] are free from all error.
> **(Augustine)**
>
> … the Church has always venerated the scriptures as she venerates the Lord's body.
> **(Catechism of the Catholic Church)**

Disagreement arises over exactly what part God plays in the process. The variety of views range from seeing the biblical writers as playing no part other than writing down the words spoken to them by God, to viewing the Bible as inspired because it was written by inspired people – human authors. In this second understanding, God did not act in a special way to write the Bible; he acted in human history and experience. It was the human authors themselves, through the influence of Jesus and the Church, who inspire; it is not the actual words of the Bible that are inspired.

Different understandings of inspiration

Objective views of inspiration

> **Specification content**
> Different understandings of inspiration (the objective view of inspiration; the subjective view of inspiration)

Many of the early Church Fathers emphasised the objective side of inspiration. God directly moved the biblical writers to write certain texts. Indeed, there are many passages in the Bible that present God as speaking directly to or through a prophet. Some of these earlier theologians took the view that the biblical writers were possessed in a special way by God's spirit, led into some kind of ecstasy so that their complete utterance could be seen as coming directly from God. The second-century theologian Athenagorus described God using the prophets 'as a flautist might blow into a flute'. In other words, inspiration is a kind of divine dictation.

However, other early Church Fathers disagreed with assigning merely a passive role to the human authors. Origen, a second- to third-century thinker, believed the authors of the Bible were fully conscious of the process of inspiration and were able to express their own views. Though many Church leaders viewed God as the author of the Bible, or referred to the Bible as 'dictated by the Holy Spirit', they had a different notion than we do today when we say the words 'author' or 'dictation'. In Latin, the word for 'author' could also mean 'producer'. Furthermore, in the ancient world, dictation of letters could go beyond a word-for-word approach, with those dictating giving their scribes the general idea of what to write, rather than the exact words. 'The ancient amanuensis was not a slavish copyist but often played an active role in giving final form to a composition' (RD Williams). When it comes to the biblical writers receiving divine dictation, this could be seen as something rigidly done (emphasising the objective role of inspiration) or a process that gave them relative freedom to say the things they thought best – giving a larger role to the subjective mode of inspiration.

Subjective views of inspiration

The European enlightenment put an emphasis on human knowledge and understanding: traditional belief in God; miracles; and the Bible as God's word were challenged.

Some thinkers of this period, who were sympathetic to Christianity, viewed inspiration as a human rather than a divine activity. They believed that the Bible could still have meaning for Christians as the witness of writers inspired by God's work in the world and the life of Jesus. In other words, there is a link between the Bible and God, not through the words of the Bible, but in the inspired experience of the writers. Some Christians objected to this approach, since it left the door open to other books being regarded as equally inspired as the Bible.

Inerrancy and plenary verbal inspiration

In the late nineteenth and early twentieth centuries, there was a reaction to the enlightenment's focus on human wisdom and knowledge, in the form of Christian **fundamentalism**. It attempted to defend the *fundamentals* of Christian faith. At least five fundamental teachings were identified:

1. the inerrancy of the Bible (that is, it is free from error)
2. the virgin birth and deity of Christ
3. the substitutionary atonement of Jesus Christ (Jesus died on behalf of humanity)
4. the bodily resurrection of Jesus
5. the authenticity of Jesus' miracles and the literal second coming of Christ.

> **Key term**
>
> **fundamentalism:** the movement from the late nineteenth century dedicated to defending key biblical doctrines, later becoming associated with a literal approach to the Bible

At the heart of fundamentalism was an objective view of revelation: God gave each word of the Bible to the human writers, so that there would be no error, contradiction or falsehood. In other words, the Bible is not merely a testimony to an experience of God by inspired writers; its very words are inspired. The technical phrase that describes this view is inerrancy or *plenary verbal inspiration. Plenary* means 'complete', 'entire' or 'absolute': God spoke verbally to the authors so that every single word in the Bible is true. The logic behind this position is:

- God is not associated with falsehood or error.
- God has inspired the Bible.
- Therefore, there are no falsehoods, contradictions or errors in the Bible. (Some fundamentalists distinguish between the original text of the Bible, which is perfect and without error, and later copies into which some errors may have crept).

Certainly, some passages suggest the writers of the Bible each received a verbal message (that is, messages of God spoken by the prophets), but most biblical writers make no mention of this process and appear to write personally. For instance, Paul writes 'To the rest I say this (I, not the Lord)' (1 Corinthians 7:12). Also, the Gospels seem to make use of multiple sources (Luke 1:1–4). As a result, many Christian theologians have rejected plenary inspiration.

More subjective theories of inspiration

Other subjective theories of inspiration include Karl Barth's view that Jesus (and not the Bible) is the 'word of God'. Many argue that if a Christian listens to the Bible with humility and a spirit of obedience, then certain passages can become transformed into the word of God in a reader's experience. This implies that inspiration is not the quality of the text, but of a reader's experience with the text under certain circumstances.

Other theologians have said that divine inspiration is much more complex than a text being produced by one individual. This insight has led to social theories of inspiration, which view the Bible as the product not of an individual working with God but as an entire faith community being impacted by God and passing that impact on to an author.

Balancing subjective and objective views

Many theologians aim to balance objective and subjective viewpoints: they affirm that God is the author of the Bible, but also that God has worked through unique human authors, each with their own style, personality and historical situations. What is important for these theologians is not that the Bible conforms to some view of perfection that we can define in logical or scientific terms, but that it is 'true' when it comes to matters of salvation, faith and morality. As 2 Timothy 3:16 says, the Bible is 'useful for teaching, rebuking, correcting and training in righteousness'.

John Calvin's use of accommodation

One way that some theologians have explained how God's authorship of the Bible can co-exist with historical or scientific errors is by using the concept of accommodation. They see expressions about history or science in the Bible as God's way of accommodating those who were writing and reading the Bible long ago; the expressions were made at a level people could understand them.

> **Key quote**
>
> Legitimate accommodation can be more accurately called 'adaptation'. God, because of infinitude, adapts himself to our finite understanding in order to reveal himself.
>
> (J Calvin)

This idea comes from the reformation theologian **John Calvin** who, through his early work as a humanist scholar, was aware of the possibilities and limits of language. 'We must never forget', said Calvin, 'that God is above and beyond our language'. The transcendent God chooses to lower himself to become intelligible in our experience. Calvin used the analogy of a nurse making 'baby talk' to a young toddler – the nurse is able to make far more sophisticated expressions, but chooses to communicate in a way that encourages interaction. For Calvin, that God has decided to accommodate his 'language' to us in a book is a cause for thanksgiving.

Calvin also speaks about the human authors of the Bible choosing to speak in a language that would be easily intelligible to their readers. For instance, Genesis 1:16 says, 'God made two great lights – the greater light to govern the day and the lesser light to govern the night ...'. This is a reference to the Sun and the Moon. However, Calvin is aware of the discovery of other planets such as Saturn that are, technically, a greater light in the sky than the Moon. So is this an error? No. Not at all: Moses (who Calvin believed to be

---

Specification content

John Calvin's doctrine of accommodation

Key person

John Calvin (1509–64): a French pastor, theologian and reformer in Geneva during the Protestant Reformation

the author of Genesis) was simply adapting truth to the common person. Moses could have referred to other planetary bodies, but this would detract from communicating the essential message of the passage.

Calvin believed the Bible to be without error. In this case, he said Genesis 1:16 is actually true: the Moon is the light that rules the night sky, *from the point of view of someone on Earth*. So, according to Calvin, even when biblical writers are accommodating their language to the reader, the scriptures are wholly true.

Some contemporary theologians who do believe that there are errors in the Bible also use the idea of accommodation. These theologians believe that the biblical writers made scientific, cultural and historical assumptions that are incorrect. These errors are examples of God accommodating to human language. However, the Bible's main message for our lives is still relevant, since it is not mainly about these scientific, cultural and historical assumptions. These errors detract little or nothing from the theological message of God's sovereignty and provision of salvation through faith in Jesus.

Portrait of John Calvin (1509–1564) attributed to Hans Holbein (1497–1543)

Summary

- An agreed and authoritative list of books is called the canon.
- The Hebrew Bible of Judaism consists of the Law (Torah), the Prophets (Nevi'im) and the Writings (Kethuvim).
- Christianity, unlike Judaism, claims that Jesus is the long-awaited Messiah, who instituted the New Covenant Jeremiah prophesied. Therefore, Christians refer to the Hebrew Bible as the Old Testament. Both Judaism and Christianity regard the writings as sacred texts.
- The Catholic Old Testament contains additional writings known as the *Apocrypha*.
- The New Testament consists of 27 books, including the Gospels, Paul's letters and the Book of Revelation, and became accepted as sacred texts.
- Most Christians believe that the Bible is inspired but disagree over the part God played in the process. Objective inspiration is the belief that God directly moved the biblical writers to write certain texts.
- In contrast, subjective inspiration is the belief that humans experienced God at work in history and expressed their thoughts without God directly guiding their words.
- Calvin argued that any apparent errors in the texts were explained by God accommodating his language to a level people could understand.

AO1 Activity

a Explain the differences between:
   i   the Hebrew Bible and the Christian Bible
   ii objective inspiration and subjective inspiration.

   This helps with your understanding of some key terms.

b Create a simple dialogue between a fundamentalist and John Calvin on the topic of error and objective inspiration.

   This helps with your understanding and presentation of the key features of the different views on error and objective inspiration.

T1 Religious figures and sacred texts

> **This section covers AO2 content and skills**

> **Specification content**
> The extent to which the Bible can be regarded as the inspired word of God

Issues for analysis and evaluation

The extent to which the Bible can be regarded as the inspired word of God

Possible line of argument	Critical analysis and evaluation
Many Christians regard the Bible as the word of God – it is 'God-breathed' (2 Timothy 3:16). Some believe the writers wrote only the words spoken to them by God. God spoke directly to the prophets and to Jesus.	This objective view of verbal inspiration surely fails, considering the errors or contradictions in the Bible, for instance two different creation accounts and disputed material at the end of Mark's Gospel.
John Calvin supported the idea of 'accommodation' to explain the historical and scientific errors. The biblical author is trying to communicate at the level of their audience.	Such a view raises questions about the trustworthiness of the Bible, for instance are the miracles historically true or are they merely accommodating to beliefs in New Testament times?
Others argue for a more subjective view in which the writers were inspired by God's work in the world and the life of Jesus. This view sees inspiration as a human rather than a divine action.	This approach would explain the errors and contradictions as well as the outbursts against God in some of the Psalms. However, it does raise the problem of no longer being confident about what the Bible says, since it is written by human beings.
The subjective view of the Bible sees God as the producer rather than one who dictates what is in the Bible. However, errors do not distract from the theological message of God's sovereignty and provision of salvation through faith in Jesus.	If the Bible is the work of human authors (for example Acts 1:1), then why should we be confident that we have the truth about salvation? Paul admits that he is writing some of his thoughts and views rather than those of God.
Is there another way of understanding 'inspiration'? Karl Barth argued that Jesus (and not the Bible) is the word of God. Friedrich Schleiermacher argued that inspiration was about the reader's experience with the text. Some have favoured 'social theories of inspiration'.	These alternative understandings of 'inspiration' imply that other books could equally be 'inspired'. Many Christians claim that the Bible is the truth from God and so reject these alternative views of inspiration.

> **AO2 Activity**
> a Analyse three possible conclusions that could be drawn from the critical analysis and evaluation of the extent to which the Bible can be regarded as the inspired word of God. What are their strengths? Which conclusion do you think is the weakest?
> b Evaluate three lines of argument to show which is the strongest argument. Explain why you find these lines of argument convincing.

Exam practice

Sample question
Evaluate whether the Christian biblical canonical orders are inspired, as opposed to just the texts they contain.

Sample answer
Christians believe, in varying ways, that God inspired the authors of individual books. But to what extent did God inspire the Christian biblical canonical order? The Bible is composed of books, starting with Genesis and ending with Revelation. The issue is whether God established that order of books or whether it was purely a human phenomenon.

Certainly, many Christians believe that the Bible contains the inspired word of God and faithfully records God's word. Therefore, it would seem reasonable to conclude that if the content of the books of the Bible is God-inspired, then the order in which the books are collated in is equally the work of God. That seems to imply that some books are more important than others, or more foundational than others. However, order does not necessarily reflect importance; the first chapter of a book is not necessarily more important than the last chapter. Many Christians see the progressive revealing through the Old Testament of the promise of a Messiah who would save his people. This revelation is made clear and fulfilled in the New Testament, so supports the view that the order of the books is significant.

However, this does not fit in with there being different orders between Bibles. For example, there are different orders in the Jewish and Christian Bibles, with the Hebrew scriptures ending with the books of Ezra/Nehemiah and Chronicles, which seem to indicate that God has fulfilled his promises to Israel after the exile with a new start in Judea. In contrast, the Christian Bibles end their Old Testament with the Minor Prophets, which suggests something entirely different: the sense of anticipation for deliverance. Surely, these differences are better accounted for by human selection rather than by God.

Furthermore, Catholic Bibles contain a group of writings accepted by neither Protestants nor Jewish people – Jewish literature written in Greek in the few hundred years before the opening of the New Testament (for example Tobit, Judith and Wisdom), as well as additions to Daniel and Esther. Some Jewish people and many Christians considered these books inspired, but Jewish believers ultimately rejected them as canonical after the first century.

It seems it is a straight choice between the ordering of the books being a human or divine process. The disagreement on the status of the books supports the argument that the process was human; the belief that it is a divine process is based on the Bible being the word of God and God ordering the books deliberately to shape his revelation that Jesus is the promised Messiah. Overall, there does seem to be a significant disagreement about which books to include and in which order to place them. Even though there is some consensus, the consensus is not wide enough to suggest that the hand of God was at work in ordering the Bible.

This section covers AO2 content and skills

Specification content
Whether the Christian biblical canonical orders are inspired, as opposed to just the texts they contain

News reporter
A good clarification of the issue, making clear the difference between the order of the books being inspired as opposed to the authors being inspired.

Tennis player
Detective
Critical thinker
This answer puts forward an argument, reflects on it and then gives a reply. It is a clear path of thinking through the issue. Some answers tend to give the arguments 'for' and then the arguments 'against'. This answer has a more integrated approach. There is a thread of thinking through and questioning how convincing a particular argument is.

Tennis player
Detective — **Judge**
The answer now focuses on approach with good examples to support the various arguments. A good summary conclusion, consistent with the arguments discussed.

Detective
This paragraph further supports the previous paragraph's argument with good examples.

Judge
This final paragraph clearly spells out the options and reaches a conclusion that is consistent with the rest of the answer. The essay is well exemplified in support of the arguments.

T1 Religious figures and sacred texts

Over to you

Below is a summary of two different points of view concerning the formation of the Bible. It is 150 words long. Your task is to use these two views and lines of argument for an evaluation; however, just to list them is not really evaluating them. Present these two views in a more evaluative style, firstly by condensing each argument and then, secondly, commenting on how effective each one is (weak or strong are good terms to start with). Write about 200 words in total.

Summary

The formation of the Bible can be seen as a haphazard process that makes it easy for it to be seen as a purely human book. Alternatively, there is evidence of a widely held consensus that these are inspired books that come from God. In favour of the first point of view is that there are lost books of the Bible and that the canon was in constant development. Furthermore, there were many books of the Bible that were debated as to their divine status. It took, literally, centuries for believers to agree on the canon. On the other hand, it appears that most believers have agreed on the 'canon within the canon' that have guided the choices for most of the books. There actually has not been significant disagreement on most of the books that compose the Bible. Finally, these books have inspired the faith of believers through the centuries.

When you have completed the task, refer to the band descriptors for A2 (WJEC) or A Level (Eduqas) and, in particular, look at the demands described in the higher band descriptors, which you should be aspiring towards. Ask yourself:

- Is my answer a confident critical analysis and perceptive evaluation of the issue?
- Is my answer a response that successfully identifies and thoroughly addresses the issues that the question raises?

E: The early Church (in Acts of the Apostles)

Make sure you have read and understood the set texts: Acts 2:14–39; 3:12–26.

Some scholars have questioned whether the Christian Church accurately represented Jesus' teaching. When the Church representatives proclaimed their message about Jesus, did they twist and distort his message to suit their purposes?

Herman Samuel Reimarus was the first enlightenment thinker to accuse the disciples of changing the views of Jesus. Reimarus said that Jesus accepted a Jewish viewpoint, popular in his time, that the world was about to end. This is known as Jewish *apocalypticism*. The noun *apocalypse* means 'a revelation' or 'disclosure', and has come to be associated with the sudden end of the world by God in an act of judgement. Reimarus believed that the disciples removed the apocalyptic viewpoint of Jesus, changing his message into timeless and spiritual truths. They did this because the world didn't end and they faked Jesus' resurrection and founded a new religion.

At the heart of the debate is the kerygmata – the proclamation of Jesus' message by the early Church. What was the proclamation and is it trustworthy?

The message of the early Church: the kerygmata

Kerygmata (singular: *kerygma*) is a Greek word meaning 'proclamation' or 'preaching'. It refers to the content and message of the preaching of the early Church, rather than to the actual activity of preaching. It is an announcement, rather than a set of teachings or doctrines. The term is used many times in the New Testament, for example Luke uses it to describe the ministry of Jesus: 'He has sent me to proclaim freedom for the prisoners and recovery of sight for the blind' (Luke 4:18).

The specification uses the plural form (*kerygmata*) because you are asked to study two passages in the Book of Acts. However, the singular term (*kerygma*) will be used in this book, as it is the standard term to refer to the proclamation of the Apostles in the New Testament.

CH Dodd on kerygma

The British New Testament scholar **CH Dodd** said that we should be careful not to confuse kerygma with teaching or with historical facts – though it can include both of these. We should also, he said, not think of the New Testament as a 'memoir' because at its heart it is a bold set of claims that confront its readers with a decision. Finally, he warned about seeing the New Testament as merely a call to moral improvement. The speeches in Acts are about being confronted with truths and experiencing a transformation of our lives.

Acts 2:14–39 and 3:12–26

The Book of Acts shows the progression of the Christian message from Jerusalem, throughout the Roman Empire and then ends with the Gospel message coming to Rome itself. In Acts 2 and 3 we are confronted by the first of many speeches (proclamations) by the Apostles in the Book of Acts. These speeches share the main idea that God's plan for salvation, unfolding through the Jewish scriptures, has reached fulfilment in the life, death and resurrection of Jesus.

This section covers AO1 content and skills

Specification content
The early Church: Its message and format: the kerygmata

Key person
Herman Samuel Reimarus (1694–1768): a German philosopher who denied the supernatural origins of Christianity

Specification content
The kerygmata as presented by CH Dodd, with reference to Acts 2:14–39; 3:12–26

Key person
CH Dodd (1884–1973): a Welsh theologian who identified a basic narrative outline underlying the apostolic message as found in the New Testament letters and in the speeches in Acts

CH Dodd

T1 Religious figures and sacred texts

> **Key quote**
>
> The main burden of the kerygma is that the unprecedented has happened: God has visited and redeemed His people
>
> (CH Dodd)

What makes the speeches in Acts 2 and 3 especially interesting is that these are presented as the first public messages of a tiny group of Jewish Christians in Jerusalem. It is noteworthy that this small movement prevailed and became a major world religion when there were so many other small movements that died out after the first generation.

The main elements of the kerygma

CH Dodd identified six main elements of the kerygma in these speeches; they are announcements that:

1 **the age of fulfilment has dawned:** The Apostles use the words of the Hebrew prophets about the coming of the new age to explain the miracles that the crowds have witnessed

2 **this new age has come about through the ministry, death and resurrection of Jesus:** The power of Jesus is behind these events is confirmed by: (a) his Davidic descent, (b) the works of power during his ministry, (c) God using his unfair death at the hands of men and (d) the raising of Jesus from the dead

3 **Jesus has ascended to the right hand of God:** This confirms that he is the Messianic head of the new Israel

4 **God's Holy Spirit has been poured out on the Church:** It is now the sign of Christ's power and glory

5 **Christ will return to bring the messianic age to its full consummation**

6 **everyone should repent:** Then their sins can be forgiven and they can receive the Holy Spirit to participate in the special, new life of the Church.

The challenges to the kerygmata

Is the Book of Acts a trustworthy historical document?

> **Key quote**
>
> The possibility of eschatological fanaticism was no doubt present in the outlook of the primitive Church, but it was restrained by the essential character of the Gospel as apprehended in experience.
>
> (CH Dodd)

Some scholars have viewed Acts as more a literary product rather than a historical account, with its speeches not having been delivered by Peter, Stephen or Paul but representing summaries of the author's point of view. The main arguments supporting this view are:

- Luke (if this is indeed the author) is a Gentile. Therefore, he was not present at some, or probably any, of the events he is reporting – certainly not for the events of Acts 2 and 3.
- Luke–Acts was probably written in the 80s CE up to 40–50 years after the events reported.

Specification content

The challenges to the kerygmata (with reference to the historical value of the speeches in Acts and the work of Rudolf Bultmann); the adapting of the Christian message to suit the audience

- It seems that the Book of Acts is a highly organised work, which may be evidence that its material has changed from its original form. For instance, there are 11 speeches (*Apostolic kerygma*); each of these has similar elements, and they are the centrepiece of a scene described by the author.
- The language used by the author is more characteristic of Luke–Acts than of what we know of Paul's theology expressed elsewhere in the New Testament. In other words, the 'voice' of Paul in the later speeches of Acts sounds more like the 'voice' of Luke–Acts than it does the 'Paul' of the early letters scholars agree were written by him.
- The events portrayed in the Book of Acts contain reports of miraculous events and sudden, dramatic reversals of points of view, which we associate with ancient literature and legends and not with a modern scientific age.

Many scholars strongly disagree with the assumption that there is no historical value in Acts. The main arguments are:

- The early Church never questioned the Book of Acts. Since Acts reports on public events known to many, surely if they had been misrepresented there would have been an outcry from those who knew of different traditions. In fact, the Book is affirmed by the Muratorian Canon, Tertullian, Clement, Origen and others.
- There is a clear tradition that Luke accompanied Paul on his missionary journeys in Colossians 4:14, Philemon 24 and 2 Timothy 4:11. Thus, he would have had access to first-hand accounts of the events he describes.
- In terms of the style and language Luke uses, it is common for any writer to arrange material in a certain order – this does not mean that the material does not have historical roots. It is also expected that the author will bring their own vocabulary and language into their writing.
- We can account for the differences between the presentation of Paul in Acts and of Paul's own writings by Paul having different aims in his speeches to the public in Acts than he did for his letters, which were more pastoral in nature.
- When CH Dodd examined the letters of Paul, he found they contain the main elements of the kerygma as they are presented in Acts.
- Dodd also argues that the author of Acts is a careful historian.

These arguments led many to conclude that Luke was personally acquainted with the Apostles and witnessed their preaching; he had no need to make anything up because he had direct access to the messages of the early Church. He had spent time with Paul and he knew those who had witnessed the birth of the Church in Jerusalem.

Is the kerygma irrelevant?

Some have argued that both the kerygma of the Apostles and Jesus are irrelevant since the historical Jesus believed that the world would end in his lifetime with the sudden and cataclysmic coming of God. In other words, we should view Jesus as an apocalyptic or **eschatological** figure (eschatology refers to the study of the 'end times').

According to this view, Jesus' aim was to bring his own generation to God before the coming judgement – he never envisioned that he was founding an ongoing movement, a Church that would endure for centuries. Jesus himself said, 'There are some standing here who will not taste death before

> **Key term**
>
> **eschatology:** the study of end things, including the soul, death, resurrection, the final judgement, immortality, heaven and hell

they see the Son of Man coming in his kingdom' (Matthew 16:28). There is evidence that the early Church also believed this: 'You too, be patient and stand firm, because the Lord's coming is near' (James 5:8). This may suggest that in the Book of Acts, the early Church was still in the grip of this apocalyptic view and believed the world was about to end.

The theologian and medical missionary Albert Schweitzer (1875–1965) declared that the one thing that could be known about the historical Jesus was the very thing that made him irrelevant for today: his belief in the imminent end of the world. The Apostles were awaiting Jesus' return and perhaps were beginning to lose hope as time passed.

CH Dodd: the relevance of the kerygma

CH Dodd said that the preaching of Jesus and the life of the early Church were much more than just concern about the possible imminent end of the world. In fact, most of it was concerned with the experience of forgiveness and living in the power of the Holy Spirit in the present, rather than the future. Early Christians were focused more on the joy they had in their experience of the risen Jesus and in the community of the Church than they were about the life to come. This is why the Church did not die out but grew as time went on.

Dodd said that Jesus himself believed not only in the coming of God at the end of the world, but that God had already broken into the world through his own life and ministry. Dodd calls this **realised eschatology**. In other words, Christians do not have to wait for the end of the world to experience the fullness of God – this can be 'realised' now, in the present. The focus of the early Church was on the power that God brings with forgiveness, community and renewed hope, much more than on the theme of the world's sudden demise.

However, there are apocalyptic passages in the New Testament, such as Mark 13, Matthew 24 and the Book of Revelation. Dodd said that some of these passages should be viewed as interpretations of the challenges that come to all people when they are faced with the power of the kerygma. Others would argue that these apocalyptic passages are pictures about final judgement, which is part of the preaching message and the kerygma. For instance, in Paul's speech to the Athenians he says: 'For God has set a day when he will judge the world with justice by the man he has appointed. He has given proof of this to everyone by raising him from the dead' (Acts 17:31).

At the heart of Christian belief is the saving power of Jesus, which can be experienced in this life. The kerygma is what Jesus himself announced in Mark 1:15: 'The time has come ['realised']. The Kingdom of God has come near. Repent and believe the good news'. Jesus and the Apostles, Dodd claims, were united by the same kerygma, a message relevant whether or not the end of the world was about to occur.

Bultmann; hearing kerygma in the myth

German theologian Rudolf Bultmann had an existentialist approach to the Christian faith. He was motivated to make the Christian message intelligible and relevant and, like Dodd, believed that the kerygma was an announcement rather than a doctrine or a teaching.

However, he saw the New Testament as full of myths that are irrelevant to people living in a modern age. There are three possible responses to the mythological language in the Bible:

- Believe the myths of the Bible literally.

> **Key term**
>
> **realised eschatology:** the notion that Christians can experience in the present a quality of life they expect after death

- 'Cut out' the mythological sections from the Bible and take a rationalistic approach, where Christianity is about moral behaviour.
- Explore the myths to discover the truths about humanity and existence they are expressing through the mythological language.

Key quote

We must ask whether the eschatological preaching and the mythological sayings as a whole contain a still deeper meaning which is concealed under the cover of mythology.

(R Bultmann)

Bultmann took this third approach, trying to find the underlying truth (the kerygma) expressed by the myth. He believed that 'an existentialist interpretation is necessary, since the real purpose of myth is not to present an objective picture of the world as it is, but to express a person's understanding of themselves in the world in which they live' (WM Arnett).

Bultmann saw Christ's life and death, as proclaimed in the kerygma, as an existential event that formed the catalyst for the existential crisis that reconciles humanity to God. The kerygma confronts individuals with an existential decision about their faith. An individual is called upon to decide for or against obedience in faith.

Key quote

The proclamation is not about … a doctrine or a dogma, but the opening up, through God's act, of the possibility of having faith.

(R Bultmann)

Bultmann called this method of interpretation of the New Testament, which tries to recover the deeper meaning behind the mythological conceptions, *demythologising* (see page 20). Therefore, the truth of the kerygma expressed in a mythical world-picture needs to be demythologised to understand its universal truth and its significance for faith.

However, demythologising is not one stage in a progression from a mythologised kerygma to a demythologised, naked, 'pure' kerygma. The kerygma will always be expressed for each generation in a particular cultural form, with its particular myths. The purpose is to translate the kerygma from an alien world-picture into a familiar one, which means that the task of demythologising must continue as long as the Christian faith endures.

The mythologies Bultmann identified

Bultmann identified two main mythologies at work in the New Testament:

- **The apocalyptic myth:** of the sudden and cataclysmic end of the world, brought about by the miraculous power of God.
- **The high-status-of-Jesus myth:** of a pre-existing being, born of the Virgin Mary; a heavenly being who descended to Earth to redeem humanity.

Key quote

Theological propositions – even those of the New Testament – can never be the object of faith…

(R Bultmann)

> **Key term**
>
> **Gnosticism:** a movement that taught that we are trapped in an evil material world; we must find special knowledge to be redeemed

Of the apocalyptic myth, Bultmann claims that history has triumphed over it, since 2000 years later the world still exists.

The high-status-of-Jesus myth he sees as having Gnostic influences. **Gnosticism** pictured all the created world in a spiritual battle. Each person is essentially a 'spark of light' that has become trapped in the world through demonic forces. A being of light has been sent down from the highest God to bring people special knowledge (*gnosis* is the Greek word for 'knowledge') so that our 'sparks' can be liberated. Bultmann believed that Christians adapted this mythology to their own beliefs in Jesus, and this led them to believing in a high status of Jesus.

Bultmann contended that only faith in the kerygma, or *proclamation*, of the New Testament was necessary for Christian faith; not any particular facts regarding the historical Jesus. He argued that when the disciples encountered Jesus, they had something new awakened in them – not beliefs in doctrines about Jesus, but an experience of God. This is because the kerygma itself expresses some basic truths about humanity:

- There is a transcendent power in the universe.
- It is false to think that we can and should control life.
- Our plans and powers are finite.
- There is forgiveness.
- It is possible to find a spirit of openness to the future.

When the Apostles proclaimed their message, individuals felt a power behind their words; a power we can still hear today. The most important aspect of Acts 2 and 3 for Bultmann is expressed in 2:37: 'When the people heard this, they were cut to the heart and said to Peter and the other apostles, "Brothers, what shall we do?"'.

The verse indicates there was a deep personal confrontation for those who heard the words of the Apostles. They did not want to analyse the truths they heard, study them or explore their historical foundations – but, instead, they made a decision. For Bultmann, the kerygma is a personal message that proclaims truth and elicits a response. It is the proclamation of salvation to a fallen humanity in terms of the possibility for authentic human existence. Above all, the kerygma is the event of God's personal address to sinners. Because the kerygma is above all an event of address here and now, it cannot simply be equated with any permanent formulation of it. Each generation will have to express it in its own cultural form or myth, so that it speaks to that generation.

Criticisms of Bultmann

- There are good reasons to believe that Christian claims about Jesus are historically reliable. Many would argue that to remove the historical Jesus challenges the very foundation of Christianity. For Bultmann, the cross simply defines God's love, but achieves nothing more than what God has always done.
- He rejects the supernatural and miraculous and reduces Christianity to a religious humanism.
- He interprets from the standpoint of existentialism and demythologises to fit the pattern.
- He creates a new myth for 'modern people'. That is, he has replaced one set of myths (apocalyptic and Gnostic) with another (his ideas about meaning).

- His existentialist interpretation suggests that Christianity is redundant since there are other ways to get the truths about the meaning of our existence than in the kerygma.
- The Book of Acts is about public declaration of the good news and a public response leading to the formation of a new community. Bultmann has distorted the setting by turning the kerygma into a personal and individualistic message.

Summary

- The kerygmata (singular kerygma) refers to the content and message of the preaching of the early Church.
- CH Dodd identified six elements of the kerygma:
    1. The age of fulfilment has dawned.
    2. This has happened through the life, death and resurrection of Jesus.
    3. Jesus is confirmed as Messiah by ascending to the right hand of God.
    4. God's Spirit has been poured out on the Church.
    5. Christ will return.
    6. Everyone should repent.
- There is debate as to whether the Book of Acts is historically reliable or whether it is a literary product.
- Albert Schweitzer argued that Jesus mistakenly believed in the imminent end of the world, while CH Dodd said that Jesus and the early Church believed in realised eschatology.
- Bultmann argued that the truth of the kerygma expressed in a mythical world-picture needs to be demythologised to understand its universal truth and its significance for faith.
- Bultmann's existentialist interpretation meant that faith did not rely on historical facts about Jesus but on a personal experience of God that demanded a response.
- The counterargument is that to remove the historical Jesus is to challenge the very basis of Christianity.

AO1 Activity

a   By referring to Acts 2:37, 'Now when they heard this, they were cut to the heart ...', explain how:
   i   Dodd
   ii Bultmann
   would explain this reaction to the kerygma.

   This helps you develop the ability to select and present the key, relevant features of Dodd's and Bultmann's understanding of the kerygma.

b   Read Acts 3:12–26. List all those elements that refer to the supernatural. Explain how Bultmann would defend the relevance of these passages even though he rejected the supernatural.

   This helps you provide examples from the kerygma of how Bultmann interprets aspects of the kerygma that are expressed in supernatural language.

T1 Religious figures and sacred texts

> **This section covers AO2 content and skills**

> **Specification content**
> The extent to which the kerygmata (within the areas of Acts studied) are of any value for Christians today

Issues for analysis and evaluation

The extent to which the kerygmata (within the areas of Acts studied) are of any value for Christians today

Possible line of argument	Critical analysis and evaluation
It is recorded in the first public speeches in Acts 2 and 3. It reveals the first glimpse into the theology of the early Christians.	The description of the early Church seems very different from most Churches today. Acts refers to mass conversions and miraculous healings, which must raise questions as to its relevancy for today.
The growth of the Pentecostal Church shows that the content of the kerygma is believed and experienced today.	Many Christians have moved away from non-scientific beliefs, such as miracles and the supernatural.
It is a model for the Church's message of salvation.	It is mythological language that needs interpreting for the twenty-first century.
In a multicultural society where many faiths exist, it is vital for the Christian message to be heard, as many Christians regard it as revealing the only way to God.	Many Christians accept that the different faiths are just different pathways to God, and are of equal importance as the Christian message of the kerygmata.
The kerygmata is the word of God and therefore of value.	The kerygmata contains a belief in the imminent return of Jesus. This wrong belief points to the unreliability of the content of the kerygmata and so is of little value.
	To highlight these speeches is to suggest that some passages in the Bible are more important than others. But if all the Bible is the word of God, then it lessens the value of the other passages.
CH Dodd argued that the end times were not merely in the future but could be experienced (or realised) for the Church today (realised eschatology) – so the kerygma is not wrong or outdated.	Rudolph Bultmann saw the kerygma as bound up with myths and needs to be understood in terms of Christian existentialism. It was the experience, not the words, that led people to be committed to the Church.

> **AO2 Activity**
> a Analyse three possible conclusions that could be drawn from the critical analysis and evaluation of the extent to which the kerygmata (within the areas of Acts studied) are of any value for Christians today. What are their strengths? Which conclusion do you think is the weakest?
> b Evaluate three lines of argument that persuaded you to think that this is the weakest conclusion. Think of any questions you could raise in response to these arguments.

Exam practice

Sample question
Evaluate whether the speeches in Acts have any historical value.

Sample answer

An important factor to consider in addressing this issue is to identify the author of the speeches in Acts. Tradition certainly seems to support it being Luke, the same author as the Gospel of Luke. According to Luke's Gospel, the author makes clear he is writing an account using material that has been handed down from eyewitnesses and that he has 'carefully investigated everything from the beginning'. At best, it still means his work is second hand, rather than being an eyewitness himself.

Although there is probably a 40–50-year gap between the events and the writing of Acts, early Christian sources vouch for its authenticity – such as the Muratorian Canon, which is dated to the second century. It was confidently placed into the biblical canon.

Perhaps an even stronger claim to historical value is that Luke was a travel companion to Paul, so Luke could have had access to eyewitnesses to those events. Indeed, the speeches would have been heard by many and well known in a Church and culture that had a tradition and ability to hold an accurate verbal tradition. The accounts in Acts would have been open to challenge, but there seems no evidence of them being disputed.

However, it has to be acknowledged that when the speeches are compared to Paul's other writings, there does seem to be a difference in style, vocabulary and subject matter. In response, it could be argued that Paul, in his letters, was writing to a different audience and for a different purpose. Also, Luke, as author of Acts, may have phrased things in his own style, but this would not preclude its content being historically accurate.

CH Dodd identified six elements in the speeches of Paul in Acts. He referred to the content as *kerygma* ('proclamation'). When Paul's letters are examined, these six elements are present and form the basis of the beliefs that he preached to the churches he wrote to in his letters. This does add further weight to the historical value of the speeches in Acts.

Rudolf Bultmann drew attention to the worldview and mythological viewpoint contained in the speeches and the supernatural events that Luke records happening leading up to the speeches (for example Pentecost and the speaking in tongues, and healings). Such events seem far removed from our scientific understanding of the workings of the universe and apocalyptic descriptions of the end of the world.

Bultmann focused on the energy and power of the early Church and the encounter that people had with Jesus that led them to renewed hope and vision. He felt this is something that could be experienced today, whether or not the speeches have any historical value.

This section covers AO2 content and skills

Specification content
Whether the speeches in Acts have any historical value

Tennis player
Detective
Critical thinker

Having put across an argument for Acts having historical value, it is immediately challenged as Luke was not an eyewitness to all the events in Acts. There is good reference to the text of Acts.

Detective

The challenge is dealt with at some length, showing very good knowledge. The answer develops a case to support the historical value of Acts.

Tennis player
Critical thinker
Detective

A doubt is then raised but is swiftly answered; the answer then resumes the argument supporting historical value.

Detective

The answer now introduces reference to a scholar and further develops support for historical value.

Tennis player
Detective **Judge**
Critical thinker

The final paragraph refers to Bultmann, who challenged the historical value on the grounds that Acts reflected a non-scientific worldview. However, through his existentialist beliefs, Bultmann argued that Acts was of value even if not of historical value. The final conclusion has been argued consistently throughout the answer.

T1 Religious figures and sacred texts

Overall, it is a good answer. It has a consistent argument supporting historical value and has scholarly references. There is good knowledge displayed, with relevant examples supporting the arguments.

However, the weight of the evidence must surely be that Luke was an accurate author who travelled with Paul at times and researched his material well. Therefore, it is reasonable to believe that the speeches of Acts are of historical value.

Over to you

Below is a brief summary of two different points of view concerning the historical value of the speeches in Acts. You want to use these two views and lines of argument for an evaluation. However, they need further reasons and evidence for support to develop the argument fully. Re-present these two views in a fully evaluative style by adding further reasons and evidence that link to their arguments. Aim for a further 100 words.

Summary

There are many reasons to accept the speeches in Acts 2 and 3 as having a historical basis. First, all the early Church Fathers accept the reports in Acts as true. Furthermore, if Luke had fabricated these speeches, there would have been many in the early Church who could have refuted this. In fact, it would not have served Luke's purposes to invent these stories, as he was attempting to write a history of the early Church. Luke would have had access to eyewitnesses to these events.

On the other hand, most scholars believe that Acts was not written until many decades after the events it describes. Luke is a Gentile and not a Jewish Christian, so therefore represents a different part of the Church than the one described. There is a similarity between the speeches in Acts that betrays the influence of an editor. Finally, the presence of the miraculous is something that we do not accept today as pointing to a historically accurate document.

When you have completed the task, refer to the band descriptors for A2 (WJEC) or A Level (Eduqas) and, in particular, look at the demands described in the higher band descriptors, which you should be aspiring towards. Ask yourself:

- Is my answer a confident critical analysis and perceptive evaluation of the issue?
- Is my answer a response that successfully identifies and thoroughly addresses the issues that the question raises?

F: Two views of Jesus

Nicholas T Wright: worldviews make a difference

A *worldview* is a collection of attitudes, values, stories and expectations about the world around us, which inform our every thought and action – it is the way a culture looks at the world.

English New Testament scholar Nicholas T Wright believes that we have all been affected by an **enlightenment** worldview. According to this story, only sense perceptions give us sure and certain knowledge about the world. In this context, history and faith are split off from each other, with *history* as part of a public discussion about evidence; *faith* is considered only as a private realm of personal, spiritual beliefs. One of the unfortunate things about this story, for Wright, is that it forces people either to live in the 'attic' of a faith that is divorced from history (faith becomes highly personal and less attached to public life) or the 'dungeon' of history (history is a sterile activity in which we find no meaning or importance).

Wright argues that an enlightenment worldview is completely different from the worldview we find at work in the New Testament. There, we find belief in a god who cares passionately about the world in general and the Jewish people in particular. God establishes a **covenant** with God's people and thinks that it is important that people live out their faith. It is a worldview where history, faith, politics and spirituality are not separated from one another. Jesus was born into that worldview and speaks from it.

> **Key quote**
>
> … worldviews, and the stories that characterise them … claim to make sense of the whole of reality
>
> **(NT Wright)**

Critical realism

In the enlightenment worldview, we think that facts or sense perception come before a worldview. Wright questions this assumption. He believes that the worldview precedes everything: it is the lens through which we make sense of data. He argues that this modern enlightenment worldview can lead to a positive knowledge of the world, as long as any claims for knowledge can be verified through the senses. However, it can also lead to a pessimistic view of human knowledge, in that anything we think we know in the external world is only knowledge of our sense data, since physical objects and the external world are only mental constructions out of phenomenal appearances (sense data). So reality is unknowable.

> **Key quote**
>
> History, then, prevents faith becoming fantasy.
>
> **(NT Wright)**

Wright combines insights from each of these views. He argues for **critical realism**, which claims that there are objects that exist apart from ourselves that we can understand through sense experience (*realism*), yet we can distort our understanding via our own standpoints and biases (so we need to be *critical* of our realism).

This section covers AO1 content and skills

Specification content

A comparison of the work of two key scholars, including their views of Jesus with reference to their different methods of studying Jesus: John Dominic Crossan and NT Wright

Wright: Jesus the true Messiah; critical realism; texts as 'the articulation of worldviews'; seeks to find the best explanation for the traditions found in the Gospels

Key terms

enlightenment: a European intellectual movement emphasising reason as the basis of knowledge over religious revelation and superstition

covenant: an agreement between two or more parties based on obedience and involving promises

Key term

critical realism: the idea that there are real objects beyond ourselves, but that we know these objects through our own experiences; therefore, we need to be critical about the objectivity of our point of view

T1 Religious figures and sacred texts

> **Key quote**
>
> ... the only access we have to this reality lies along the spiralling path of appropriate dialogue or conversation between the knower and the thing known.
>
> (NT Wright)

We bring our own biases to anything we know, the conditioning of our psychological, historical, sociological and political context. We therefore need to be critical about the objectivity of our point of view.

The first step to finding the truth is recognising this fundamental insight that a worldview precedes facts. Instead of 'writing off' other points of view (for instance those we find in the New Testament), we must accept that there might be truth beyond our own viewpoint. There is no such thing as a completely neutral detached observer.

The next step is to be willing to enter a dialogue between our point of view and the object we are encountering. In this dialogue, we may become aware of our own biases and of truth in a new story. As a result, our worldview:

- might be confirmed
- might need to be modified
- might need to be abandoned.

Therefore, Wright advocates such a process as we study the life and teachings of Jesus.

Wright's view of Jesus: the true Messiah

Entering into this process of dialogue means, on the one hand, that faith in Jesus must meet the facts of history. Christians cannot build images of Jesus that are divorced from information gleaned from historical sources. On the other hand, Wright says, we must not assume that history will disprove Christian claims. We must not turn historical scepticism into a paranoia that rules out the possibility that events have happened in history that can be of meaning and value for our lives today. When Wright enters a historical study of Jesus, he finds these points significant:

> **Key quote**
>
> ... the Gospels are what they are precisely because their authors thought the events they were recording – all of them, not just some – actually happened ... These stories were never designed to express or embody a dehistoricised spirituality ...
>
> (NT Wright)

- **Jesus was a Jewish prophet announcing the Kingdom of God:** This should be the starting point for any historical study of Jesus: his Jewish context, the perception of those around him that he was a prophet, and the political declaration of the coming of the Kingdom of God. Wright claims that Jesus should be seen as someone who was initiating a movement, not a 'wandering preacher giving sermons'.
- **Eschatological expectation:** Jesus shared the view that Jewish people were the chosen people of God and that history was going somewhere. He believed the Kingdom was breaking into history. The Kingdom was about to come.

- **Messiah:** There were other Jewish figures at the turn of the first millennium announcing the Kingdom of God (Judas the Galilean and Simeon ben Kosiba). Many people considered these figures to be messiahs; Jesus acted and spoke in ways that showed he believed that he was the **Messiah** – the one in whom God would accomplish his decisive purpose.
- **A Messiah who gave his life:** The Jewish Messiah was popularly thought of as being a victorious figure. His defeat was therefore the sign that he was not the Messiah. However, there are at least two important facts about Jesus' life that reveal he was reinterpreting the meaning of *Messiah*:
    1. He rejected violent revolutionary behaviour.
    2. He drew upon Jewish traditions about God using the suffering of his people to bring about redemption.

Wright believes that Jesus thought of his own death as a part of his messianic task.

All the other movements around messiahs of Jesus' era ended with that figure's death. Not so with Jesus, claims Wright. This means that the reinterpretation of messiahship to include the idea of dying for sins was an idea that caught on. Jesus' resurrection confirmed to his followers that he was the true Messiah. Furthermore, the writers of the Gospels were convinced that these events were historical events: Israel's God was acting in history through the life, death and resurrection of Jesus. Wright argues that due to the intention of writers to present history in a public context, and because of the compelling nature of the claims themselves, we should take the Gospels seriously.

Crossan's method

John Dominic Crossan is a historian and New Testament scholar who has come to views about Jesus very different from NT Wright's. Crossan attempts to find this historical Jesus by pursuing three areas:

1. **Cross-cultural anthropology:** What we can know about the ancient Mediterranean culture, agrarian society, gender relations, colonialisms, ethnicity, class, taxes, and so on at the time of Jesus.
2. **Jewish and Greco-Roman history:** The land where Jesus lived was a colony of the Roman Empire and there are many sources that can be used to understand what Jewish life under Roman rule might have been like. The challenge of this kind of study is that historical sources are mainly written by elite, wealthy and powerful males. Therefore, we have to think critically to attempt to understand what life might have been like for lower classes or peasants.
3. **Literary and textual study** of the New Testament and books outside the New Testament that might also inform us about Jesus' life.

Jesus is a Mediterranean peasant

Crossan sees Jesus as a Mediterranean Jewish peasant. Each of these three areas of study is very important. To know what it means for Jesus to be Jewish involves literary and textual study; studying Jewish and Greco-Roman history gives insight into Jesus' life and teaching as a peasant; and understanding social and psychological relationships in the Mediterranean context at that time through studying cross-cultural anthropology sheds valuable light on Jesus' life and times.

> **Key term**
>
> **Messiah (literally 'anointed one'):** a figure who is expected to unite Jewish people and save them from their oppressors, ushering in an era of peace

> **Specification content**
>
> Crossan: Jesus the social revolutionary; using apocryphal gospels; seeing Jesus as a product of his time; what the words of Jesus would have meant in Jesus' time

> **Key person**
>
> **John Dominic Crossan (b. 1934):** an Irish-American New Testament scholar and a former Catholic priest; he argued for a non-eschatological view of Jesus, and saw more value in some non-canonical gospels as superior and earlier than the canonical ones

John Dominic Crossan

When it comes to working with texts that appear to report directly on Jesus' life, Crossan has two main strategies:

1. To use only materials that he dates between 30 CE and 60 CE Crossan considers the four Gospels reached their final form after 60 CE, so he is cautious to discern between earlier and later layers in the Gospels.
2. Never to base any insight on Jesus' life that has only a single independent attestation. That is, there needs to be more than one early source for the same saying or event before Crossan will consider it possible evidence for Jesus' life.

Using apocryphal Gospels

Crossan believes that there are other texts that may provide sources for the life of Jesus independent of the New Testament: the **apocryphal Gospels**. This is the term given to non-canonical Gospels rejected by the Christian Church because they are considered heretical, legendary or of only secondary importance. Many of these Gospels are also called *pseudepigrapha* ('falsely inscribed') because they are written by anonymous authors who gave the name of an Apostle to their writings. These Gospels, in their present *form*, are from the second to fourth centuries BCE, dating much later than the majority of the New Testament writings. Some, such as the **Gospel of Thomas** and the *Apocryphon of James*, are found in the Nag Hammadi library, a collection discovered in the Nag Hammadi valley in Egypt in 1945. This collection dates from the fourth century and reflects a view called *Gnosticism* – that truth from the universe is known through secret knowledge (see page 48). Other apocryphal Gospels, such as the *Gospel of the Hebrews*, are preserved in the quotations of Church Fathers.

However, the Church and many New Testament scholars believe that these Gospels neither give reliable information on the life of Jesus nor independent sayings from Jesus. American John P Meier (1942–2022), who was regarded as one of the leading scholars of the historical Jesus and early Christianity, commented that what we see in these later documents are 'imaginative Christians reflecting popular piety and legend, and Gnostic Christians developing a mystical speculative system'. Needless to say, Crossan disagreed.

Key terms

apocryphal Gospels: writings about Jesus not accepted by the Church; some exist as complete documents, others as fragments or as quotations in early Christian writings

Gospel of Thomas: a book of 114 sayings of Jesus in the fourth century CE, discovered in Egypt in 1945

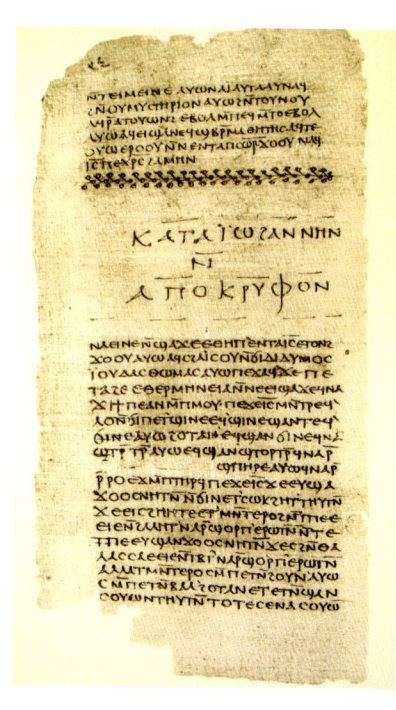

The Nag Hammadi Codex II, which includes the Gospel of Thomas

Key quote

I understand the virginal conception of Jesus to be a confessional statement about Jesus' status and not a biological statement about Mary's body.

(JD Crossan)

Crossan believes that even though many of these sources are later than the New Testament, they may contain traditions that are independent of the New Testament. Also, he believes that there may be early layers within some of these books that predate the four Gospels.

Q and the Gospel of Thomas

Crossan believes that there are two Gospels that should especially concern everyone who wants to know about the historical Jesus:

1. **'Q' (based on the German word *Quelle*, meaning 'source'):** This is not actually an apocryphal Gospel, but is 'hidden' in Matthew and Luke. Scholars have long thought that behind the shared sayings in Matthew and Luke is a source they both used; a simple collection of sayings from Jesus. Crossan believes that this is a good source for giving information

on the historical Jesus because it predates the Gospels and does not contain birth narratives, resurrection narratives or other material that Crossan feels may have been added later by Christians but does not stem from the historical Jesus.

2. **The Gospel of Thomas:** This Gospel, like Q, is a collection of sayings (114) attributed to Jesus without a birth or resurrection narrative. Crossan argues that the Gospel of Thomas dates from a much earlier period because a list of sayings is what we might expect from an early attempt to remember Jesus, and also because several fragments from the Gospel of Thomas may pre-date the four Gospels.

Crossan's picture of Jesus

Crossan rejects the view that the birth and resurrection narratives happened in history. He sees them as later additions that expressed the importance of Jesus for his followers and, in the case of the resurrection, established community leadership after the crucifixion. The reason that Jesus' movement continued after his death has nothing to do with the miraculous 'bookends' of his life, but with other factors you can see in the earliest layers of tradition:

- **He intended a social revolution:** It appears that Jesus may have begun as an apocalyptic preacher, following John the Baptist's example, but that he did not stay this way. Instead of staying in the desert and living as an **ascetic**, calling for God's judgement on the world, Jesus became known for sharing meals with others – even the gossip about him reflects this: 'Here is a glutton and a drunkard, a friend of tax collectors and sinners' (Matthew 11:19).

- **He advocated a Kingdom lifestyle:** Crossan believes that Jesus turned from an apocalyptic future to the idea that the Kingdom of God can be experienced now through a wise lifestyle that even peasants could live out. This would lead to an open community without distinction of gender status. Jesus had a dream of a just and equal world.

- **He served at an open table:** A study of the ancient Mediterranean world (or almost any culture) reveals that sharing food involves a complex set of rules to do with maintaining and reinforcing social boundaries. Jesus' pattern was to disrupt those boundaries by eating with people regardless of gender, rank or social acceptability; this is preserved in his teaching about inviting those off the street to the table.

- **He performed miracles of social healing:** Rather than seeing Jesus' miracles of healing as medical cures, we should understand that the people healed were viewed as impure and were socially ostracised. Jesus healed illnesses without curing the disease by welcoming outcasts back into society and encouraging his followers to do the same. In this way, he challenged traditions both within his religion and wider society – and awakened criticism and fear about this 'Kingdom of God'.

> **Key term**
>
> **ascetic:** someone who lives a sparse and disciplined lifestyle

> **Key quote**
>
> Here is the heart of the Jesus movement, a shared egalitarianism of spiritual (healing) and material (eating) resources.
>
> (JD Crossan)

> **Key quote**
>
> ... Jesus, who did not and could not cure that disease or any other one, healed the poor man's illness by refusing to accept the disease's ritual uncleanness and social ostracisation ...
>
> (JD Crossan)

T1 Religious figures and sacred texts

- **He practised an itinerant lifestyle:** Jesus kept on the move to prevent individuals and villages from profiting from his activity. In fact, Jesus wanted others to become itinerant teacher-healers as well, encouraging them to stay on the move and introduce others to the Kingdom lifestyle.
- **He can be compared to the Cynics:** *Cynicism* was a Greek philosophical movement pre-dating Jesus that flouted basic human social codes and ordinary cultural values. Cynics rejected a materialistic way of life, and were often itinerant, carrying as few possessions as possible. However, they operated in urban centres and were largely individualistic. Jesus, by contrast, was active in rural areas and was dedicated to growing a community with like-minded values.

When Jesus was put to death, these ideas lived on in many of his followers – they experienced the continuing 'power' of Jesus as they lived his lifestyle, without the need to experience the physical resurrection of Jesus. Yet, at the same time, some of his followers were changing his ideas to modes of power and authority more familiar in a Greco-Roman world. This included having clear leaders in the Church and changing the open meal to a closed Eucharist ruled over by an 'approved' authority. Later on, Constantine became a 'Christian' emperor and presided over an all-male clergy who, in turn, helped him unite a Christian kingdom. For Crossan, nothing could be more opposed to Jesus' lifestyle of radical equality.

Summary

- Wright and Crossan argue for two very different views of Jesus.
- Wright's approach is critical realism, and regards the Gospels as reliable historical accounts.
- Jesus believed he was the Messiah, but reinterpreted its meaning with the idea of a sacrificial death.
- Crossan's approach sees the Gospels as non-historical accounts, and he favours instead the non-canonical gospels and 'Q'.
- Crossan sees Jesus as a Mediterranean Jewish peasant and a social revolutionary who challenged Mediterranean culture with its complex rules around social boundaries.

AO1 Activity

a Explain why NT Wright thinks critical realism is the right approach to evaluating a worldview.

This helps you develop the ability to select and present the key, relevant features of critical realism and ensure that you are making accurate use of specialist language and vocabulary in context.

b On small revision cards, summarise the key reasons for Crossan concluding that Jesus is best described as a Mediterranean Jewish peasant. Support this view with extracts from quotations.

This helps you select the key, relevant information for an answer to a question that expects knowledge and understanding of Crossan's view of Jesus.

Issues for analysis and evaluation
The validity of using critical realism to understand Jesus

Possible line of argument	Critical analysis and evaluation
NT Wright applies critical realism to understand the historical Jesus so that we must be open to challenge our worldview.	Science and the testimony of sense experience is how we arrive at our worldview. It is tried and tested and has led to great technological achievements.
Wright argues that in the West we have largely abandoned the supernatural worldview of the New Testament, but such assumptions need to be challenged.	There has always been dialogue between science and religion. The result has been the rejection of the supernatural world of the New Testament after a long period of challenge – exactly what Wright demanded!
Wright defends pursuing a critical realism approach since if we can trust only our sense experience then it suggests we can't be sure of anything beyond it!	Even if we acknowledge that we understand reality only through our own point of view, it is then quite a leap to accept the realities that Jesus spoke of.
There is another way to understand the New Testament: John Dominic Crossan draws on historical, anthropological and textual studies that focus on the time of Jesus, including apocryphal Gospels.	This explains miracles in sociological and psychological terms that he refers to as social miracles. Jesus is best understood as a social revolutionary. Therefore, there is no challenge to a scientific worldview that rejects the supernatural.
Wright challenges Crossan's approach, arguing that it is closed-minded. We should remain humble about our claims about the truth of reality since we look at things through the lenses of our culture and experience.	Crossan supports his views by arguing that the document 'Q' (made up of sayings) lies behind the layers of the New Testament and this has no supernatural elements in it. This document is consistent with our present understanding of a non-supernatural reality.
Wright appeals to the testimony in the Gospels and the growth of the Christian Church.	However, many would accuse Wright of not being critical enough about the Gospels and their historical reliability. He comes from a position of faith, having been raised in the Christian 'story'.
Wright sees critical realism as the path to finding the balance between faith and history.	Crossan doesn't assume that the supernatural cannot occur. He just doesn't find any evidence and so has no reason to reject a post-enlightenment worldview.

> **This section covers AO2 content and skills**

> **Specification content**
> The validity of using critical realism to understand Jesus

> **AO2 Activity**
> a Analyse three possible conclusions that could be drawn from the critical analysis and evaluation of the validity of using critical realism to understand Jesus. What are their strengths? Which conclusion do you think is the strongest?
> b Evaluate three lines of argument that persuade you to think that this is the strongest conclusion. What questions can you raise in response to these arguments?

T1 Religious figures and sacred texts

This section covers AO2 content and skills

Specification content
The validity of using apocryphal Gospels to understand Jesus

News reporter
Tennis player
Detective

The answer clearly sets out the two different views about the sources of the life of Jesus. It makes good reference to the scholar JD Crossan, explaining his support of using the apocryphal Gospels and why the Church rejected them.

Detective

This paragraph cites a number of good, clear arguments defending Crossan's views, concluding that the presentation of Jesus as a wise teacher better fits our contemporary study of history than that presented by the New Testament Gospels.

Tennis player
Philosopher

This paragraph gives a response to Crossan, citing another scholar (N.T. Wright). It raises some questions as to the extent the New Testament Gospels do actually contain an accurate account.

Tennis player
Detective
Critical thinker

The answer considers further arguments of Crossan's, posing questions as to how convincing they are.

Exam practice

Sample question
Evaluate the validity of using apocryphal Gospels to understand Jesus.

Sample answer

The Church has based its understanding of the life of Jesus on the documents that make up the New Testament – namely, the four Gospels, Acts of the Apostles and the epistles of the New Testament. However, John Dominic Crossan draws attention to other documents that also claim to provide information about the historical Jesus. These documents include the apocryphal Gospels that the Church rejected for inclusion in the canon because it considered them heretical or of secondary importance. All of them are dated from the second to the fourth centuries, and so much later than the books of the New Testament. In addition, most of them exist only as fragments or quotations preserved in other, even later writings. So, given these facts, it is hard to see why they should be considered when attempting to understand Jesus.

In reply, Crossan argues that these later documents reflect traditions independent of mainstream Christianity and may well contain earlier layers or views. Crossan particularly refers to the Gospel of Thomas as an apocryphal Gospel because it is a complete gospel of 114 sayings and presents Jesus as a teacher of wisdom, without any reference to a birth or resurrection narrative. In addition, an early fragment of this fourth-century document has been found that suggests that this Gospel could be dated earlier. This image of Jesus, Crossan argues, presents Jesus as a wise teacher rather than some supernatural miracle-worker, which better fits our contemporary study of history and is much more believable than the view of Jesus in the Gospels.

Not surprisingly, this view and approach has been challenged, especially by conservative scholars such as NT Wright. He warns against a scientific worldview that rules out positions without taking their claims seriously. There is a danger that only sources that do not contain the supernatural are considered trustworthy, however much later they postdate the events. But actually, the Gospels of the New Testament were written sometime after the events, and they differ in detail between them, which surely brings into question their reliability. For instance, only two of the Gospels refer to the birth narratives, and even though the resurrection is reported, there are significant differences between the accounts. So, to what extent do the Gospels give an accurate account?

Crossan argues that, to get a true picture of Jesus, you need to get behind the New Testament Gospels. He claims that behind the four Gospels is the document 'Q', which contains just the sayings of Jesus. It contains no supernatural accounts. However, that does not necessarily mean that there were no accounts of supernatural events in Jesus' life. The supernatural accounts in the Gospels were circulating at a time when eyewitnesses were still alive, and there is no evidence that these accounts were challenged.

WJEC/Eduqas Religious Studies for AS & A Level Christianity

In conclusion, it does seem that the arguments are more persuasive to use the New Testament Gospels rather than the apocryphal Gospels to understand Jesus.

> **Judge**
> This is a good answer that displays a thoughtful, reflective approach to Crossan's arguments for using apocryphal Gospels. It reaches a conclusion that is consistently argued throughout the answer.

Over to you

Below is an argument concerning traditional views of Jesus as mistaken. Respond to this argument by thinking of three key questions you could ask the writer that would challenge their view and force them to defend their argument.

Argument

Traditional Christian doctrine concerning Jesus is completely misguided. This is because attributing a miraculous birth, life and resurrection to Jesus obscures the most interesting historical facts about his life – that he was a peasant living in an unpleasant backwater of the Roman Empire who somehow, in spite of this, founded a social movement that challenged others to transcend their social limitations. By placing the emphasis on the miraculous nature of his life, we miss the astounding fact that Jesus presided at an 'open table'; had a radically inclusive movement; brought those who were condemned as impure back into the community ('healing'); and challenged those who aspired merely to have riches and an easy life. Too bad that all of this was forgotten and Jesus was turned into a 'King' by a state Church that was eventually run by powerful elites. If only the Church would now consider sources for Jesus' life that do not focus on the miraculous aspects, then there might be hope that Christianity could return to its roots. We must not simply accept that the New Testament reflects the only view of Jesus, but must examine the life of Jesus using other sources (like the Gospel of Thomas), as well as determining the earliest layers in the New Testament.

When you have completed the task, refer to the band descriptors for A2 (WJEC) or A Level (Eduqas) and, in particular, look at the demands described in the higher band descriptors, which you should be aspiring towards. Ask yourself:

- Is my answer a confident critical analysis and perceptive evaluation of the issue?
- Is my answer a response that successfully identifies and thoroughly addresses the issues that the question raises?

T1 Religious figures and sacred texts

T2 Religious concepts

This section covers AO1 content and skills

Specification content

Is God male? The issue of male language about God; the pastoral benefits and challenges of the model of Father; Sallie McFague and God as Mother

A: The nature of God

Is God male?

The portrayal of God as male in the Bible

The original languages of the Bible (Hebrew and Greek) consistently speak of God as *Father*. They also refer to God by the masculine personal pronoun *he*. Jesus, the Son of God, is male, and the Holy Spirit of God is traditionally spoken of as *he*.

> **Key quote**
>
> Christians think that God himself has taught us how to speak of Him.
> **(CS Lewis)**

God is compared to a human father. He provides for his children, disciplines them and loves them. This does not mean, however, that he is male, any more than referring to *Mother Earth* means that the Earth is female. God exists in a form that defies male and female categories.

Jesus is spoken of as the *Son of God* and the *Son of Man*. During his life on Earth, he was clearly a man. However, Christians believe that before he ever became incarnate, he was with God and was God (John 1:1) and so was neither male nor female.

The Holy Spirit is also referred to in masculine terms (John 15:26), depicted as a person with insight, knowledge and a will, who can be lied to and grieved. This does not mean the Holy Spirit is male since it is called Spirit.

There are also several passages in the Bible that portray God in female terms. In Isaiah 66:13, for example, God is described as a comforting mother. In Matthew 23:37, Jesus uses a motherly illustration of himself: 'Jerusalem, Jerusalem ... how often have I longed to gather your children together, as a hen gathers her chicks under her wings, and you were not willing'.

The pastoral benefits and challenges of the model of Father

Becoming a follower of Jesus means that we become adopted into the Father's family (Romans 6:23). We are his sons and daughters (2 Corinthians 6:18).

The image of an earthly father gives us just a partial glimpse of God and his character. However good the human father is, the essence of fatherhood is found in God, not in human beings. Nevertheless, the human-father image does highlight some of the same characteristics as God the Father, and so can be of help and comfort to people, for instance:

- Just as a good human father provides for his children's needs, so even more so does the Heavenly Father. He cares for his children and loves them to an even greater depth than a good earthly father.
- The human father is protective and strong. The Heavenly Father is creator of the world and is trustworthy.

- The Heavenly Father always has his very best in mind for his children. His patience and kindness never runs out and he is always approachable.
- A human father, out of love for his children, disciplines them. In the same way, the Heavenly Father disciplines and corrects us (Hebrews 12:3–11). God is forgiving and welcomes us back when we repent.
- God is ever present with us and wants us to develop and deepen our relationship with him.

All these aspects of God the Father can be a great encouragement and comfort to those feeling alone or rejected or suffering in some way.

Although the model of God as Father can be helpful, many would argue that it can also be unhelpful. Many people's experiences of a human father have been destructive and abusive. They have had terrible fathers.

Father language also is patriarchal language and shapes our image of God, which, in turn, shapes our relationship with God and other people. If we think of God only in terms of 'fatherly' characteristics, such as power and authority, we may think of exploitation of women and abuse of the Earth. Patriarchy has become linked to sexism, misogyny, inequality and abuse. Many see the Bible as conveying a violent, militaristic, male God, which is claimed to have led to male domination of women. It is seen as a book written by men for men. The association of masculinity with divinity makes male supremacy a fact that cannot be challenged and is not inclusive of women.

Sallie McFague: God as Mother

Although the Bible is clear that God values both men and women equally, some theologians have expressed concern about its consistent use of male language about God.

Sallie McFague was an American theologian who wrote from an **ecofeminist** perspective. In her *Metaphorical Theology: Models of God in Religious Language* (1982), she maintains that all language about God is metaphorical. Names and titles (Father, King, and so on) are simply ways in which we think about God. They say very little about God's true nature.

The metaphors used in the Bible often turn into idols: we end up worshipping the metaphor instead of God. However, all metaphors become outdated with time.

McFague wants to provide new metaphors for understanding God in ways that are meaningful today. By using the **metaphor** of God as Mother, she is not saying that God is a Mother (or even female) but that the image of 'mother' highlights certain characteristics of God (such as love for the world).

McFague develops a metaphor of the world as God's body and goes on to develop three metaphors for God's relationship with the world. The metaphors correspond to three Christian doctrines, three ethical elements and three types of love:

1. **Mother:** corresponding to the traditional title 'Father'; the doctrine of creation; the ethical element of justice; and *agapé* love ('selfless' love), the type of love God has for the world.

> **Key person**
>
> **Sallie McFague (1933–2019):** an American theologian who saw the Earth as 'God's body'

Sallie McFague

> **Key terms**
>
> **ecofeminist:** someone who is interested in both the environment and women's rights
> **metaphor:** something that represents or is a symbol for something else

> **"Key quote"**
>
> I do not know who God is, but I find some models better than others for constructing an image of God.
>
> (S McFague)

2. **Lover:** corresponding to the traditional title 'Son'; the doctrine of salvation; the ethical element of healing; and *eros* ('desire'), the way in which God's love works in the world.

3. **Friend:** corresponding to the traditional title 'Spirit', the doctrine of eschatology; the ethical element of companionship; and *philia* ('companionship'), the way in which human beings should interact in the world.

According to McFague, 'the feminine side of God is taken to comprise the tender, nurturing, passive, healing aspects of divine activity, whereas the activities in which God creates, redeems, establishes peace, administers justice and so on, are called masculine'.

She also warns against sentimentalising maternal imagery. For McFague, the metaphor of God as Mother focuses 'on the most basic things that females (as mothers) do ... give birth, feed, protect the young, want the young to flourish'. Hence, McFague focuses on God as female, not in feminine terms, which she sees as mere social constructs (what society wants women to think that they are biologically programmed to be).

While some theologians have welcomed McFague's concept of God as Mother, others have rejected it as unbiblical. Jesus asserted that God was 'Father'. Also, in relation to Jesus, the terms *father* and *mother* are not interchangeable terms, because clearly Jesus' mother was Mary.

Can God suffer?

The traditional Christian view

Traditional Christian theology has always taught the impassibility of God.

Impassibility means 'unable to suffer' or 'incapable of emotion of any kind'. It asserts that God is unable to experience emotion or suffering or pain, and therefore has no feelings that are similar to human feelings. This attribute is closely related to God's *immutability* (his unchanging nature). Equally, God's omnipotence means that he is not subject to anything, including suffering.

However, the Old Testament reveals a god who displays a range of emotions – love, grief, compassion, anger – which often cause him to 'repent' or 'change his mind'. The New Testament reveals a god who has become incarnate in Jesus. Jesus, in his human nature, is *passible*. He is able to feel emotion and pain, particularly in his passion and cross. It could be argued, however, that this did not affect the impassibility of his divine nature, as it was always God's plan to overcome suffering with resurrection.

Recent events, such as two world wars, the Holocaust and continuing conflicts and genocides, have prompted several prominent theologians to challenge this traditional view of God's impassibility. They argue that Christians cannot have faith in a god who is immune to suffering. Therefore, they conclude that God is passible, that he does undergo emotional change and that he can suffer.

Jürgen Moltmann: The Crucified God

Jürgen Moltmann was one such theologian, a German who, in his own life, faced the problem of God and suffering. He was confronted with the reality of Auschwitz as a conscript in the German army.

In his book *The Crucified God* (1972), he argues that God suffers with humanity and grounds his theology on Jesus' cry from the cross, 'My God, my God, why have you forsaken me?' (Mark 15:34).

> **Specification content**
>
> Can God suffer? The impassibility of God; the modern view of a suffering God illustrated by Jürgen Moltmann (*The Crucified God*)

> **Key person**
>
> **Jürgen Moltmann (1926–2024):** an influential German theologian famous for his 'theology of hope', in which he asserts that God suffers with humanity and has promised humanity a better future based on the resurrection

Moltmann sees Jesus Christ as the human face of God, so the crucified Christ really is God. Therefore, the cry of abandonment by Jesus from the cross takes place within God. In Jesus, God has identified himself with those abandoned by God. Moltmann uses the story of a Jewish boy the Nazis hanged in Auschwitz. God, he asserts, hanged with him on the gallows, for God suffers with those who suffer.

> **Key quote**
>
> Which God motivates Christian faith: the crucified God or the gods of religion, race and class?
>
> (J Moltmann)

However, God cannot suffer unwillingly or because of any deficiency in his being. But he can suffer actively. He can suffer in love, which is not a deficiency in his being. He is affected by human suffering because he loves his creation.

> **Key quote**
>
> In the cross, Father and Son are most deeply separated in the forsakenness and at the same time are most inwardly one in their surrender.
>
> (J Moltmann)

For Moltmann, Christians identifying with the crucified Christ means solidarity with poor, oppressed and alienated people. The power of the crucified Christ comes from the agapistic love with which Christ suffers. By joining forces against oppression, Christians truly identify with the cross. In this way, following the crucified Christ 'is no longer a purely private and spiritualised matter, but develops into a political theology ... The church of the crucified Christ must take sides in the concrete social and political conflicts going on about it and in which it is involved, and must be prepared to join and form parties' (Moltmann).

Jürgen Moltmann

Summary

* The Bible portrays God as male.
* The model of God as Father can be both pastorally beneficial while also leading to views of male supremacy.
* Sallie McFague argues that language about God is metaphorical. It tells us little about God's nature.
* She develops a new interpretation of the Trinity (with each aspect containing a type of love and an ethical quality): God as Mother (*agapé* meaning 'selfless love'), Lover (*eros* meaning 'healing'), Friend (*philia* meaning 'companionship').
* Jürgen Moltmann challenges the traditional view that God cannot suffer or experience emotion.
* The crucified Christ shows that God suffers with those who suffer. Love demands being open to suffering.
* Christians identifying with the crucified Christ oppose oppression and show solidarity with poor people.

AO1 Activity

a Explain what Moltmann means when he states that Christian identity is 'an act of identification with the crucified Christ'. Give two quotations that illustrate Moltmann's view.

This helps you develop the ability to select and present the key, relevant features of Moltmann's understanding of Jesus' cry from the cross 'my God, my God, why have you forsaken me?'.

b Find the Book of Common Prayer online and go to 'The Collects' (short prayers). Make a list of all the ways that several of these prayers describe God.

This helps you provide examples on the maleness of God in Christianity when answering questions on the male imagery in relation to God.

T2 Religious concepts

> **This section covers AO2 content and skills**

> **Specification content**
> The theological implications of a suffering God

Issues for analysis and evaluation

The theological implications of a suffering God

Possible line of argument	Critical analysis and evaluation
God cannot suffer (impassibility). It is one of God's attributes, along with immutability and omnipotence. Immutability means that God cannot respond to pain, since it entails change. Therefore he cannot suffer.	It solves the problem of evil if God can suffer. However, it might lead to a panentheistic (present in every part of the universe and extending beyond space and time) God, who is therefore part of the natural world and not omnipotent. To many, the idea of a passible God leads to atheism.
The Old Testament speaks of God as showing compassion and being angry. God cares for his creation, is upset when the covenant is broken and rejoices when 'his children return to faith'.	Some would argue that these stories should not be taken literally.
In the New Testament, Jesus feels pain at his rejection and weeps at the death of Lazarus. The Trinity cannot be understood without understanding the suffering God, since Jesus is the Son of God.	If the accounts are true, then perhaps Jesus' divine nature retained its impassibility attribute as it was his human nature that felt suffering. Alternatively, perhaps Jesus was not God incarnate, but just a human being. This assumes Jesus is God incarnate, which many would question. Others may appeal to Jesus' human nature, rather than his divine nature, that experiences suffering.
Both the idea of impassibility and the idea of God who is emotionally involved with his creation are not contradictory.	The contradiction seems to rest on the assumption that our understanding of our experiences of emotion equate to those of God. God's emotions are consistent with God's perfect character, and so are different from ours.
The Bible is the word of God so there must be a solution that explains God's impassibility.	Moltmann's God is empathetic. God understands and shares the suffering of others, but does not have ownership of the experience itself.

> **AO2 Activity**
>
> a   Analyse three possible conclusions that could be drawn from the critical analysis and evaluation of the theological implications of a suffering God. What are their strengths? Which conclusion do you think is the weakest?
>
> b   Evaluate three lines of argument that persuade you that this is the weakest conclusion. Think of questions you could raise in response to these arguments.

Exam practice

Sample question
Evaluate the validity of referring to God as 'Mother'.

Sample answer

If the Bible is the word of God, then surely God should be referred to as 'Father'. The Bible uses the masculine pronoun to refer to God, and Jesus uses the affectionate term *Abba* that children in Palestine would use for their father ('Daddy'). The Lord's Prayer begins with 'Our Father, who art in heaven …'

Clearly, the early Christians addressed God in a similar way, as in Romans Paul writes that those who believe in Jesus can also now call God Abba. That suggests a personal relationship that goes beyond acknowledging God as creator.

There is a possible biblical case for referring to God as a 'Mother', since Isaiah 66 has God with female qualities (*wisdom*). Indeed, Isaiah describes God as a comforting mother, and Jesus compares God to a woman searching for a lost coin. John's Gospel refers to God as Spirit, which reveals a god who is beyond gender.

The argument that McFague uses is that God is beyond language. She claims that theology has confused human language with God language. It should be viewed more as human metaphors rather than direct words given by God. The Bible appears to have been written by men for men. The problem is that the patriarchal language also shapes our image of God, which, in turn, shapes our relationship with God. This could be a persuasive argument for referring to God as 'Mother', since if people think of God only in terms of male characteristics (for example power and authority) they may ignore the motherly, nurturing characteristics of God.

The Father–Son bond between God and Jesus is a relationship that appears to exclude women. As a result, it does not convey traditionally feminine characteristics such as compassion, grace and love. Yet these characteristics are obviously present in the Father–Son bond.

There does seem to be a valid case for referring to God as 'Mother'. To see God only as Father is to limit the metaphors for God and risk the concept of God becoming captive to a male-dominated culture. It ignores the poetry and multiple images of God in the Bible. Maybe the concept of God as 'Mother' of the world was deliberately avoided because of the possible links with Near Eastern cults where the mother-goddess gives birth to the Earth. However, in the twenty-first century, such a link is unlikely to be made, so there is no reason to avoid referring to God as 'Mother'.

Anyway, does it have to be one or the other? Why not embrace both understandings, which will develop our understanding of God?

This section covers AO2 content and skills

Specification content
The validity of referring to God as 'Mother'

News reporter
A clear introduction that illustrates how the Bible uses patriarchal language to describe God, and so sets up the debate about whether it is valid to refer to God as 'Mother'.

Detective
This further illustration shows the biblical approach to God language.

Tennis player
Detective
This paragraph introduces an alternative view, with illustrations to support it.

Philosopher — **Explorer**
This paragraph raises a new approach to the whole debate on the grounds that God is beyond language, and the use of human metaphors creates problems. The argument is linked to a scholar.

Detective
The answer now reflects back on further problems posed by the use of patriarchal language for God; namely, the lack of traditionally feminine characteristics the language conveys.

Judge
The conclusion is consistent with the argument throughout the answer.

Philosopher
The answer ends with reflective questions that could be developed further. However, overall it is a good answer and clearly engages with the issues.

Over to you

Below is a weak answer that a student has written in response to a question requiring evaluation of the extent to which a suffering God is a contradiction in terms. In a group, using the band level descriptors, place this answer in a relevant band that corresponds to the description inside that band. (It is obviously a weak answer and so would not be in bands 3–5.) To do this, it will be useful to consider what is missing from the answer and what is inaccurate. The accompanying analysis will assist you. When analysing the answer's weaknesses, think of five ways you would improve the answer to make it stronger. You may have more than five suggestions, but try to negotiate as a group and prioritise the five most important things lacking.

Question

Evaluate the extent to which a suffering God is a contradiction in terms.

Answer

Theologians who argue in favour of a passible God (1) are panentheists (2). If God is just part of the natural world, he cannot be its creator. And if he is infected with the evil of the world, he cannot be omnibenevolent. A passible God can suffer with all who suffer, but he can no longer free humankind from sin and death (3). Stripped of his omnipotence and omnibenevolence, he is no more powerful than we are (4). However, God is also said to be omniscient. He cannot be omniscient unless he is able to experience human emotions. In the Old Testament, God does not show any emotional involvement with his people (5), but in the Gospels, Jesus often shows his compassion (6) for suffering humanity. (7)

Analysis of answer:

1. What does the word passible mean?
2. What does the word panentheist mean?
3. Why? The answer needs to explain that the panentheist God appears to have lost his transcendence.
4. What about the incarnation, when God became one of us?
5. This statement is inaccurate. There are many examples in the Old Testament of God reacting to events on Earth with anger, compassion, etc.
6. No examples are given.
7. There is no reasoned conclusion.

B: The Trinity

The need for the doctrine of the Trinity

Christianity is a monotheistic religion. For most Christians, the Christian God exists as three persons: Father (Creator), Son (Redeemer) and Holy Spirit (Sustainer). The doctrine of the Trinity was needed to define the relationship between these three persons.

The doctrine asserts three things:

1. The Father, Son and Holy Spirit are three distinct persons.

> **Key quotes**
>
> Hear O Israel, the Lord our God, the Lord is one
> **(Deuteronomy 6:4)**
>
> Thomas answered him [Jesus], 'My Lord and my God!'
> **(John 20:28)**

2. Each person is fully God; the three are co-existent, co-eternal and co-equal.
3. There is only one God; the doctrine does not split God into three parts.

It was Tertullian in the third century CE who coined the word *Trinity* and the doctrine was formalised in the Nicene Creed (325 CE), which stated that the Son was 'of one substance' (Greek: *homoousios*) with the Father.

> **Key quote**
>
> Trinity – a bespoke word, tailored to express both three-ness and oneness.
> **(S Bullivant)**

The formula was designed to counteract what Tertullian saw as three contemporary heresies:

1. **Adoptionism:** The belief that Jesus was an ordinary man who became the Son of God only at his baptism.
2. **Sabellianism:** The belief that Jesus was divine but not human.
3. **Arianism:** The belief that Jesus was the highest of all created beings but not of the same substance as God.

One of the theologians present at the Council of Nicea in 325 CE was Athanasius. His name was given to the Athanasius Creed but it is generally agreed that he did not write it since it was probably composed during the fifth century. Most regard the Athanasius Creed as the early Church's most comprehensive picture of the Trinity.

The biblical foundations of the doctrine of the Trinity

> **Key quote**
>
> … the doctrine of the Trinity stems directly from the early Christians' experiences of God
> **(S Bullivant)**

This section covers AO1 content and skills

Specification content

The need for the doctrine of the Trinity: the nature and identity of Christ (issues of divinity and pre-existence) and Christ's relationship with the Father (co-equal and co-eternal); the origin of the Holy Spirit: the filioque controversy

T2 Religious concepts

The Trinity

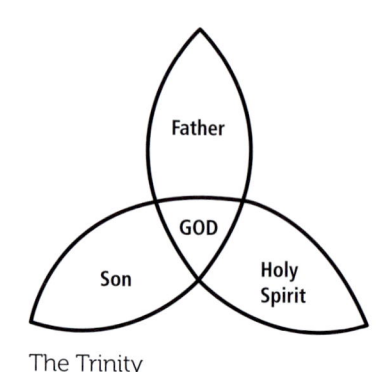

The belief is based on the Bible, though the word *Trinity* does not appear in the Bible. However, some Christians argue that the concept that it represents – God as three co-existent, co-eternal and co-equal persons – does.

In the Old Testament, God the Father is often referred to in the plural:
- The first Hebrew word used for God (Genesis 1:1) is *Elohim*, a plural noun (with a singular verb). The same word is used many times throughout the Old Testament.
- In Genesis 1:26–27, God refers to himself in the plural: 'Let us make humankind in our image'.
- In Isaiah 9:6–7, there is a prophecy about a child who will be born who will be called Mighty God, Prince of peace and will reign on David's throne forever.

In the New Testament, Jesus is often referred to as God:
- John 1:1–2 says that Jesus was the word and that word was God and that all things were created through him.
- In Colossians 1:15, Paul states that 'The Son is the image of the invisible God', and in 2:9 writes 'For in Christ all the fullness of the Deity lives in bodily form'.
- Thomas, when Jesus appears after his resurrection, addresses him as 'My Lord and my God' (John 20:28).

The Holy Spirit too is referred to as God:
- In John 14:23, the indwelling of the Holy Spirit is linked to the indwelling of Jesus and his Father.
- In 1 Corinthians 6:19, Paul asks the Corinthians: 'Do you not know that your bodies are temples of the Holy Spirit, who is in you, whom you have received from God?'

There are some passages where all three are mentioned together:
- In the Great Commission in Matthew 28:18–20, Jesus sends the disciples to baptise all nations 'in the name of the Father and of the Son and of the Holy Spirit'.
- In 1 Corinthians 13:14, Paul ends his letter by saying 'May the grace of the Lord Jesus Christ, and the love of God, and the fellowship of the Holy Spirit be with you all'.

The Bible teaches throughout that God is one:
- In the Old Testament, Deuteronomy 6:4–5 states that God is one.
- In the New Testament, the statement is repeated by Jesus in Mark 12:29 ('the Lord our God, the Lord is one').

The Christian Church has never been able to explain adequately how God can be one, and at the same time three. It regards the Trinity as a mystery that reflects that:
- no human words can express the reality of God
- God is a community; a family of three in one.

Most Christians accept the Trinitarian formula, with the exception of a few denominations, such as the Unitarian Church, which teaches that Jesus was human and not God.

The filioque controversy

The creed agreed at the Council of Nicea in 325 CE simply stated that Christians believe in the Holy Spirit. This was amended in 381 CE at the Council of Constantinople to '[believe] in the Holy Spirit, the Lord, the Giver of life, *who proceeds from the Father'*. All the Churches represented at the Council agreed to the new wording. It reflected the teaching in John 15:26, 'when the Advocate comes, whom I will send to you from the Father – the Spirit of truth who goes out [proceeds] from the Father.'

The Council of Nicea (325 CE)

In 589 CE, at the Third Council of Toledo, however, there was another change. The clause about the Holy Spirit was extended: '... who proceeds from the Father *and the Son*'. It was added to reflect the thinking of several influential theologians and possibly to make clear that Jesus (the Son) had equal divinity as the Father.

The three English words 'and the Son' are one word in Latin: *filioque*. Inserting this into the Nicene Creed caused controversy. Although the Latin-speaking West had already widely accepted this addition, the Greek-speaking East had not accepted it. Therefore, the word had been added without the agreement of the five patriarchs of Jerusalem, Antioch, Alexandria, Rome and Constantinople.

The dispute over filioque continued for six centuries. Matters came to a head when, in 1014, Pope Benedict VIII agreed to use the word for the first time at a Mass in Rome. Eventually, this and other issues led to the Great Schism of 1054, which divided the European Christian Church into the Western Roman Catholic Church, with the pope as its head, and the Eastern Orthodox Church, with a patriarch as its head. The Eastern Orthodox Church includes national Churches such as the Greek Orthodox Church and the Russian Orthodox Church.

T2 Religious concepts

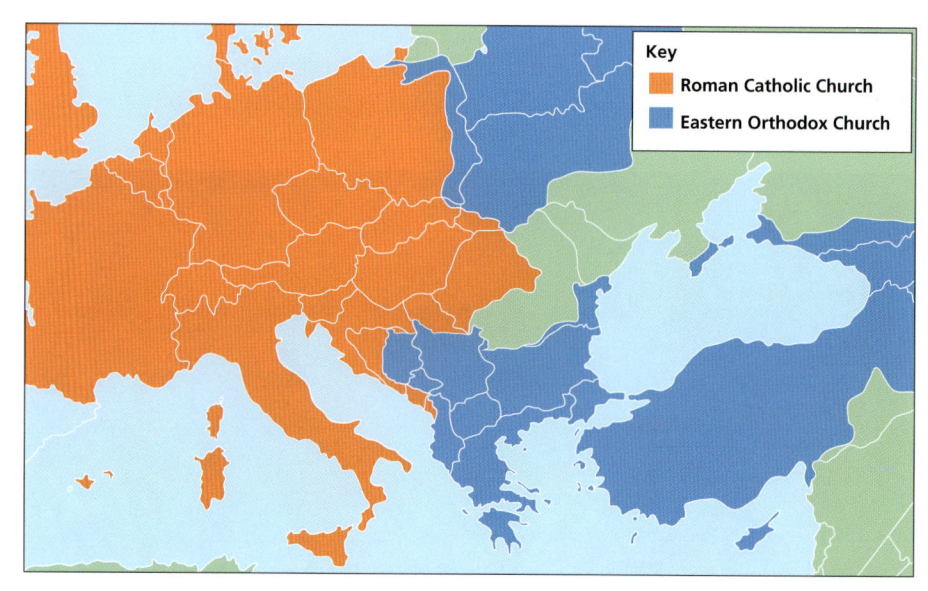

Great Schism (1054 CE)

The Western Church argued that since the Holy Spirit acts within the Trinity as the bond of love between Father and Son, it follows that the Holy Spirit must proceed from both. Also, since the Holy Spirit acts within human beings to unite them with the Father and the Son, and with each other, in this bond of love, it follows that human beings can derive the nature of God from this experience.

The Eastern Church rejected the idea that the doctrine of the Trinity can be based on human experience. All the Bible reveals is that the Spirit 'proceeds' from the Father.

Although the division between the two Churches remains to this day, there have been attempts at reconciliation, and dialogue continues over what the word *proceeds* means. Pope Francis, on his 2021 pastoral visit to Greece, deliberately did not include the word *filioque* when he recited the creed.

Modern developments of the Trinity

Controversy has surrounded the doctrine of the Trinity. Enlightenment theologians (see page 57) found it problematic, as did Friedrich Schleiermacher (1768–1834). He tried to reconcile enlightenment theology with traditional beliefs, and gave little space to the doctrine in his theological work *The Christian Faith* (1821).

Later, **Karl Barth** (1886–1968) placed the doctrine of the Trinity at the centre of Christian theology. He understood it as the basis of how God revealed himself to human beings:

- **In the Son:** this is an **objective** 'unveiling' of what God is.
- **In the Spirit:** this is a subjective reception, or 'imparting' how God is working for us.

Barth illustrates what he means by this by imagining two men witnessing Jesus' crucifixion.

- The first says, 'There is a common criminal being executed'. This man has not recognised the unveiling of God in Jesus.
- The second man says, 'There is the Son of God dying for me'. To this man, the Holy Spirit has imparted that God is in Jesus.

> **Key person**
>
> **Karl Barth (1886–1968):** a Swiss theologian whose work had a deep influence on 20th-century theology

Karl Barth

> **Key term**
>
> **objective:** factual, not based on personal belief

Barth argues that human beings are incapable of responding to the objective revelation of God in Jesus unless the Holy Spirit imparts that revelation. This imparting by the Spirit proceeds from both the hidden Father and the revealed Son. Therefore, Barth endorses the use of the word *filioque*.

Barth also selects the German word *seinweise*, translated as 'modes of being' or 'ways of being', to replace the word *person*. He argued that *person* in the nineteenth century came to mean 'personality', so there was a danger that God would be understood as having 'three personalities'. So for Barth, the Trinity formula is 'one God in three modes of being'.

The main criticism of Barth's view is that he falls into the heresy of modalism. *Modalism* is the belief that the Father, Son and Holy Spirit are three different modes of God, rather than three distinct persons within the Godhead. In other words, there are no personal distinctions within the Godhead. It is as though God wears three different masks, which he puts on depending on whether he is operating as Father, Son or Holy Spirit. Such a view means that the Father, Son and Holy Spirit exist one after the other, never at the same time, which destroys the eternal unity of the Godhead.

Barth responds that his aim is to highlight the unchanging nature of the one eternal Trinity. There are three modes but one personality.

Summary

- The Christian God exists as three persons: Father, Son and Holy Spirit.
- The formula for the Trinity defines the relationship between the three persons and counteracts heresies.
- The word *Trinity* does not appear in the Bible. However, the concept of God as three persons can be found in both the Old and the New Testaments.
- The filioque controversy arose over adding the phrase 'and the Son' to the creed from 'proceeds from the Father'.
- The addition made clear that Jesus (the Son) and the Father had equal divinity.
- This controversy was part of the cause of the Great Schism of 1054 CE.
- Enlightenment theologians found the doctrine of the Trinity problematic, but Karl Barth sees 'in the Son' as an 'unveiling' of what God is, while 'in the Spirit' is the 'imparting' of how God is working for us.
- Barth therefore endorses the filioque addition to the creed as the basis of how God revealed himself to human beings.

AO1 Activity

a   Explain why the addition of the filioque clause to the Nicene Creed sparked controversy.

This helps you develop the ability to select and present the key, relevant features of the relationship of the Holy Spirit to the Father and the Son.

b   Design a flowchart highlighting the biblical references to the concept of the Trinity.

This helps you select the key, relevant information for an answer to a question that expects knowledge and understanding of the biblical foundations of the doctrine of the Trinity.

> **This section covers AO2 content and skills**

> **Specification content**
> Whether the doctrine of the Trinity is necessary to understand the God of Christianity

Issues for analysis and evaluation

Whether the doctrine of the Trinity is necessary to understand the God of Christianity

Possible line of argument	Critical analysis and evaluation
The doctrine of the Trinity is fundamental to the understanding of God in Christianity.	The Trinity is merely an abstract idea that makes no logical sense.
The doctrine of the Trinity clarifies Christian teaching about God. It states that God must be simultaneously both Three and One.	The doctrine has confused things and given rise to several theories that have been pronounced as heresy, e.g. modalism and adoptionism.
The doctrine has been the cause of a schism between the Churches of East and West, so has been unhelpful.	The disagreement over the addition of the word *filioque* is important as it made a change to the Creed, which is a statement of the Churches' beliefs.
The doctrine is important as it expresses the truths found in the Bible about God.	The Bible is not reliable and it has led to Christians creating a doctrine that makes no sense. Jesus refers to himself as 'son of man' rather than 'Son of God'.
The doctrine plays an important part in worship, e.g. baptism is in the name of the Father, Son and Holy Spirit.	The first commandment is to love God, and Jesus taught that we should love God and love our neighbour. The doctrine of the Trinity is an addition by the Church.
The doctrine of the Trinity is clearly in the Bible.	It is true that God is referred to by plural nouns and there are references to Jesus as 'God's Son' and also to 'the Spirit of God'. But nowhere is the actual doctrine stated in the Bible. It was formulated much later.
The Trinity is a guide for all human relationships: a family in which all the members are distinct but have a unity.	It may be a helpful image and guide but it doesn't mean the Trinity doctrine is true.
Given there is no coherent or universal agreement about understanding the doctrine of the Trinity, it seems difficult to argue that the doctrine is necessary to understand God.	Perhaps what is necessary to understand and know about God is to understand and know that God is love. The Trinity is a mystery and we should just accept it as such and not try to understand it.

> **AO2 Activity**
> a Analyse three possible conclusions that could be drawn from the critical analysis and evaluation of whether the doctrine of the Trinity is necessary to understand the God of Christianity. What are their strengths? Which conclusion do you think is the strongest?
> b Evaluate three lines of argument that persuade you to think that this is the strongest conclusion. Think of questions you could raise in response to these arguments.

This section covers AO2 content and skills

Exam practice
Sample question
Evaluate the monotheistic claims of the doctrine of the Trinity.

Specification content
The monotheistic claims of the doctrine of the Trinity

Sample answer
The doctrine of the Trinity asserts that there is one God; that each person of the Trinity is fully God; that the Father, Son and Holy Spirit are not the same. It was Tertullian who coined the word trinity ('tri-unity') but the doctrine of the Trinity is not explicitly in scripture. The Bible states that there is only one God – for instance, in the Jewish shema. Likewise, the three persons of Father, Son and Holy Spirit are all presented, in the Bible, as persons who are divine.

News reporter
A good introduction that sets out clearly the actual doctrine of the Trinity and its monotheistic claims.

For instance, Jesus forgives sin; uses the divine name 'I am' and accepts Thomas calling him 'God'. Jesus refers to the Holy Spirit as another comforter – a personal replacement of himself, and uses the personal pronoun 'he'. Therefore, the Holy Spirit is a person. The three persons are also distinct in that they appear together at the end of Matthew's Gospel when he commands Christians to baptise in the name of the Father, and of the Son and of the Holy Spirit.

Detective
This paragraph gives further evidence from the Bible to support the actual doctrine and that Jesus is referred to as 'God'.

It seems clear that the Bible presents one God, yet three distinct persons who are all divine. Yet it seems nonsense to claim that God is both one and three! Surely, that is a logical contradiction. If so, then the monotheistic claim is not valid.

News reporter
Critical thinker
Having summarised the biblical view, the answer now questions its coherency and so challenges the monotheistic claims.

Not surprisingly, theologians and philosophers have attempted to solve the apparent contradiction but it has always resulted in the Church claiming the attempted solution as a heresy, in that one aspect of the Trinity doctrine is denied.

Philosopher
This paragraph raises further difficulties about monotheistic claims. It argues that no clear explanation of how one God can be three distinct divine persons has been given.

For instance, one God (monotheism) can be maintained if the three persons are seen as God acting in three different forms or functions, like a single actor using different masks. However, the doctrine of the Trinity demands the three members of the Trinity are beings who are separate, though related.

Another attempt at a solution is to argue that Jesus was a human being who was adopted as God's son at his baptism. But this has difficulties in that it still leaves the problem of two divine beings (the Father and the Holy Spirit), as well as seemingly having to dismiss the birth narratives as myth added later.

Try as Christians do, it seems there is no way that 'three' can be the same as 'one'!

Critical thinker
Detective
This paragraph further demonstrates the problem of finding a solution with examples of failed attempts, so supporting the view that the monotheistic claim is wrong.

T2 Religious concepts

> **Tennis player**
> **Judge**
>
> For many, the monotheistic claims of the doctrine of the Trinity are therefore not valid. They are simply mathematical nonsense. However, for others, they are valid, while admitting that human wisdom does not know, and cannot know, all the mysteries of God. As human beings, they acknowledge their limitations in understanding and embrace the doctrine in faith.

The final paragraph argues the alternative view, with appeals to the limits of human knowledge and understanding, while acknowledging that no clear conclusion can be reached. A good answer that addresses the issue, with the balance of the argument against monotheistic claims. Perhaps there could be more development of the argument concerning limited human knowledge.

Over to you

Below is a reasonable answer, although not perfect, that a student has written in response to a question requiring an examination of whether or not the doctrine of the Trinity is unbiblical. Using the band level descriptors, compare this with the relevant higher bands and the descriptions inside those bands. (It is obviously a reasonable answer, and so would not be in bands 5, 1 or 2.) To do this, it will be useful to consider what is both strong and weak about the answer, and therefore what needs developing.

When analysing the answer, in a group, identify three ways to make this answer a better one. You may have more than three observations – and indeed suggestions – to make it a near-perfect answer!

Question

Examine whether or not the doctrine of the Trinity is unbiblical.

Answer

The word 'Trinity' does not appear in the Bible, and the Trinitarian doctrine is not set out in a single biblical verse or passage. On the contrary, the Bible insists that there is only one God. The Old Testament has no awareness of a Trinity, and neither, apparently, does Jesus in his teaching.

In the Old Testament, the Book of Deuteronomy states unequivocally that 'the Lord our God, the Lord is one', and this is endorsed in the New Testament, both by Jesus and by Paul. In the Gospel of John, Jesus calls God the Father 'the only true God'. This cannot be the case if Jesus and the Holy Spirit also claim to be God. Jesus also tells his disciples in John that he is going to the Father, 'because the Father is greater than I'.

On the other hand, it is true that in the New Testament Jesus is often referred to as God. John 1 says that Jesus was the Word and the Word was God and that all things were created through him. In Philippians 2, Paul writes that Jesus 'though he was in the form of God, did not regard equality with God as something to be exploited'.

The Holy Spirit too is referred to as God. In John 14, Jesus speaks of the Holy Spirit as equal with himself and the Father. In the Great Commission in Matthew 28, he sends the disciples to baptise all nations 'in the name of the Father and of the Son and of the Holy Spirit'. Paul, in his Letter to the Romans, tells his readers that if the Spirit of God dwells in them, God will give them life.

The Old Testament is therefore clear that God the Father is the only one God. However, the New Testament, with its references not only to Jesus as God's Son but also to the Holy Spirit as the Spirit of God, seems to suggest that God consists of three persons: Father, Son and Holy Spirit. It thus became necessary to formulate the doctrine of the Trinity to explain the relationship between the three.

C: The Atonement

The Atonement: definition

Most religions have rituals, often involving sacrifice, to reconcile people with the deity. Christianity teaches that the death of Jesus allows reconciliation. This process is called the **Atonement**.

Reconciliation is necessary because all people have sinned. Genesis 3 records how sin first came into the world, when the devil successfully tempted Adam and Eve to disobey God. Christianity teaches that, as a result, we all have a bias to rebel against God, and this disobedience results in our separation from God. Unless we are reconciled, we will be eternally separate from God.

The word *atonement* has been used in the English language since the sixteenth century to express the significance of Jesus' death. It was coined from the two words 'at one' by **William Tyndale**. *At-one-ment* simply means 'to set at one' or 'to reconcile'. Most modern versions of the Bible use the word *reconciliation*.

The New Testament seems to use several different models to convey how God reconciled humankind to himself through Jesus' death.

The Christus Victor theory

In the first 1000 years of Christianity, the predominant view on Atonement was that Jesus thought of his death in terms of a ransom payment to redeem men and women from sin. The Gospels certainly give some support to this view. Matthew 20:28 quotes him as saying that 'the Son of Man came ... to give his life as a ransom for many'. The idea is repeated elsewhere in the New Testament, such as in 1 Timothy 2:5–6, where Paul speaks of 'Jesus ... who gave himself as a ransom for all'.

Origen maintained that Jesus' death was a ransom payment to Satan, to free humankind, who Satan had enslaved following Adam and Eve's sin. However, many objected to this theory on the grounds that it gives Satan more power than God has. How could Satan have the power to demand a ransom from God? Surely God can just do and take what he wants.

> **Key quote**
>
> The payment could not be made to God, because God was not holding sinners in captivity for a ransom, so the payment had to be to the devil.
>
> (Origen)

In 1931, **Gustaf Aulen** repopularised the ransom model in his influential book *Christus Victor*, where he argues that the idea of 'ransom' should not be seen in terms of a business transaction, but as a rescue or liberation of humanity from the slavery of sin. In Aulen's words, 'the work of Christ is first and foremost a victory over the powers that hold mankind in bondage, sin, death, and the devil'.

The *Christus Victor* view is rooted in the incarnation and how Christ entered into human misery and wickedness to redeem it. Jesus became what we are so that we could become what he is. Colossians 2:15 refers to Christ 'having disarmed the powers and authorities ... triumphing over them by the cross'. Christ's victory over evil brings opportunity for the Kingdom of God to be established on Earth.

This section covers AO1 content and skills

Specification content

Three theories of the Atonement (which are not mutually exclusive): the death of Jesus as Christus Victor (with reference to the liberation of humanity from hostile powers); the death of Jesus as a substitution (both the belief that Jesus died as a substitute for humanity, and the belief that only the divine-human Jesus could act as a sacrifice by God for the sake of humanity); the death of Jesus as a moral example (of how to live and die)

The underlying assumptions about the need for divine forgiveness and the conflict between the wrath and love of God in theories of the Atonement

Key term

Atonement: to make 'at one' or reconcile

Key persons

William Tyndale (1494–1536): one of the first translators of the Bible into English

Origen (c.185 CE–253 CE): a second- to third-century theologian

Gustaf Aulen (1879–1977): a Swedish theologian who wrote the book *Christus Victor*

T2 Religious concepts

Jesus as a substitute

The idea of a substitute appears in the Old Testament and was a common practice aimed at restoring a broken relationship between people and God. For instance, Leviticus 16:20–22 describes a process where the priest symbolically lays the sins of the community upon a goat, which is then cast out into the wilderness.

Jesus died as a substitute for humanity

Anselm rejected the belief of his day that Jesus paid a ransom to Satan, publishing his *Cur Deos Homo?* ('Why was God a man?') around 1097. Anselm argued that human sin defrauds God of the honour he is due. This debt to God was greater than humans were able to pay. However, Christ's death – the ultimate act of obedience – brings God great honour and is beyond the call of duty for Christ. It is more honour than he was obliged to give, and his surplus repays our deficit. In other words, Christ, instead of us, pays the honour to the Father. According to Anselm, that is why God became a man – so that he could pay the debt to himself.

> **Key quote**
>
> Through a tree we were made debtors to God; so through a tree we have our debt cancelled.
>
> (Irenaeus)

Sixteenth-century Protestant reformers considered Anselm's theory inadequate because it was based on the concept of God's honour rather than on that of God's justice. They argued that Jesus set human beings free from being punished for their sins by taking that punishment upon himself on the cross, thus satisfying the justice of God.

They based their argument on the Suffering Servant Songs in the Old Testament Book of Isaiah, where there are famous descriptions of vicarious suffering, for example 'the Lord has laid on him the iniquity of us all' (Isaiah 53:6), and some passages in Paul's letters, for example:

> **Key quote**
>
> Christ redeemed us from the curse of the law by becoming a curse for us.
>
> (Galatians 3:13)

Only Jesus could take the place of humanity

Asserting that human beings had nothing of sufficient value to sacrifice to God for their sins, Christian theologians argued that God himself had provided the sacrifice for them, as he had done in the story of Abraham and Isaac (Genesis 22:8). In about 420 CE, **Augustine** wrote in *The City of God* '[Jesus] offered sacrifice for our sins. And where did he find that offering, the pure victim that he would offer? He offered himself'. If it is God's justice that must be satisfied, his righteous anger against sin, then only the divine-human Jesus could take the place of humanity.

The Epistle to the Hebrews states that through the perfect sacrifice of Jesus, human sin was dealt with 'once for all' (Hebrews 7:27). Jesus' death on the cross paid the penalty – a final atonement for sin.

In both the Old Testament prophets and the New Testament, the cup is used as a symbol of God's wrath, for example Revelation 14:9–10, and in the

> **Key persons**
>
> **Anselm (c.1033–1109):** Italian-born monk, theologian and philosopher who became Archbishop of Canterbury
>
> **Augustine (354 CE–430 CE):** a theologian, philosopher and bishop of Hippo; one of the most important figures in early Western Christianity

Augustine of Hippo

Garden of Gethsemane Jesus prays to the Father, 'Take this cup from me. Yet not what I will, but what you will' (Mark 14:36).

The moral-example theory

This approach to understanding the Atonement was first formulated by Augustine and restated by **Peter Abelard** at the beginning of the twelfth century as a reaction against Anselm's theory. Modern liberal theologians favour it.

> ### Key quote
>
> ... to teach us by both word and example even to the point of death, thus binding us to himself through love.
>
> (P Abelard)

Key person

Peter Abelard (1079–1142): a French theologian and philosopher

This model proposes that Jesus died, not to appease or placate God, but to show human beings the depth of God's love for them. The purpose was to lead people to repentance. Jesus' sacrifice provides a perfect moral role model that can influence us to act more morally ourselves. Therefore, atonement is not to appease God's honour or justice, but aims to improve human morals. The passages referring to final judgement, like the parable of the sheep and goats, link atonement to moral conduct, implying that salvation depends on how we act.

Underlying assumptions of Atonement theories

The theories of the Atonement attempt to explain what Jesus' death achieved. All the theories acknowledge that there is a broken relationship between God and human beings, caused by sin, but as to how Jesus' death brings reconciliation is debated.

In the case of Christus Victor, it emphasises the triumph of the cross over evil and bringing opportunity to establish God's kingdom on Earth. Reconciliation seems automatic for all regardless of a person's action. There is little emphasis on human sin and its consequences. Many Christians have felt that this is rather triumphalist, does not take sin seriously enough, and depicts God as in some way beholden to Satan and his power.

The substitution theory focuses on the unique divine-human nature of Jesus in order to explain the reconciliation. For Anselm, it was linked to honour, but this was later criticised as an unbiblical model that was a central concept in the feudal system of Anselm's day. The Protestant reformers argued that it was God's righteousness and justice that lies at the heart of Jesus' death. God's wrath against sin and God's love come together with the death of the Son of God. In some way, through his death, Jesus absorbed the penalty of sin and made it possible to be reconciled with God. John Stott summarised this understanding as 'God himself gave himself to save us from himself'.

This theory has been criticised on the grounds that no loving God would offer his only Son as a sacrifice to satisfy his own sense of justice. Also, it separates the Father and the Son. It is as if the Son saves us from the Father. Indeed, why would God need or want a sacrifice before he could be merciful? It implies that God is an angry tyrant who must be appeased before he forgives.

The moral-example theory avoids these problems, but it has been criticised for not explaining the crucifixion. Jesus did not need to die to provide people with a perfect moral example. He could have done so through his life and teachings. It denies the supernatural effect of Jesus' death and teaches that salvation is through works not faith.

Are the theories of the Atonement contradictory?

Scholars such as NT Wright claim that the different Atonement theories are not necessarily contradictory. However, they do have different preferred theories, but claim that the other theories only make sense in light of that. William Craig argues that each theory of the Atonement has its contribution to make, since they are all based on themes and motifs that are found in the Bible. Along similar lines, NT Wright argues that we cannot fully specify the exact meaning of the Atonement in a single theory.

Other scholars would disagree and reject the view that all the theories 'fit together'. For instance, some see the moral-example theory as advocating salvation by works that they regard as firmly rejected in New Testament writings.

Another approach is to draw attention to the fact that the substitution theory, focusing on justice, did not appear until the sixteenth century, while the moral-example theory can be dated to as early as the third century. The implication is that the early view should be preferred.

Summary

- There is a broken relationship between God and human beings, caused by sin.
- Jesus' death makes reconciliation with God possible; this process is called the *Atonement*.
- There are different theories of the Atonement:
    - **The Christus Victor theory:** Jesus' death liberates humanity from the slavery of sin. Christ is victorious over evil by disarming the powers of evil.
    - **The substitute theory:** The focus is on God's justice and his righteous anger against sin. The divine-human Jesus took the place of humanity to make the reconciliation possible.
    - **The moral-example theory:** Jesus' sacrifice provides a perfect moral role model, which will lead people to repentance and improve human morality.
- Each of the theories has been challenged in terms of consistency with God's nature.
- Some scholars see the different theories as contradictory, while others argue they each make a contribution, since one theory alone cannot give the exact meaning fully.

AO1 Activity

a   Explain the key features of each model of the Atonement. Support the explanations with extracts from quotations.

This helps you select and recall a core set of points to develop an answer explaining each model and ensure that you are making accurate use of specialist language and vocabulary in context.

b   Decide on an image to represent each model of the Atonement. Draw this image and, beneath it, list how the image illustrates the model.

This helps you recall the key points of each of the models of the Atonement and the differences between them.

Issues for analysis and evaluation

The extent to which the three images (theories) of the Atonement are contradictory

> **This section covers AO2 content and skills**
>
> **Specification content**
> The extent to which the three images (theories) of the Atonement are contradictory

Possible line of argument	Critical analysis and evaluation
Three theories (images) have been proposed to explain the biblical teaching about atonement: Christus Victor, substitution and moral examples.	They contradict since the first two are supernatural transactions while the moral theory is about personal moral effort.
The moral example is not biblical and so removes the contradiction between natural and supernatural.	Some argue that the moral example is consistent with New Testament teaching about the need for repentance but clashes with Paul's rejection of salvation through works. However, it is possible that Paul was referring to Jewish ritual 'works' (e.g. circumcision) not moral good works such as faithfulness to Jesus' teaching.
The Christus Victor and the substitution theories agree that salvation can be achieved only through the death of Christ and faith in him.	The Christus Victor and the substitution theories each have a very different focus. The former is about liberation from power of sin and death and our subjective experience, while the latter is about the objective fact of God's justice by the punishment for sin himself on the cross.
Can all three theories be seen as part of the substitution image?	John Stott has supported this view. He sees the substitution theory focused entirely on the death of Jesus, while linking the moral example to Jesus' death in the wider context of his ethical teaching.
Other approaches to non-contradiction of the three theories:	1 They are not mutually exclusive nor contradictory but help bring out different aspects of the Atonement. 2 Each understanding serves to support the other rather than contradict it outright. 3 They are complementary – Jesus and the cross are central; the death of Jesus is potentially life-changing for people. 4 The Atonement is a mystery and we should just accept it as such.

> **AO2 Activity**
> a   Analyse three possible conclusions that could be drawn from the critical analysis and evaluation of the extent to which the three theories (images) of the Atonement are contradictory. What are their strengths? Which conclusion do you think is the weakest?
> b   Using the strongest conclusion, select three lines of argument that you would use to support this conclusion. Try to explain why you have selected these.

T2 Religious concepts

This section covers AO2 content and skills

Specification content
The extent to which the three images (theories) of the Atonement suggest the Christian God is cruel

---

News reporter

A good introduction to the background of Old Testament sacrifices, which is linked to Jesus as a sacrifice. The conclusion is that God is cruel since an alternative system could have been created.

Tennis player / Detective

The answer now considers the doctrine of the Trinity. It could be argued that God offered himself, in which case God cannot be seen as cruel.

Tennis player / Detective / Critical thinker

The answer addresses the second image of Atonement and sees this as supporting the idea of God as cruel. It then considers some alternative understandings of the satisfaction image, which vary between viewing God as a god of vengeance and a god of love. The arguments are reflective and clearly expressed.

Tennis player / Detective

The final image is considered and briefly examined.

Explorer / Detective / Critical thinker

The answer links the three images well, viewing them not as distinct and separate, but each as part of the whole picture. It also draws attention to beyond the actual death, to the results achieved: resurrection and reconciliation.

Exam practice

Sample question
Evaluate the extent to which the three images of the Atonement suggest the Christian God is cruel.

Sample answer

The Old Testament is full of rules and descriptions about the Temple sacrificial system where Jewish people made a sacrifice of animals to make reconciliation with God. Blood was a metaphor or symbol for life. It was equivalent to life itself. So it is not surprising that the images (theories) of the Atonement are rooted in the images of the Temple sacrifices.

The sacrificial image of the Atonement, with Jesus' death portrayed as a scapegoat or Passover lamb, are derived from the Old Testament. It depicts a god who offers his own son as a sacrifice to satisfy his own sense of justice – like an angry tyrant who must be appeased before he forgives. He is indeed cruel, since he could have created some other system that avoided suffering and death.

However, the doctrine of the Trinity makes clear that Jesus is God, so God offered himself as a sacrifice willingly, to die for humanity – his enemies – to make it possible for them to avoid divine judgement. Understood in this way, God can hardly be seen as cruel.

Perhaps the satisfaction image is more difficult to escape this charge of God's cruelty. It depicts God as a feudal overlord concerned with honour. Human sin, according to Anselm, had so offended God's honour that it could be satisfied only by the death of the God-man Jesus. Many Christians feel this is a dated and very unbiblical model. Protestants proposed that satisfaction was not based around honour but justice, and so advocated the penal substitution model. Jesus sets human beings free from divine judgement by taking that judgement upon himself on the cross, satisfying the justice of God. Again, this seems a model rooted in violence. It portrays God as a god of vengeance who insists that his own son suffer spiritually and physically. However, by Jesus dying the death that sinners deserved, then it could equally be seen as the ultimate example of divine love.

The moral-example model could be seen in the same light, demonstrating God's love. God is seen as cruel only if the purpose of Jesus' death was to provide people with a perfect moral example.

Perhaps the claim that God is cruel is valid only when we consider part of the picture. The Bible argues there was a need for sinful humanity to be reconciled with God. These different models, in different ways, indicate God's way of achieving this reconciliation. Also, the events of the cross need to be seen in their entirety. The cross was not the end. After three days, Jesus was resurrected. The end justified the means. Atonement was made.

---

86 | WJEC/Eduqas Religious Studies for AS & A Level Christianity

So although the three images of Atonement suggest that the Christian God is cruel, that is only because the full and complete picture and understanding do not emerge until the resurrection. It is love, not cruelty, that the images point to.

Over to you

Below is a reasonable answer, although not perfect, that a student has written in response to a question requiring an examination of whether or not the moral-example theory is a convincing model of the Atonement. Using the band level descriptors, compare this with the relevant higher bands and the descriptions inside those bands. (It is obviously a reasonable answer, and so would not be in bands 5, 1 or 2.) To do this, it will be useful to consider what is both strong and weak about the answer and therefore what needs developing.

When analysing the answer, in a group, identify three ways to make this answer a better one. You may have more than three observations – and indeed suggestions – to make it a perfect answer!

Answer

At first glance, the moral-example theory is a very convincing model of the Atonement.

First, it removes the risk of portraying God in a negative light, as most other theories do. For example, the early theories that Jesus died as a sacrifice for human sin (Hebrews), or that his death was a ransom payment to Satan (Origen), present God either as a tyrant or as a debtor and deceiver, and the sixteenth-century reformers' penal substitution portrays him as an unjust child abuser.

Second, it gives human beings responsibility for following Jesus' moral example. With other models, human beings have no part in the process of salvation. All the work is done by Jesus.

Third, it does not allege that Jesus' death had any 'supernatural' effect. This makes the Atonement more acceptable to those who call for the demythologisation of the supernatural aspects of the Gospel message.

On further examination, however, the moral-example theory is not so convincing.

First, it does not explain why Jesus had to die. He could have given his followers the necessary moral example in his life and teaching.

Second, it teaches salvation through works, not faith. Human beings can now secure their own salvation simply through their own moral effort by following Jesus' example. This goes against the idea of justification through faith; one of the cardinal beliefs of the Protestant Reformation.

Third, it diminishes God's anger against sin. If Jesus' death was not in some way a vicarious death for the punishment of human sin, then the fall has not been erased and God's justice has still not been administered and satisfied.

Judge

A strong conclusion that it is love not cruelty that the images point to. The answer consistently supports this conclusion throughout, and examines all three images.
A very good answer that fully addresses the question and answers alternative views.

T2 Religious concepts

T2 Religious life

This section covers AO1 content and skills

Specification content
Luther's arguments for justification by faith alone (with reference to Romans 1:17; 5:1; Ephesians 2:8–9; Galatians 2:16; and Luther's rejection of James 2:24)

Key term
absolution: declaration by a priest that a person's sins have been forgiven

Martin Luther

Key person
Martin Luther (1483–1546): a German monk whose writings inspired the Protestant Reformation

D: Faith and works

Make sure you have read and understood the set texts:
Romans 1:17, 5:1; Ephesians 2:8–9; Galatians 2:16; James 2:24.

Luther and justification by faith alone

Justification and purgatory

Justification means being made righteous in the sight of God.

In the Middle Ages, the Roman Catholic Church linked justification with baptism and penance. In baptism, God began the process of making an individual righteous in his sight by removing original sin. The process was continued by confession and penance. People confessed their sins to the priest, who granted them **absolution** for any actual sins they had committed and imposed a penance that they must perform. The idea was thus formed that penance led to righteousness, and that justification was an appropriate reward for good works.

Closely associated with the doctrine of penance was that of purgatory. The Roman Catholic Church taught that if Christians died without having done adequate penance for their sins, they had to spend time in purgatory to complete that penance. Only then would they be accepted into heaven. Purgatory, therefore, was a place of suffering where the souls of believers absolved their sins.

Martin Luther

Martin Luther was a German Augustinian monk and professor of theology at the University of Wittenberg who felt a deep sense of sinfulness and a profound anxiety for his soul's salvation. Despite doing everything that the Church required of him and spending long hours in prayer, confession and penance, he felt he was losing touch with God, and fell into a deep spiritual despair.

Eventually, he concluded that human beings did not play a part; justification was entirely the gift of God. Sinners are not saved by good works; they are saved by faith alone (which Luther termed *sola fide*) – by absolute dependence on God's promise of forgiveness. God then makes them righteous. Luther based this conviction on:

- **Romans 1:17:** 'The righteous will live by faith'
- **Romans 3:28:** 'For we maintain that a person is justified by faith apart from the works of the law'
- **Romans 5:1:** 'We have been justified through faith'
- **Ephesians 2:8–9:** 'For it is by grace you have been saved, through faith – and this is not from yourselves, it is the gift of God – not by works, so that no one can boast'
- **Galatians 2:16:** 'know that a person is not justified by the works of the law, but by faith in Jesus Christ'.

> **Key quote**
>
> Luther added the word *alone* [to his German translation of Romans 3v28] lest anyone see faith as one among a number of causes of justification – including works.
>
> **(Alister McGrath)**

However, other biblical passages seemed to contradict these statements. For instance, the Letter of James maintains that 'a person is considered righteous by what they do and not by faith alone' (James 2:24). Luther failed to reconcile this with the other biblical verses, but concluded that James' letter was 'an Epistle of straw' that had 'nothing of the nature of Gospel about it'. For Luther, faith was a vital, transforming power; a new and invigorating personal relationship with God.

Indulgences

In 1517, Luther was able to apply his new theory of salvation to a Church practice that was an obvious abuse. This was the sale of indulgences. An indulgence was a piece of paper a sinner could buy from the Pope to avoid a penance. The proceeds from the sale of indulgences went towards building the church of St Peter in Rome, although in Wittenberg half the money went to the Cardinal Archbishop of Mainz to offset what he had paid to be appointed archbishop.

Johann Tetzel, a Dominican monk, was a commissioner for this collection. Tetzel overstated Catholic doctrine on indulgences, alleging that they not only liberated the living from doing penance, but also that the souls of the dead could be released from purgatory on payment of a few coins by their surviving relatives. A well-known saying was attributed to him: 'As soon as a coin in the coffer rings/the soul from purgatory springs'.

To Luther, convinced that salvation was a matter of a right personal relationship with God, Tetzel's teaching was an abomination. Luther preached against the abuse of indulgences, and on 31 October 1517 posted on the door of the castle church in Wittenberg his famous Ninety-five Theses against clerical abuses in the Roman Catholic Church. This was the spark that ignited the Protestant Reformation.

The Council of Trent as a response to Luther

From 1545 to 1563, the Roman Catholic Church held an important council, known as the *Council of Trent*. Trent or Trento is a city in what is now northern Italy. The council was set up to consider its responses to the Reformation.

It concluded that:

- God does not just make people righteous; they must become righteous.
- Good works are required as a condition for ultimate justification.
- People cannot bring about their own salvation; they must co-operate with the grace of God.

> **Key quote**
>
> You see that a person is considered righteous by what they do and not by faith alone.
>
> **(James 2:24)**

Specification content

The Council of Trent as a response to Luther

> **Key quote**
>
> We do not become righteous by doing righteous deeds but, having been made righteous, we do righteous deeds.
>
> **(M. Luther)**

- Justification works in two phases: in the first place, righteousness is mediated through baptism, which is God's gift of grace; in the second, righteousness is increased by participating in the Eucharist and penance, and by doing good works.
- There is a middle position between assurance of salvation and despair: people can have a relative (not absolute) certainty of justification.
- Neither faith nor works merit justification: initial justification is by grace, but works are necessary for progressive salvation.
- They would reform the practices of selling indulgences, but they asserted that the Church had the power to grant them.
- The doctrine of purgatory was upheld.

The decrees of the Council of Trent have never been revoked and are confirmed by both the Second Vatican Council (1962–65) and the official 'Catechism of the Catholic Church' (1992).

Protestant criticism of the Council of Trent

Protestants reasserted that the true biblical view was that justification is declared by God through his grace. He acquits sinners of guilt in the sense of not counting their sins against them. They quoted such texts as 2 Corinthians 5:19, where Paul says 'that God was reconciling the world to himself in Christ, not counting people's sins against them'.

They claimed that believing good works merit grace contradicted the Bible, which teaches that 'the gift of God is eternal life' (Romans 6:23) and that eternal life is available right now to those who believe (John 5:24).

Equally, Protestants did not agree that good works were necessary for salvation, but rather that salvation inevitably produces good works. Good works are the result of salvation, not the cause of salvation.

A modern view: EP Sanders

In his book *Paul and Palestinian Judaism* (1977), **EP Sanders** rejects the view that Paul's Jewish religion was simply a 'salvation by works' religion. This had been the popular view. Instead, Sanders argues that it was **covenantal nomism** (a term he coined). Jewish people believed that God had instigated a covenant of grace with them, which made them 'a chosen nation' and gave them a special status. They maintained their special status in that covenant, however, only by obeying God's commandments. The status itself was a gift, not a reward for obedience. So Jewish people entered the covenant by grace and remained in it by works. This, Sanders argues, was the Jewish view in Paul's time. In other words, it was not a 'salvation by works' belief.

Sanders sets Paul's theology against this background, which is much closer to the New Testament view of justification. Paul asserted that in Jesus, God has acted to save the world. Therefore, Paul concluded that the Mosaic Law was not the means of saving the world. He realised that people are justified, not through the Mosaic Law, but through the cross of Jesus.

The justification that Jesus achieved for humanity was an act of God's grace. It was not earned by humankind. It can only be maintained, however, when people respond in gratitude, keeping God's commandments and entering into a mystical participation in Jesus. The covenant did not limit who could be included. In Sanders' words, 'Christ came to provide a new Lordship for those who participate in his death and resurrection', be they Jewish or Gentiles. Thus, Christians enter the new covenant by baptism, but must then be made righteous by faith. It is union with Christ that leads to justification.

Key quote

Faith is a living, daring confidence in God's grace.

(M. Luther)

Specification content

EP Sanders and the role of works in justification

Key person

EP Sanders (1937–2022): an American New Testament scholar who challenged the negative view of rabbinic Judaism and gave a new perspective on Paul

Key term

covenantal nomism: God's election of Jewish people as a chosen nation provided they obeyed his commandments

Therefore, Sanders argues that the Jewish understanding of justification was much closer to the New Testament teaching than was previously thought.

Some have criticised Sanders' view of Jewish beliefs of justification at the time of Paul. They maintain that the rabbinic literature of Paul's time contains ample evidence of a Jewish belief in righteousness by works. It also ignores clear evidence that many Jewish people believed themselves morally superior to their peers because they adhered strictly to God's commandments through their works.

> **Summary**
> - *Justification* means 'being made righteous in the sight of God'.
> - Martin Luther argued that sinners are justified by faith alone and not by good works.
> - In 1517, he posted on the church door at Wittenberg his Ninety-five Theses against clerical abuses in the Roman Catholic Church. This sparked the Protestant Reformation.
> - The Council of Trent met to respond to the Protestant Reformation.
> - The Council affirmed that we are justified by faith, but not faith alone. We must also keep God's commandments.
> - EP Sanders argues that the Jewish understanding of justification was much closer to the New Testament teaching than previously thought.

> **AO1 Activity**
>
> a   Explain how Martin Luther's understanding of justification differs from that of the Roman Catholic Church. Support the two views with extracts from biblical texts.
>
> This helps you develop understanding of the different aspects of doctrines of justification and awareness of the key terminology involved, and helps you demonstrate accurate use of specialist language and evidence using biblical texts.
>
> b   Draw a diagram to illustrate the similarities and differences between EP Sanders' view of justification and that of:
>
> i   the Roman Catholic Church
>
> ii Luther.
>
> This helps you select and recall the key points and the relationship between the different views of justification.

T2 Religious life

> **This section covers AO2 content and skills**

> **Specification content**
> The extent to which both faith and works are aspects of justification

Issues for analysis and evaluation

The extent to which both faith and works are aspects of justification

Possible line of argument	Critical analysis and evaluation
Most Roman Catholics would see justification as a process involving both faith and works.	The process would start with baptism to remove original sin and then maintained by repentance, penance and good works.
The Bible supports the Roman Catholic view.	James 2:24 refers to justification being by works and not faith alone. People can be declared righteous only when they are righteous.
An alternative view sees justification as a one-off moment – Martin Luther was of this view. He saw justification as a divine act where God declares them righteous.	There is nothing that sinners can do that can justify them before God. God has done once for all, through Jesus' death on the cross.
The Bible supports this view.	James 2:24 refers to 'dead faith', which is worthless. Faith is not just about intellectual acceptance – it should cause a change in a person's life. Real faith produces good works. But good works are the result of justification, not the cause of justification.
Faith alone as the means of justification compromises God's justice since he declared people to be righteous when they are not.	God's justice has not been compromised because Jesus took our sin and its consequences on himself. Justification is a declarative act of God's grace.
Grace is more important than either faith or works.	Grace comes before both faith and works according to Catholic teaching. For Luther, grace comes to a person first through faith, and this results in good works.
It is a matter of emphasis and interpretation.	Neither side of the debate suggests that a person is saved by good works alone.

> **AO2 Activity**
> a Analyse three possible conclusions that could be drawn from the critical analysis and evaluation of the extent to which both faith and works are aspects of justification. What are their strengths? Which conclusion do you think is the weakest?
> b Evaluate three lines of argument that persuaded you to think that this is the weakest conclusion. Think of questions you could raise in response to these arguments.

Exam practice

Sample question
Evaluate the extent to which the New Testament letters support arguments for justification by faith alone.

Sample answer
Many Christians argue that justification is by faith alone and seemingly do not include works as an aspect of justification. They view salvation as a single moment or event when faith is discovered and one is 'saved'. The text of Romans 3:28 is often quoted as clear evidence of this view of salvation. However, the often-quoted verse of Romans 3:28 ('that man is justified … alone through faith') does not contain the word 'alone' in the original. Martin Luther added it when he translated the text into German.

The only time the words faith alone appear is in James 2:24, which states that we are not justified by faith alone but by what we do. So it seems hard to argue that the New Testament letters support justification by faith alone.

In Romans, Paul claims that it will be the doers of the law who will be justified.

Most New Testament letters link the two together, with works along with faith as the path to salvation.

So can 'by faith alone' be supported? The emphasis in the New Testament seems to be on faith as the gateway to human reconciliation with God. It is through faith, which then leads to works, that we are saved. The James quotation does not rule out faith, but sees works linked to faith. Paul also makes clear that grace comes before faith or works. In that sense, grace is more important since it inspires both faith and works.

Many would argue that the way of reconciling the verses in James and Romans is to understand them as not being about how people attain righteousness. Rather, it is about how they prove to others that they are justified. Faith without works is dead. We could interpret James as meaning that people are not proved or made just by a dead faith, but that righteousness must be proved by their works. Genuine faith will result in actions and obedience.

1 John 2 states that if someone says they believe in God but does not keep the commandments, they are lying. Does this imply that faith alone is not enough? Maybe there is no contradiction if 'faith' is not referring just to intellectual assent, but more about a living faith and trust in God, which leads to a life of Godly obedience and good works.

So, if by the statement 'you are justified by faith alone' means intellectual faith with no following good works or any call for discipleship, then the New Testament does not support that. However, if 'faith' refers to a living faith and trust in God, then the whole of the New Testament, including the letters, are supportive of that understanding.

This section covers AO2 content and skills

Specification content
The extent to which the New Testament letters support arguments for justification by faith alone

News reporter / Detective
The answer introduces and explains the idea of salvation being by faith alone. It shows good knowledge of the problems of the text Romans 3:28.

Detective
A strong case with some examples from biblical text further the view that the New Testament letters do not support justification by faith alone.

Detective / Critical thinker
The answer considers whether there is any case for justification by faith alone. It is a thoughtful and reflective treatment, showing good knowledge and understanding of the biblical text.

Explorer / Detective
The answer attempts to reconcile what might appear as two contradictory verses. Again, it shows good understanding of the biblical text.

Critical thinker / Explorer
The debate introduces another biblical text, which gives rise to some critical reasoning and a possible harmonising of the texts.

Judge
The answer consistently argues for and reflects on the conclusion in the light of some Bible verses that might challenge such a conclusion.
A good answer that shows thoughtful reasoning and good knowledge and understanding of biblical texts.

Over to you

Below is a below-average answer that a student has written in response to a question requiring an evaluation of whether EP Sanders' view of justification is convincing. (It is obviously a below-average answer and so would be about lower band 2.) It will be useful, initially, to consider what is missing from the answer and what is inaccurate. The accompanying list gives you some possible observations to assist you. Beware that not all points may be relevant!

When analysing the answer's weaknesses, in a group, choose five points from the list that you would use to improve the answer to make it stronger. Then write out your additions, each one in a clear paragraph. Remember: It is how you use the points that is the most important factor. Apply the principles of evaluation by making sure that you:

- identify issues clearly
- present accurate views of others, making sure that you comment on the views presented
- reach an overall personal judgement.
  You may add more of your own suggestions, but try to negotiate as a group and prioritise the most important things to add.

Answer

EP Sanders argues that in the Jewish religion, which St Paul was brought up in, there was a 'pattern' based on the Jewish belief that God had instigated a covenant with them, which made them a 'chosen nation'. They maintained this covenant by obeying God's commandments. The covenant itself was a gift, but it was maintained by obedience.

Sanders sets Paul's theology in this light. Paul realised that people are justified, not through the Mosaic Law, but through the cross. The justification that Jesus achieved for humanity was an act of God's grace, which can only be maintained when people respond in obedience. Christians enter the new covenant by baptism, but must thereafter be made righteous by faith.

Some theologians have criticised Sanders' theory on the grounds that it uses non-biblical sources to override biblical teaching. However, his position is valid because it reflects traditional thinking.

Observations

1. What is the title of Sanders' book on the subject?
2. What is Sanders' technical term for this 'pattern'?
3. Where exactly does Paul say these things?
4. What are the non-biblical sources Sanders uses?
5. Are there other arguments against Sanders' views, e.g. evidence of a Jewish belief in justification by works, that it fails to address the problem of self-righteousness?
6. The one-sentence conclusion is superficial and invalid. The conclusion should be balanced, reflecting the argument presented and clearly linking to the question.

E: The community of believers

Make sure that you have read and understood the set text: Acts 2:42–47.

The New Testament community of believers

The Acts of the Apostles is the earliest account we have of the spread of Christianity during the first century CE. There is a general consensus that Acts was written by Luke, the same author of the third Gospel, some 40 years after Jesus' crucifixion.

The life of the early Christian community is characterised mainly by its enthusiasm under the guidance of the Holy Spirit. From the beginning, however, it demonstrates elements of an organised structure, reflected in its practices, communal life, worship and discipline. These are described in Acts 2:42–47.

'They devoted themselves to the apostles' teaching and to fellowship' (v42)

The apostles' teaching (*didache* in Greek) was preached in the early Church in what the New Testament scholar CH Dodd and others termed the *kerygma*, which means a 'proclamation'. The aim of the kerygma was to proclaim the key acts of the Gospel. It followed a particular pattern:

- Old Testament prophecies had been fulfilled; the Messiah had come.
- This has happened through the life, death and resurrection of Jesus.
- He was born of the house of David, and died to save humankind.
- He was buried, but resurrected on the third day, according to the scriptures.
- He ascended to heaven and sits at the right hand of God.
- He will come again to be humankind's Judge and Saviour.
- Therefore, all are called to repent and be baptised in his name.

The early Christian community was 'devoted' to this teaching. It was united in its belief that Jesus was the Messiah, that he had been raised from the dead, that he now sits at the right hand of God and that it is through him that people's sins are forgiven. Believers accepted this teaching, and baptism, which led them to a 'fellowship', a special relationship with God through Jesus Christ and with each other, expressed in partaking of communion, holding fast to the apostolic doctrines and following a particular way of life.

> **Key quote**
>
> The Bible knows nothing of solitary religion.
> (J Wesley)

'[They devoted themselves] to the breaking of bread' (v42)

The phrase 'breaking of bread' can refer to two different things:

- The breaking of the bread at the Lord's Supper, the sacrament that Jesus established at his final meal with his disciples the night before his crucifixion.
- The dividing of the loaves at a communal meal; in apostolic times, such meals were held regularly in some Jewish communities.

This section covers AO1 content and skills

Specification content
The New Testament community of believers

The meaning of the phrase is determined by its context.

- In Acts 2:42, where it is used in the context of worship, it probably refers to the sacramental meal.
- In Acts 2:46, it probably refers to an early Church practice that may well have been a means of providing sustenance for the poorer members of the family, or just sharing a meal as friends together.

Both practices demonstrated the unity of the early Christian community; the first because it was a sacrament reflecting the members' communion with each other and with God; and the second because it allowed them to deepen their relationship with each other.

'[They devoted themselves] to prayer' (v42)

Jewish men in Jerusalem went to the Temple to pray at least three times a day. The apostles and their followers still adhered to this custom. Acts 5:12 records that they met in 'Solomon's portico', which formed part of the Court of the Gentiles, so called because Gentiles were allowed to enter it.

However, the early Christians met also to pray in private homes. There may have been several reasons for this:

- The Pentecost experience had been so intense that it compelled them to seek constant fellowship with God and with each other.
- The practice of prayer brought them into contact with pious Jewish people, who the Christians could then talk to about Jesus as the long-awaited Messiah that the Jewish people were anticipating.
- They were aware that prayer was the main source of their strength as individual Christians and as a Christian community.

The word *prayers* includes praise, adoration, thanksgiving, petition, confession and giving God glory.

Modern church at prayer

'They had everything in common' (v44)

Acts 2:45 states that all those who believed 'sold property and possessions to give to anyone who had need'. This does not mean that the early Christian community taught some kind of religious communism, where 'everything in common' meant a redistribution of wealth. Nowhere in Acts is there any suggestion of class warfare or confiscation of property. The communal life is not seen as compulsory for all Christians, because we read elsewhere in Acts that some believers owned property (for example in 12:12, the disciples meet in a house that belonged to Mary, Mark's mother).

What Luke is testifying to is the voluntary, loving and selfless disposition of the early Christians. The Holy Spirit acting in their lives caused them to care for their less fortunate colleagues. Not everyone received a distribution of what was laid at the apostles' feet. The proceeds were distributed 'as any had need'. There was no general distribution of wealth.

The New Testament makes no mention of any similar communities, so it may have been during only the earliest years of Christianity, and limited to the Christian group in Jerusalem.

The New Testament community of believers as a model for the contemporary Church

Today's Christian Church is the 'body of Christ' on Earth. It exists to worship God, to administer the sacraments, to teach, to make disciples, to serve and to have fellowship.

> **Key quote**
>
> Wherever we see the word of God purely preached and heard, there a church of God exists …
>
> (J Calvin)

> **Specification content**
>
> The New Testament community of believers as a model for churches today (with reference to Acts 2:42–47); the role of churches in providing worship and sacraments, religious teaching, mission, service and outreach, and fellowship for the community of believers

Religious teaching

Over the centuries, the Church has split into many denominations. The Eastern Orthodox and Western Roman Catholic Churches separated in 1054. The sixteenth-century Reformation saw the Protestant Lutherans leave the Catholic Church. It split further when Protestants divided into Baptists (who reject infant baptism), Congregationalists (whose individual congregations are autonomous), Presbyterians (who are generally governed by assemblies of Church elders) and others.

All contemporary Christian denominations claim that, like the early Christian community, they adhere closely to the basic teaching of the apostles. They all share the basic beliefs, even though there are some differences.

Worship, sacraments and fellowship

The Church administers the sacraments. A *sacrament* is 'an outward and visible sign of an inward and invisible grace' (Augustine). They are ordained by Christ and entrusted to the Church to administer. There are seven sacraments in the Roman Catholic Church and in many Orthodox Churches (baptism, confirmation, the Eucharist, penance, anointing of the sick, ordination and marriage). Most Protestants recognise only two (baptism and the Eucharist). Partaking in the sacraments of the Church, accepting its doctrines and following an appropriate way of life leads believers into a 'fellowship', which is a special relationship with God through Jesus Christ, and with each other.

T2 Religious life

Some denominations have religious orders made up of monks and nuns, who live, work and pray together and hold everything in common.

Mission, service and outreach

Others practise *tithing*, where members agree to give one-tenth of their income towards the Church's work. All denominations do what they can to serve others, especially to assist sick and poor people.

Christians believe that, through the Church, people can make contact with the risen Jesus, who exists today in the Christians in the Church. The Church is a sign of God's grace, and it is also an instrument of God's grace. It works for peace, charity, overseas mission and so on to bring about the justice and mercy that God intends for all creation. The Church is the agent of God's mission to the world. Christian charity organisations, such as Tearfund or CAFOD (Catholic Agency for Overseas Development), respond to natural disasters such as famine and earthquakes, as well as crises caused by humans such as wars. They give tangible support to survivors. Churches have helped with foodbanks, and reached out to refugees to help them rebuild their lives. In poorer countries, the Church has often set up programmes for health and child development.

> **Key quotes**
>
> There is no real religious experience that does not express itself in charity.
> **(CH Dodd)**
>
> Jesus gave us a model for the work of the church at the Last Supper … [He] began to wash their feet.
> **(P Yancey)**

To tell people the Good News of Jesus Christ and his offer of forgiveness and eternal life is a key part of the work of the Church. In Matthew 28:18–20, Jesus said to his disciples, 'Go and make disciples of all nations, baptising them in the name of the Father and of the Son and of the Holy Spirit, and teaching them to obey everything I have commanded you'. Therefore, outreach ministry is a critical part of the work of the Church, to spread God's word and share his love with the community and the world at large. Church services of worship and teaching help bring people into a deeper relationship with Jesus Christ.

The New Testament Church in some ways is an excellent model for contemporary Christian Churches. It was united in worship and belief and its life was founded on prayer. It operated under the guidance of the Holy Spirit but, in the beginning, limited its outreach only to Jewish people. Paul's letters also reveal the various problems experienced in the early Churches, with disagreements, jealousy and a leadership that was often autocratic.

> **Summary**
> * Five activities of the early Church:
>   1. Listening to apostles' teaching (*didache*) and preaching (*kerygma*)
>   2. Fellowship
>   3. Breaking of bread
>   4. Prayer
>   5. Held material possessions in common
> * Seven activities of Churches today:
>   1. Religious teaching
>   2. Worship
>   3. Sacraments
>   4. Fellowship
>   5. Mission
>   6. Service
>   7. Outreach

AO1 Activity

a. Explain the life of the early Christian community as portrayed in Acts 2:42–47.

This helps you identify elements of the organised structure of the practices of the early Christian community, using Acts 2 as the main source.

b. Draw a line down the middle of a revision card. In the left-hand column, list all the activities the early Church undertook. In the right-hand column, list all the activities of churches today. Draw a line between those that are shared and circle those that belong only to the early Church OR to the contemporary Church.

This helps you to recall and see the extent that the activities of the contemporary Church are modelled on those of the early Church.

> **This section covers AO2 content and skills**

> **Specification content**
> The extent to which contemporary Christian Churches should follow the New Testament model

Issues for analysis and evaluation

The extent to which contemporary Christian Churches should follow the New Testament model

Possible line of argument	Critical analysis and evaluation
Just as we should follow the early teaching of the Church, so we should follow the early Church's model of a Church. Both are given in the Bible – which is the word of God, and given for our guidance.	The teaching of the Church is fixed and contains eternal truth, while the model for the Church is not fixed and changes with the needs of the age. Today, we live in a pluralistic society. Acts 2 worked for a specific group of Jewish Christians in a specific location. Surely the Holy Spirit can lead Churches into new forms to speak to new generations.
The New Testament Church is the ideal model: united in beliefs, practices, worship and communal life; led by the Holy Spirit; had strong leadership; prayerful and mission orientated; effectively administered; attractive to outsiders.	The Church today is in decline in the UK. Its traditions no longer relate to contemporary life. The New Testament model is also flawed. It was far from being the 'Golden Age'. There was favouritism and jealousy, and the leadership was inconsistent and often led to bitter arguments (I Corinthians 1:5; 3:1).
Though the New Testament Church had faults, we can learn lessons from it, for instance the arranging of the Council of Jerusalem to resolve problems.	Today's Church faces situations that are very different from the Christians of the first century. There is very little we can learn from the New Testament model.
Our knowledge of the New Testament Church is very limited.	One of the main aspects of Church is worship, but in Acts 2 only prayer is mentioned – though Paul mentions more in his letters. Leadership varied between theocratic, autocratic and sometimes democratic.
There is no single model of the early Church.	Paul's letters reveal a variety of different structures and models of the Churches.
The early Church soon moved away from the model of a Church in Acts 2.	As the Church spread, so Churches' needs changed and they became more diverse. There is no clear New Testament model for a contemporary Church to follow.

> **AO2 Activity**
>
> a Analyse three possible conclusions that could be drawn from the critical analysis and evaluation of the extent to which contemporary Christian Churches should follow the New Testament model. What are their strengths? Which conclusion do you think is the strongest?
>
> b Evaluate three lines of argument that persuaded you to think that this is the strongest conclusion. Think of questions you could raise in response to these arguments.

Exam practice

Sample question

Evaluate whether the main role of the Church is to provide religious teaching.

Sample answer

According to the Acts of the Apostles, the first thing listed about the fellowship of believers is that 'they devoted themselves to the apostles' teaching'. If the Church does not accurately pass on the teaching of the apostles, then the Church will drift into heresy and its message of salvation and eternal life will be lost. What could be more important than the message of salvation? Paul was very concerned about passing on the message of Jesus and opposed even the apostles when they seemed to be drifting away from it.

Churches even split away from other Churches if they feel the message is being changed, for instance the great schism in 1054 between the Catholic and Eastern Orthodox Churches; then again in the sixteenth century, between the Roman Catholic and the Protestant Churches. Clearly, these groups thought the correct teaching must be upheld at any cost.

The problem is that different people have interpreted scripture in different ways. This leads to fragmentation and bewilderment to ordinary Christians who may not understand the intricate details of theology. For them, people and showing God's love matter more. It is love and reacting to humanitarian needs that should therefore be the main focus of the Church – not petty squabbles over obscure doctrine. Jesus' parable of the Good Samaritan is about God's love in action. Paul wrote 'these three remain: faith, hope and love. But the greatest of these is love' (1 Corinthians 13). True Christian love (agapé) is unselfish and unconditional.

However, it is doctrine and teaching that gives rise to the love for people. The example and teaching of Jesus has led Christians to care for weak, poor, suffering, marginalised and vulnerable people. In the parable of the sheep and goats, Jesus says, 'whatever you did for one of the least of these brothers of mine, you did for me'. So religious teaching is not in opposition to caring about people; one leads to the other.

Yet, it is not always clear what is meant by 'religious teaching'. Traditional teaching about the role of women, birth control, marriage of divorced or single-sex couples, and so on seems to be out of sync with twenty-first-century culture. Many might see this as a Church living in the past and of little relevance today.

This section covers AO2 content and skills

Specification content
Whether the main role of the Church is to provide religious teaching

Detective / News reporter

A good introduction, linking the main role back to the beginning of the Church in Acts 2. It clearly states why this role is important to the continuation of the Church. To reinforce it, it poses a rhetorical question and then develops the illustration of Paul's concern about the teaching of salvation.

Detective / News reporter

The main role of teaching is further developed by reference to Church history events. It is the dispute about teaching that is seen as the cause of the schisms, illustrating how important right teaching was to the Church.

Tennis player / News reporter / Detective

This paragraph considers an alternative view. It is not the theoretical aspect so much as the practical working of the Church 'through love' that is seen as the main role of the Church.

Philosopher / Detective

This paragraph reflects on debate that theology and practice go together; one leads to the other.

Philosopher

This paragraph raises the question of religious teaching being out of sync with present cultural views.

Detective
News reporter
Judge **Explorer**

The answer considers other roles, with an appeal to Jesus' command in Matthew 28. The final conclusion is consistent with the argument throughout the answer, which shows good biblical knowledge and well-illustrated arguments. A very good answer.

But what of other roles of the Church, for instance the giving of the sacraments such as baptism and of worship? The most important role of the Church is surely its mission to make disciples and baptise: 'Therefore go and make disciples of all nations, baptising them in the name of the Father and of the Son and of the Holy Spirit, and teaching them to obey everything I have commanded you' (Matthew 28). This is what Jesus himself commanded his followers to do.

Perhaps the best conclusion is to support the view that the main role of the Church is to provide religious teaching, but only in so far as it delivers a message that is life-changing and impacts upon those in need.

Over to you

Below is a below-average answer that a student has written in response to a question requiring an evaluation of the contention that the contemporary Christian Church is more of an instrument than a sign of God's grace. (It is obviously a below-average answer and so would be about band 2.) It will be useful, initially, to consider what is missing from the answer and what is inaccurate. This time, there is no accompanying list to assist you.

When analysing the answer's weaknesses, in a group, decide on five points that you would use to improve the answer. Then write out your additions, each one in a clear paragraph. Remember: It is how you use the points that is the most important factor. Apply the principles of evaluation by making sure that you:

- identify issues clearly
- present accurate views of others, making sure that you comment on the views presented
- reach an overall personal judgement. You may add more of your own suggestions, but try to negotiate as a group and prioritise the most important things to add.

Answer

You could argue that the Christian Church is a sign of God's grace because it administers the sacraments, of which there are seven in all. However, not many people receive the sacraments today.

The Church is more relevant as an instrument of God's grace. This is when it works on behalf of God for peace, charity, fair trade, gender equality, overseas mission, and so on.

A key quotation comes from Dodd: 'There is no real religious experience that does not express itself in charity.'

Attempts to get the worldwide Church to respond as one on global peace and justice issues have been more successful than those aimed at developing a common approach to the sacraments, particularly the Eucharist.

F: Key moral principles

Make sure that you have read and understood the set texts: Leviticus 19:34; Luke 10:25–28; Exodus 34:6–7; 1 John 4:19–21; 1 Samuel 12:24; Ephesians 4:25–27; 2 Corinthians 1:12; 1 Timothy 1:5; Matthew 6:14–15; Colossians 3:12–13.

An introduction to key Christian principles

Christian moral principles are based on God's laws regarding behaviour. Christians attempt to obey certain rules laid down by God and recorded in Old Testament law and in the New Testament teaching of Jesus.

Jesus was often challenged by Jewish leaders about his attitude to Old Testament law, and why his followers did not adhere to it more closely. He was once asked by a Pharisee (a member of a sect devoted to the study of the law), 'Teacher, which is the greatest commandment in the Law?' Jesus replied: "Love the Lord your God with all your heart and with all your soul and with all your mind." This is the first and greatest commandment. And the second is like it: "Love your neighbour as yourself". All the Law and the Prophets hang on these two commandments' (Matthew 22:36–40).

Love of neighbour

Jesus' reply to the Pharisee was echoing what had been written in the Old Testament (Deuteronomy 6:5 and Leviticus 19:18). Leviticus goes on to give a reason for this command to love your neighbour: Israelites are to welcome foreigners as fellow citizens and to 'love them as yourself, for you were foreigners in Egypt' (Leviticus 19:34).

The two commandments are repeated at the beginning of Jesus' parable of the Good Samaritan (Luke 10:25–37). When asked by a lawyer 'What must I do to inherit eternal life?', Jesus replies 'What is written in the Law?'. The lawyer answers that the law commands people to love God and to love their neighbour as themselves. 'You have answered correctly,' Jesus replied. 'Do this and you will live.' The lawyer then asks, 'And who is my neighbour?'. Jesus replies by telling the parable about a man who is attacked and robbed on the road from Jerusalem to Jericho. Two Jewish religious leaders pass him by without offering help, but a Samaritan (Jewish people considered Samaritans to be their enemies) stops, binds the man's wounds and takes care of him. Jesus then commands the lawyer: 'Go and do likewise.'

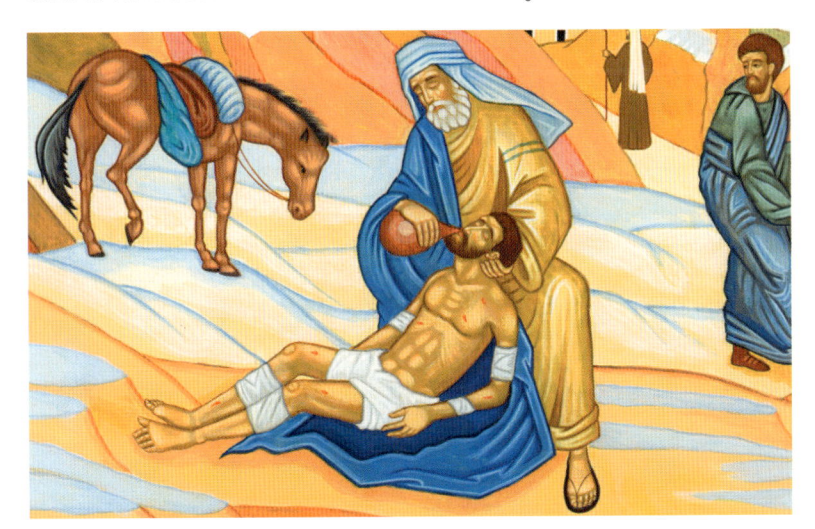

The Good Samaritan

This section covers AO1 content and skills

Specification content
Selected key moral principles of Christianity

Key quote
How many observe Christ's birthday! How few, His precepts.
(B Franklin)

Specification content
Selected key moral principles of Christianity: the importance of love of neighbour (Leviticus 19:34; Luke 10:25–28)

It is clear that, for Jesus, a 'neighbour' is not simply the person who happens to live next door, but everyone we happen to meet on life's journey, friend or enemy. In the Sermon on the Mount, Jesus tells his followers that they have heard the old saying 'Love your neighbour but hate your enemy'. 'But,' he goes on, 'I tell you, love your enemies and pray for those who persecute you' (Matthew 5:43).

To love God with heart, soul and mind is to recognise that everyone is part of God's creation. Everyone deserves respect, and for their needs and desires to be equal to everyone else's. This is a core Christian principle.

God's love as a potential model for Christian behaviour

The basic model for Christian behaviour is the love God himself shows for human beings. In both the Old and New Testaments, God is presented as a god of love.

> **Specification content**
> Selected key moral principles of Christianity: God's love as a potential model for Christian behaviour (Exodus 34:6–7; 1 John 4:19–21).

> **Key quote**
> To love another person is to see the face of God.
> (V Hugo)

In the Old Testament, in Exodus 34:6–7, God reveals himself to Moses and, in words attributed to God himself, describes his own character, proclaiming that he:

- **is compassionate:** he does not punish us, even though we deserve it
- **is gracious:** he gives us what we do not deserve
- **is slow to anger:** he is long-suffering and patient
- **abounds in love and faithfulness:** his love and faithfulness are unchanging

> **Key quote**
> Though our feelings come and go, His love for us does not.
> (CS Lewis)

- **maintains love to thousands:** he is an active love for the human race
- **forgives wickedness, rebellion and sin:** he forgives all – wickedness (our fallen nature), rebellion (deliberate and defiant revolt against his law) and sin (every wrong we do, accidental or otherwise)
- **does not leave the guilty unpunished:** he is nevertheless a God of justice; his love includes correction, and those who insist on doing evil will be punished
- **punishes the children for the sin of the parents to the third and fourth generation:** the consequences of sin are likely to be felt by the family of the guilty, but will be limited to three or four generations.

The New Testament teaches that God's steadfast love and faithfulness was revealed fully in the life and death of Jesus. Since God has so loved human beings, human beings must so love God. In 1 John 4:19–21, John insists that it is impossible to love God without also loving other people. Those who say that they love God, and hate their brothers and sisters, are liars. If they do not love their brothers or sisters, whom they have seen, how can they love God, whom they have not seen? True love of God includes a love of humanity.

A regard for truth

Christians have always considered themselves to be guardians of the truth. By *truth*, they mean the ultimate meaning and value of existence. They believe the Bible to contain God's revelation to human beings. It communicates the truth about the nature of God, the person of Jesus and the account of God's salvation plan in history to bring forgiveness and eternal life.

In the Old Testament (1 Samuel 12:24), the Israelites are reminded to 'consider what great things he has done for you'. These 'great things' included freeing them from captivity in Egypt and leading them into the Promised Land. In the New Testament, Jesus says of himself 'I am the way and the truth and the life' (John 14:6).

In the New Testament, Jesus, through his death and resurrection, frees human beings from captivity to sin and leads them to a promised eternal life.

As a result, Christians are called to put away their old, corrupt self and to 'put on the new self, created to be like God in true righteousness and holiness' (Ephesians 4:24). Paul goes on to advise Christians to 'speak truthfully to your neighbour, for we are all members of one body. In your anger do not sin. Do not let the sun go down while you are still angry, and do not give the devil a foothold' (Ephesians 4:25–27).

In other words, Paul warns Christians not to allow anger to fester in the heart because that opens the door for the devil.

> **Specification content**
> Selected key moral principles of Christianity: regard for truth (1 Samuel 12:24; Ephesians 4:25–27)

The role of conscience

The Bible teaches that human beings, because they are made in the image of God, have an innate sense of right and wrong. They are able to view life situations in a moral or ethical light and to judge that some actions are 'right' and others 'wrong'. This ability is called *conscience*. Paul writes in 1 Timothy 1:5 that love 'comes from a pure heart and a good conscience and a sincere faith'.

> **Specification content**
> Selected key moral principles of Christianity: the role of conscience (2 Corinthians 1:12; 1 Timothy 1:5)

> **" Key quote "**
>
> Conscience is the voice of the soul; the passions are the voice of the body.
>
> **(J Rousseau)**

In 2 Corinthians 1:12, Paul defends himself against the accusation that he is fickle and unreliable. He states that he has a clear conscience before God and claims that his conscience testifies that he conducts himself 'with integrity and godly sincerity'. His conscience verifies the integrity of his heart. In other words, Paul's actions and words match his moral awareness, which is based on God's standards.

Christians believe that their conscience is informed both by the Bible and the work of the Holy Spirit. When they violate the standards that they believe are expected of them, they experience guilt. They then confess their sin and experience God's forgiveness. When people repeatedly ignore their conscience, they become desensitised to moral issues and go along with things they know to be wrong.

Conscience can also become overly sensitive, condemning the believer for normal human failures, and leading to false guilt. The Christian's goal is to develop a mature conscience based on biblical teaching as illuminated by the Holy Spirit. The Bible is clear that believers must have their conscience informed by God's word.

Christians' moral behaviour must therefore satisfy their conscience so that it will not cause them guilt.

T2 Religious life

> **Specification content**
> Selected key moral principles of Christianity: the need for forgiveness (Matthew 6:14–15; Colossians 3:12–13)

The need for forgiveness

Forgiveness is a prominent theme in Jesus' teaching. In his Sermon on the Mount (Matthew 6:14–15), he tells his followers that if they do not forgive, they themselves will not be forgiven. It is a spiritual law. God wants the best for his people but, if they cannot forgive, then they cut themselves off from the blessings that God wants to give them.

> **" Key quote "**
>
> Forgiveness is the key to action and freedom.
> (H Arendt)

On another occasion, when Peter asks him 'how often should I forgive?', Jesus answers 'Not seven times, but seventy-seven times' (Matthew 18:21–22). This answer suggests that forgiveness is not easy. People who have been wronged do not naturally overflow with grace and mercy. Nevertheless, Christians must spend a lifetime forgiving.

Paul echoes Jesus' teaching. For him, the model for Christian forgiveness is the forgiveness God freely grants to sinners. In Colossians 3:13, he writes: 'Bear with each other and forgive one another if any of you has a grievance against someone. Forgive as the Lord forgave you'.

Therefore, to obey God, Christians must consciously decide to forgive. They believe that forgiveness sets them free from all feelings of anger and hurt that previously constrained them.

> **Summary**
> * Five key moral principles:
>   1. **Love of neighbour:** Love is both spiritual and practical.
>   2. **God's love as a model for Christian behaviour:** God has a loving character, is merciful and gracious, is slow to anger.
>   3. **A regard for truth:** We are to put away falsehood.
>   4. **The role of conscience:** The way to a good conscience is to recognise God as the source of goodness.
>   5. **The need for forgiveness:** Christians are to emulate the forgiveness Jesus showed on the cross.

> **AO1 Activity**
>
> a List each of the key moral principles on small revision cards. On the back of each, list the Bible verses that relate to it.
>
> This helps you provide biblical support for each of the moral principles.
>
> b Draw a mind map explaining each of the key moral principles and giving key quotes to support your points..
>
> This helps you prioritise and select a core set of points to develop an answer, and helps ensure you are making accurate use of specialist language and vocabulary in context.

Issues for analysis and evaluation

Whether love of neighbour is the most important moral principle in Christianity

Possible line of argument	Critical analysis and evaluation
Jesus' life and teaching shows the importance of love: it is illustrated in his parables and demonstrated by him in his life on Earth.	Certainly the Golden Rule points to love as the important moral principle: 'So in everything, do to others what you would have them do to you' (Matthew 7:12). But Jesus spoke much more on other themes, including 'the Kingdom of God'.
There are other moral principles, such as care for needy and oppressed people.	But these other moral principles are all driven by love.
Love of neighbour is taught in Paul's writings. 1 Corinthians 13 declares that the greatest of faith, hope and love, is love.	There are many moral principles throughout the Bible, such as honesty and forgiveness. It is not clear that love is the most important one.
1 John 4:8: 'Whoever does not love does not know God, because God is love.'	Loving your neighbour comes second after loving God. Therefore, the most important imperative is to love God (Luke 10:27).
Loving neighbour equates with loving God: 'For anyone who does not love his brother ... cannot love God' (1 John 4:20).	God is the source of that love, so God is the source of all moral principles in Christianity.
The Bible refers just to loving your neighbour, but Jesus makes clear in his parable of the Good Samaritan that your neighbour is anyone who needs help.	The Church has often ignored starving and oppressed people if they did not accept the Christian message. However, at times, it has been Christians who have helped those society has rejected.

> **This section covers AO2 content and skills**
>
> **Specification content**
> Whether love of neighbour is the most important moral principle in Christianity

AO2 Activity

a Analyse three possible conclusions that could be drawn from the critical analysis and evaluation of whether love of neighbour is the most important moral principle in Christianity. What are their strengths? Which conclusion do you think is the strongest?

b Evaluate three lines of argument that persuade you to think that this is the strongest conclusion. Think of questions you could raise in response to these arguments.

T2 Religious life

This section covers AO2 content and skills

Specification content
The extent to which God's behaviour towards humans is the basis for Christian morality.

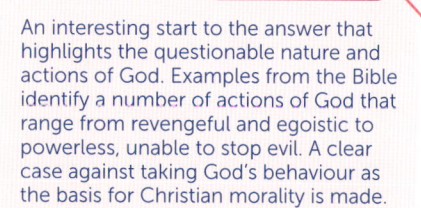

News reporter

Detective

An interesting start to the answer that highlights the questionable nature and actions of God. Examples from the Bible identify a number of actions of God that range from revengeful and egoistic to powerless, unable to stop evil. A clear case against taking God's behaviour as the basis for Christian morality is made.

Explorer

The answer is balanced with some biblical examples that highlight some positive aspects that would be a good basis for Christian behaviour.

Detective

This paragraph explores the nature of God's love as reflecting the basis of Christian morality. Again, good use is made of biblical texts.

Tennis player

Explorer

This paragraph raises another angle on the debate: the difficulty of trying to follow Jesus' example and teachings. A counterargument is given.

Judge

The answer ends with a good summary and a conclusion that the essay consistently argues and reflects on.

Exam practice

Sample question
Evaluate the extent to which God's behaviour towards humans is the basis for Christian morality.

Sample answer

Someone once commented 'I don't know whether God exists, but it would be better for his reputation if he didn't'. In other words, God's behaviour towards human beings is violent and angry, for example the vengeful killings recorded in the Old Testament, such as the ten plagues, along with the New Testament depiction of God creating hell as a place of judgement and torture. Many see God as an egoistic deity who requires worship. Even worse, he is seen as someone who killed his son to satisfy his need for atonement. Being omnipotent, he seems unable to stop evil in the world, with the good and righteous suffering while often the wicked prosper. Understandably, such a list of actions makes it hard to support the view that God's behaviour is the basis for Christian morality.

However, such a view is only a partial view. Christians would point to other characteristics and behaviour of God that are positive. In Exodus 34, God reveals himself to Moses as merciful and gracious, long-suffering and patient, forgiving and just. In the Old Testament, there are commands by God about treatment of strangers, and loving your neighbour as yourself.

Many Christians believe that God's behaviour towards human beings is fully revealed in the New Testament, particularly in the life and death of Jesus, who they believe is fully God. For instance, in John's Gospel there is the statement about the extent of God's love for human beings: 'God so loved the world that he gave his only Son, so that everyone who believes in him may not perish but may have eternal life'. This example of sacrificial love is the basis of Christian morality: 'We love because he first loved us'. The response to God's love for us is to show love for human beings by keeping his commandments. Jesus accepted all, forgave sinners, welcomed outcasts and cared for weak and sick people.

However, it is not easy to follow Jesus' examples and teachings. But Christians believe that they are helped to change by the Holy Spirit, to be more like Jesus, being transformed by the love of God.

Whether all actions of God can form the basis of Christian morality is doubtful. God is God who acts righteously and is the judge of the world. In other words, God has actions that only God can do. It is his love, teachings and commands, not his behaviour, that is the basis of Christian morality.

Over to you

Below is a list of several key points in response to a question requiring an evaluation of whether or not Jesus' teachings concerning key moral principles are the basis of Christian morality. It is obviously a very full list. It will be useful, initially, to consider what you think are the most important points to use when planning an answer. This exercise, in essence, is like writing your own set of possible answers that are listed in a typical mark scheme as indicative content. In a group, select the most important points you feel should be included in a list of indicative content for this question. You need to decide on two things:

1. which points to select
2. the order to put them in an answer.

List of indicative content

In support:
- It should be, because Jesus' teaching is the teaching of God.
- In the Sermon on the Mount, Jesus instructs his followers to adopt his interpretation of God's law.
- Many of Jesus' parables and actions illustrate the basis for moral behaviour.
- Some Christians would say that all that matters is trying to live and treat others as Jesus did.
- As it is not always easy to follow Jesus' example and teachings, Jesus has sent down the Holy Spirit to assist people in their efforts.
- With the assistance of the Holy Spirit, Christians aim to live a holy life.
- Most Christians' aim is to act as a force for good in the world.

Against:
- The basic template for Christian morality is the Mosaic Law.
- In the Sermon on the Mount, Jesus insists that he did not come to abolish the Mosaic Law but to fulfil it.
- Jesus also insisted that the first commandment was to love God.
- Christians therefore often base their morality on what they know of God and his behaviour towards humans.
- Therefore, they too must be merciful, gracious, long-suffering, patient, active in love for humanity, forgiving and just.
- Christians believe that these attributes of God were fully revealed in the life, and particularly in the death, of Jesus.
- Christians therefore love God because God first loved them.
- True love of God includes a love of humanity.
- The appropriate way to respond to God's love is therefore to show love for human beings.

T3 Significant social developments in religious thought

This section covers AO1 content and skills

Specification content

Attitudes towards wealth; the dangers of wealth (with reference to Mark 10:17–25; Matthew 6:25–34; Luke 12:33–34; 1 Timothy 6:10)

A: Attitudes towards wealth

Make sure you have read and understand the set texts:
Mark 10:17–25; Matthew 6:25–34; Luke 12:33–34; 1 Timothy 6:10.

The dangers of wealth

Believers across all religions wonder about the effect of money and wealth on their soul. However, the quest for riches seems to stand in stark contrast to the words of Jesus: 'life does not consist in an abundance of possessions' (Luke 12:15). In Christianity, there are a variety of views that are claimed to have biblical support. These range from voluntary poverty to the belief that God wants to bless his followers with wealth. In between these two positions, Christians have various convictions about how to live responsibly with money and possessions.

Mark 10:17–25

- **Context:** This passage comes in a section of Mark (8:21–10:52) where Jesus is teaching the meaning of discipleship. Jesus' answer to the question of how to obtain eternal life is 'keep the Mosaic Law'. The man asking the question is Jewish. He has been raised on the Law his entire life, but this has not led him to the answer he seeks. Then Jesus says to him, 'One thing you lack, Go, sell everything you have and give to the poor, and you will have treasure in heaven. Then come, follow me' (Mark 10:21). Traditional Jewish teaching on wealth sees it as a sign of divine favour, so that the disciples assume that entry into the Kingdom must be easier for richer people. Jesus provides an answer that is a reversal of accepted ideas: it was his wealth that was holding the man back from the Kingdom of God. Jesus asks the man to give up all possessions and join the Jesus-movement. The man goes away sad because he has great wealth.

> **Key quote**
>
> Idolatry is the heart of rebellion against God (Romans 1:18–32), and no other rival to God than Mammon appears more often or centrally in scripture.
>
> (C Blomberg)

- **Main message:** The rich man clearly sees giving up his wealth as a stumbling block to following Jesus. Then Jesus tells the disciples that it is hard for the rich to enter the Kingdom of God. The usual understanding is that affluent people are always tempted to rely on earthly things and on their own efforts than to cast themselves on the mercy of God. Jesus uses the image of a camel going through the eye of a needle to illustrate the difficulty of entering the Kingdom of God.

  Some Christians interpret this teaching to refer to all who wanted to follow him, while the majority argue that it refers just to this man. What is clear is that for Jesus the Kingdom of God is of infinitely more importance than money and wealth.

- **Scholarly detail:** The laws that Jesus lists are mostly from the second half of the Ten Commandments, which are to do with relationships to others. The commandment 'not to defraud' is not, however, a part of the Ten Commandments, but is a variation on the theme of theft. To defraud is to gain money through illegal means, for example holding back wages. Some scholars see including 'defraud' as an example of Jesus going beyond the letter of the law to insights about its spirit and perhaps even an awareness that the rich man had not stolen in the sense spoken about in the Ten Commandments, but was guilty of other financial sins.

Some early manuscripts use the word *kamilon* ('rope') instead of *kamelon* ('camel'). Some have argued that there was a passage into Jerusalem open only at night called the 'Needle Gate'; any camel needed to have its luggage removed to crouch down and get through the entry. However, there is no historical foundation for this. Sayings of other Jewish teachers have survived that speak of the impossibility of some vast object (such as an elephant) getting through the eye of a needle, which supports the idea of a camel, as the original text.

Matthew 6:25–34

- **Context:** This passage is a part of the Sermon on the Mount, where Jesus outlines what it means to live in the presence of God. One of the main themes of this sermon is that righteousness must be defined in a new way, going beyond the letter of the law to an all-embracing lifestyle of love and commitment.
- **Main message:** Jesus urges his followers to have the right priorities, with the climax of this passage being verse 33, putting the Kingdom of God and righteous living first. The enemy of any priority is anxiety; in this case, it is anxiety about food or clothing. The people in Jesus' audience are not especially rich or powerful; in fact, they were likely living a hand-to-mouth existence. Yet Jesus insists that the priority is not food or clothing, but spiritual things. He demands this because not only is anxiety useless, but also because it is a mark of faithlessness. God will provide, as reflected by God's goodness in the natural world.
- **Scholarly insight:** The term *anxiety* is used in this passage more than in any other place in the New Testament. It has to do with being afraid in such a way as to cause distress. Some passages that might have been known to the Gospel writers include Sirach 30:24: 'Jealousy and anger shorten life, and anxiety brings on premature old age'; in 1 Maccabees 6:10 and Sirach 42:9, the term is used in relation to losing sleep.

Jesus' audience would have been very familiar with the wealth of Solomon (1 Kings 3:13; 10:14–17), perhaps, even longing for God to restore their nation to that former glory. So, it might have been quite surprising to have Jesus point out that they were already surrounded by the glory of the natural world far greater than Solomon's.

Luke 12:33–34

- **Context:** Earlier in this same chapter in Luke (12:16–21) is the parable of the rich fool: a wealthy man celebrates how he has hoarded enough material wealth to secure his future. The problem is that death now comes to him and he has made the mistake of neglecting his spiritual life. The passage recommends exactly the opposite lifestyle. Jesus counsels his followers to concentrate on the real riches – heavenly treasure.

- **Main meaning:** The striking aspect about these verses is the requirement that Jesus' followers sell their possessions and give the proceeds to poor people. Jesus then uses the imagery of a spiritual bank account that is free of the anxieties and inevitable corruption of earthly bank accounts.

- **Scholarly insight:** The Book of Acts shows the followers of Jesus living out this instruction to sell their possessions (Acts 2:44–5; 4:32–5). However, most scholars do not think that Jesus was demanding that his followers sell all their possessions. Giving to poor people was very important in Jewish thought at the time of the New Testament. Jesus commanded Zacchaeus to give away only half his wealth (Luke 19:1–10), and Jesus was entertained in Martha's house (Luke 10:38), which Jesus did not rebuke her for owning.

Jesus is not excluding private ownership, but he is emphasising that believers must not be dominated by their possessions. Trust in riches prevents trust in God.

1 Timothy 6:10

- **Context:** 1 Timothy is concerned with heretical teachings and lax morality entering the Church. The author wants the Church to keep to the truth faith, avoiding obscure beliefs and developing a strong moral centre. 1 Timothy 6:10 contains the final sentence in a section describing the conduct of true Christians (5:1–6:10).

- **Main meaning:** Money is not evil in itself. The real danger is the 'love of money' or, in other words, greed. This greed has motivated false teachers to ignore the truth and drift from the faith. Wealth and faith appear to be awkward partners. Material prosperity comes with a warning label, though it is the eagerness to be rich rather than riches itself that is the real danger.

- **Scholarly insight:** The phrase 'the love of money is a root of all kinds of evil' was a common saying in the ancient world. Several centuries earlier, the **cynic** philosopher Diogenes of Sinope said, 'the love of money is the mother-city of all evils'.

Biblical teaching on stewardship

Stewardship means 'administration' or 'management'. It comes from the role of a steward in ancient times, who was someone who managed various aspects of a house. The theological concept of stewardship views human beings as having the God-given position of managing all their resources well. The concept of stewardship involves several key principles for Christians:

- God has created the Earth; it belongs, therefore, not to us but to God. Human beings have been given charge over it (Genesis 1:26–28; Genesis 2:15; Psalm 8).

> **Key term**
>
> **cynic:** a person who has a bleak outlook about others, always imagining that people are ruled by their worst instincts

> **Specification content**
>
> Apparent contradiction between biblical teaching on stewardship and the ascetic ideal

- The material world is good. Genesis speaks of God's creation as 'good'; this goodness remains even though there is sin in the world (Romans 1:20). Therefore, we should not flee from the management of the material world.
- The Bible assumes that there is private ownership (the Eighth Commandment; see also Leviticus 19:35 and Numbers 27:1–11). Therefore, stewardship applies not only to nations and groups, but also to individuals.
- As God is the defender of the poor and the oppressed (Psalm 68:4–5; Proverbs 14:31), stewardship always includes giving generously to those in need.
- Some Christians see the concept of a tithe from the Hebrew scriptures (giving ten per cent of their income) as an aspect of stewardship.

The opposite of stewardship is greed and covetousness, each of which are consistently condemned in the Old and New Testaments (for example Psalm 10). The Hebrew prophets gave searing rebukes over economic sins, even to the point of declaring that participating in religious activities such as sacrifices and festivals is meaningless for people involved in oppressing poor people (for example Isaiah 1:10–20; Amos 5:11–27). The unbridled quest for wealth is never approved; even kings are told that there are limits to their wealth (Deuteronomy 17:16–17).

Those who see their role in life as stewards do not necessarily embrace a communistic view of Christian community (that is, the monastic ideal) or voluntary poverty. Instead, they view their role as managing wisely the resources God has given them. The Methodist preacher John Wesley (1703–91) said 'Make all you can, save all you can, give all you can'.

The ascetic ideal

Asceticism comes from Greek, meaning 'exercise' or 'training'. In Greek philosophy, it referred to practising strict self-denial as a measure of personal and especially spiritual discipline. The word is used only once in the New Testament, in Acts 24:16, where it is translated as 'strive' or 'exercise' to live in such a way as to have a clear conscience towards God and others. However, the idea of undertaking a special discipline or lifestyle as a part of the Christian path permeates the New Testament.

Jesus declared, 'Whoever wants to be my disciple must deny themselves and take up their cross and follow me' (Mark 8:34). It was the way to protect his followers from being captured by the love of this world and could involve fasting, devotion to prayer and living an itinerant lifestyle. It seems it could also entail abstaining from sexual relationships – though this was not commanded. Jesus refers to this area in Matthew 9:12, and Paul discusses the appropriateness of the celibate life in light of God's return in 1 Corinthians 7. However, John the Baptist is depicted as much more an ascetic than Jesus (Matthew 3:1–6). In contrast, Jesus enjoyed hospitality and was described as a drunkard and a glutton.

Asceticism in the history of the Church

Ascetic practices became widespread among early Christians, with some renouncing marriage, home and property and turning to extreme forms of fasting and self-deprivation. The theologian Origen (185 CE–154 CE) (see page 81) dedicated himself to an ascetic lifestyle of voluntary poverty, fasting and vigils so that his soul could be purified from passion to secure true knowledge of God in this life.

> **Key term**
>
> **asceticism:** discipline or training; avoiding various desires to attain a spiritual goal or ideal

> **Key terms**
>
> **Desert Fathers:** early Christian hermits who lived an ascetic life in the Egyptian desert
>
> **self-flagellation:** striking oneself with a whip, especially as a form of religious discipline
>
> **Manichaeism:** a movement that viewed the world as a conflict between good and evil, with the soul's release found through asceticism
>
> **Montanism:** a movement that believed in asceticism and the imminent end of the world

The **Desert Fathers** renounced an increasingly worldly Church to focus on a simple lifestyle of prayer and devotion in remote locations. They viewed Jesus' 40 days in the wilderness and the lifestyle of John the Baptist as examples to follow.

In the Middle Ages, monasteries attempted, in different ways, to build Christian character through a disciplined life. Some focused on the suffering of Christ, and more violent forms of asceticism became a part of the Christian tradition – wearing hair shirts and chains, as well as **self-flagellation**. Other Christians developed spiritual disciplines such as prayer, penitence, reading spiritual works, pilgrimage and reflecting on the meaning of the sacraments. The rise of humanism and Protestantism brought questions about the value of asceticism, though fasting, prayer and concerns about 'worldly pleasures' have also been a part of Protestant piety. Asceticism can therefore refer to different practices, depending on the type and branch of Christianity being referenced.

Asceticism raises the question of the attitude a Christian should take towards the world. Christians are aware of the dangers of their hearts being captured by the love of this world, and so need to take care how rightly to participate in this world. On the one hand, Hebrew religion is known for embracing the world, celebrating the bounty of nature and enjoying festivals. At the other extreme, movements such as **Manichaeism** and **Montanism** considered the world to be evil, and advocated extreme forms of discipline. Though these movements were judged to be heretical, most Christian Churches believe that some training and discipline is essential to live a God-orientated life. It is about trying to find the best way to be in the world without being of the world.

The prosperity Gospel

> **Specification content**
>
> The prosperity Gospel of the Word-Faith movement

> **Key terms**
>
> **prosperity Gospel:** the teaching that faith and giving to the Church will bring health and wealth
>
> **Pentecostal denominations:** independent churches that emphasise the gifts of the Spirit
>
> **charismatic churches:** churches that may differ from their denomination by emphasising religious experiences and miracles of healing

The **prosperity Gospel** is the teaching that Christians have the right to expect wealth and good health. They can achieve this by making a positive confession of faith as well as 'sowing seeds' through paying tithes and donating to religious causes, with the belief that God will give back a multiplied harvest or return of their initial offering. This approach became popular through prominent television evangelists at the end of the twentieth century, such as **Oral Roberts**. It now has a following among some **Pentecostal denominations** and **charismatic churches**. It is also known as the *Word-Faith movement*, because of the teaching that it is not good enough merely to believe what the Bible says about well-being; health and wealth must be proclaimed or confessed out loud. This approach has been called the 'name it and claim it' teaching – that by using the power of your words combined with the faith force, a person will be able to name whatever they want into existence. They also believe that 'negative confessions' will create a negative reality, so when healing does not happen it is because of a lack of faith.

> **Key person**
>
> **Oral Roberts (1918–2009):** a pioneering televangelist who built a financial empire that included several homes, a university and a hospital

> **" Key quote "**
>
> God wants you well. God wants you prosperous. God wants you a whole person.
>
> (O Roberts)

Biblical support for this includes such passages as 'You do not have, because you do not ask God' (James 4:3) and 'If you have faith as small as a mustard seed, you can say to this mountain, "Move from here to there," and it will move. Nothing will be impossible for you' (Matthew 17:20). The theme of faith is combined with the view that the covenant that God made with Israel included a promise of material blessing.

Does God want his followers to be wealthy?

The patriarchs in the Hebrew scriptures did experience, at times, enormous wealth. In addition to this, God's instructions for the tabernacle include costly materials. There are powerful images of the people of God inheriting a land that is 'flowing with milk and honey'. There are references to the apostles owning homes, and Jesus and the disciples having an appointed treasurer (Judas Iscariot). These insights seem to portray a god who is not prescribing an ascetic ideal.

The prosperity Gospel is popular in economically deprived places, offering Christians hope for upward mobility. It is also popular in more affluent areas. For instance, the book *The Prayer of Jabez*, which centres on a prayer for material blessing, topped the *New York Times* bestseller list soon after its publication. The prayer of Jabez is from 1 Chronicles 4:10: 'Jabez cried out to the God of Israel, "Oh, that you would bless me and enlarge my territory! Let your hand be with me, and keep me from harm so that I will be free from pain." And God granted his request.'

Problems with prosperity

Biblical scholar **Craig L Blomberg** made a series of critical observations on using the Bible to establish a gospel of prosperity:

- God never promised prosperity to all individual Israelites based on their personal levels of faithfulness or obedience to Torah. This promise was given to the nation as a whole. It was clear that godly Israelites could remain poor, in part, through oppression by others.
- God never made similar arrangements with any of the other countries surrounding Israel; therefore it is a mistake to apply promises made in the Old Testament to modern-day nations.
- No New Testament text ever makes the promise of peace and prosperity contingent on faith or obedience.
- In fact, the blessing that believers receive for their faith is not wealth, but the spiritual qualities of hope and love to achieve more good works in the world (2 Corinthians 9:8).
- The Bible warns about the corrupting influence of wealth: 'Those who want to get rich fall into temptation and a trap and into many foolish and harmful desires that plunge people into ruin and destruction. For the love of money is a root of all kinds of evil' (1 Timothy 6:9–10).
- Many biblical passages speak about God's power being perfected in weakness and suffering. The hardships Jesus endured in his life and his manner of death do not seem to confirm the prosperity Gospel.

Praying-hands sculpture, Oral Roberts University

Key person

Craig L Blomberg (b.1955): an American New Testament scholar whose academic expertise includes parables, miracles, financial stewardship and gender roles

"Key quote"

What Paul promises to the generous giver is not wealth-in-return but all that you need and also sufficient for every good work (2 Corinthians 9:8).

(P Barnett)

T3 Significant social developments in religious thought

> **Summary**
> - There are four main passages about wealth:
>   1. The Kingdom of God is infinitely more important than money and wealth. (Mark 10:17–25)
>   2. Jesus urges his followers to have the right priorities – which are spiritual rather than secular. They have no need to be anxious. (Matthew 6:25–34)
>   3. A secure future and real treasure is heavenly treasure not material wealth. (Luke 12:33–34)
>   4. Money is not evil in itself; the real danger is the love of money. (1 Timothy 6:10)
> - Human beings have the God-given position of managing all their resources well.
> - The idea of undertaking a special discipline (asceticism) or lifestyle as a part of the Christian path runs throughout the New Testament.
> - The prosperity Gospel is the teaching that Christians have the right to expect wealth and good health.
> - However, the blessing that believers receive for their faith is not wealth but the spiritual qualities of hope and love to achieve more good works in the world. (2 Corinthians 9:8)

AO1 Activity

a. Explain what is actually condemned, prohibited or discouraged in each of the biblical verses listed in this theme.

This helps you develop the use of biblical texts to illustrate and explain attitudes towards wealth.

b. Make a list of:
   i. ascetic practices found in the Bible (including the life of Jesus)
   ii. ascetic practices today in the lives of Christians and programmes of the Church.

c. Beside each list, answer this question:

Could this practice be seen as good stewardship – or not?

This helps you develop organisation skills by selecting and ordering evidence and examples for exam questions on both asceticism and stewardship.

Issues for analysis and evaluation

The extent to which wealth is a sign of God's blessing

Possible line of argument	Critical analysis and evaluation
Some Christians argue that having an abundance of material possessions/money is a sign of being blessed by God, and Christians should expect to have this in their lives.	This has become known as the *prosperity Gospel* (also known as the *Word-Faith movement*). If you walk in faith and give generously to religious causes, God will give you wealth.
This teaching of the prosperity Gospel is biblical, especially in the Old Testament, e.g. the Patriarchs who responded to God's call in faith were often blessed in wealth, and Deuteronomy 28:11 states that obedience would make them 'abound in prosperity'.	However, many would argue that these promises in the Old Testament did not apply to everyone – they were to specific individuals or to the nation of Israel as a whole. It is not clear that it applies to individual Christians.
James 2:3 implies that it is a promise to individual Christians. The only reason that many Christians do not have is that they do not ask. Faith and obedience results in prosperity.	The New Testament suggests that suffering can strengthen a spiritual life and that prosperity in return for faith and obedience is under the conditions of the old covenant and does not refer to Christians today.
The Bible talks about God's blessings, and blessings can refer to material wealth.	The New Testament focuses on blessings being spiritual blessings rather than material wealth.
Health and wealth is surely what God wants for his people.	The love of money is the root of all evil. Paul states that love is greater than faith and hope. Seeking health and wealth seems a selfish desire.
John 3:2 implies that God wants us to prosper in wealth and health.	This verse has been wrongly translated. It should be translated as: 'I pray that all may go well with you and that you may be in good health, just as it is well with your soul'.

> **This section covers AO2 content and skills**
>
> **Specification content**
> The extent to which wealth is a sign of God's blessing

AO2 Activity

a Evaluate three lines of argument from the critical analysis and evaluation of the extent to which wealth is a sign of God's blessing. What are their strengths and weaknesses? Which line of argument is strongest?

b Using the strongest line of argument, try to identify three key questions that could be asked – they could be critical questions, challenges, hypothetical or direct.

This section covers AO2 content and skills

Specification content
Whether the ascetic ideal is compatible with Christianity

News reporter
The introduction focuses on arguing that Jesus lived an ascetic life and therefore it must be compatible with Christianity. Some examples are given to support this view.

Detective
Evidence from Church history is given to support the ascetic ideal as being part of Christianity.

Detective
Having examined Jesus' lifestyle to illustrate the ascetic ideal, the answer now examines Jesus' teaching. A strong case for the ascetic ideal has been developed.

Critical thinker

Detective

Tennis player
The answer now starts to question just how convincing the case is for an ascetic ideal in Christianity; firstly focusing on teaching.

Philosopher

Critical thinker

Detective
This paragraph raises more questions; this time about the arguments from Jesus' lifestyle. It is a good reflective examination of the strength of the case for an ascetic ideal that formed the earlier part of the answer.

Critical thinker

Explorer
An alternative approach now develops – that the ascetic ideal is actually contrary to Christianity. Again, good knowledge of biblical texts is shown.

Exam practice

Sample question
Evaluate whether the ascetic ideal is compatible with Christianity.

Sample answer

Jesus devoted his life to following God the Father's path and it is Jesus who is our example. If we examine the way Jesus lived, we could argue that he followed some aspects of an ascetic life. For example, he began his ministry with 40 days of prayer and fasting in the desert. In addition, Jesus experienced poverty; he taught about giving away one's possessions and lived an itinerant lifestyle.

Indeed, Christianity has attracted a number of people and movements of an ascetic ideal throughout its history. John the Baptist lived a life removed from society. His poverty and simple lifestyle attracted many early Christians. In the early centuries, many Christians lived as hermits in the Egyptian desert, devoting their lives to prayer and reflection in the context of a simple life. Such groups developed into monastic communities, whose communal living centred on rules of poverty, chastity and obedience. It is clear that Christian living requires some sort of denial of worldly pleasure and comfort, that is, an ascetic ideal.

As noted with Jesus, not just his lifestyle but also his teaching reflects the ascetic ideal. Jesus often highlighted the problem of wealth when trying to follow God's path. He indicated that we spend far too much time concerned about food and clothing and far too little time on spiritual matters. In Luke 12, Jesus told one of his followers to 'sell your possessions' and give the money to poorer people – something the early Church lived out, according to Acts 2.

However, it is one thing for Jesus to teach this but it can hardly be a law for Christians to follow. This 'selling your possessions' was a particular instruction to one individual, not a universal teaching. Indeed, Jesus approves of Zacchaeus giving up only half his wealth and the theme is not mentioned again in the Gospels. Matthew's Gospel makes clear that it is priorities that are the problem rather than wealth or money in particular. Paul tells Timothy that it is the love of money that is a root of evil, rather than money itself (1 Timothy).

To see Jesus' lifestyle as reflective of asceticism may also be a distortion. Are the events from Jesus' life too selective? There are stories in the New Testament of Jesus receiving hospitality from those who were well off and he was even referred to as 'a glutton and a drunkard, a friend of tax-collectors and sinners'. Neither is it clear that if Jesus did live an ascetic ideal, he did so because it was an ideal that Christians should follow. Some argue that Jesus thought the world was about to end and that this belief drove him to adopt an itinerant lifestyle and live an extreme ascetic life that would not have to be endured for long.

It could be that the ascetic ideal distracts from what is central in the Bible – spiritual development and helping those who are poor or oppressed. Asceticism is more about retreating from the world rather than engaging with it. The Christian ideal is surely more about stewardship and serving, rather than withdrawal and concern for self. Surely Christians should enjoy the created world, including material blessings. After all, in Genesis God declares that the world is 'good'.

WJEC/Eduqas Religious Studies for AS & A Level Christianity

Perhaps the final blow to the ascetic ideal is that Christianity does not have a clear picture of what that ideal should look like. How often did Jesus fast and pray? Should the ideal identify with the suffering of Jesus by Christians physically punishing their bodies, such as self-flagellation, as in the medieval period? Should it involve various forms of meditation? Some aspects may require some form of asceticism, such as a serious commitment to give generously. However, if Christians cannot agree on an ascetic ideal, maybe it is because there is no ascetic ideal in Christianity.

Explorer / Critical thinker / Philosopher / Judge

This paragraph raises another challenge to the ascetic ideal by means of a series of questions. The conclusion is punchy and is consistent with the previous discussion.

Overall, the essay is thorough and detailed, with a clear route of evaluation and good texts from the Bible as illustrations to support the arguments.

Over to you

Below is an evaluation of the claim that the prosperity Gospel represents biblical teaching on wealth and stewardship. At present, it has no quotations at all to support the argument it presents. Underneath the evaluation are two quotations that could be used in the outline to improve it. Your task is to rewrite the outline but make use of the quotations. Such phrases as 'according to …', 'the scholar … argues' or 'it has been suggested by …' may help.

Evaluation

The claim that God wants all believers to experience wealth and health is questionable on several grounds. First, in the Hebrew scriptures, not all of those who follow God are given these gifts (i.e. Job). They sometimes go through long periods of time of deprivation, suffering or hardship (i.e. Abraham's wandering). Clearly, the focus of the Hebrew scriptures is not that people should aspire to wealth, but that they should be compassionate with wealth, and use it to help others and take care of those experiencing social oppression.

Turning to the New Testament, there are clear teachings on the danger of wealth. Jesus himself lived an itinerant existence, relying on the welfare of others. In fact, the suffering at the end of his life seems to be the opposite to what the prosperity Gospel prescribes – does this mean that he had no faith? The early Church, as described in Acts 2, focuses on generously sharing with those in need so that all can have a degree of comfort – this is not the same as wealth.

Quotation 1

… we reject the unbiblical notion that spiritual welfare can be measured in terms of material welfare, or that wealth is always a sign of God's blessing (since it can be obtained by oppression, deceit or corruption), or that poverty or illness or early death is always a sign of God's curse, or lack of faith, or human curses (since the Bible explicitly denies that it is always so).

(The Lausanne Theology Working Group)

Quotation 2

If some measure of material comfort is inherently desirable, then all people should have the chance to gain it. If too much unnecessary wealth leads so often to sin, then those with excess amounts should divest themselves of it. These two truisms, amply demonstrated from all portions of scripture … lead inexorably to a third: God's people should give generously from their surplus (and be ruthlessly honest about how much is surplus).

(Craig L Blomberg)

When you have completed the task, try to find another quotation that you could use and further extend your evaluation.

T3 Significant social developments in religious thought

This section covers AO1 content and skills

Specification content

Migration and Christianity in the UK; the challenges of Christian migration to the UK, with reference to assimilation, provision of worship, style of worship and issues of culture; the reverse mission movement to the UK

B: Migration and Christianity in the UK

Migration and immigration

The United Nations has declared that the number of people currently displaced by conflict is the highest ever recorded. In the UK, we are aware of the needs of many from Afghanistan, Sudan, Iran, Albania, Eritrea and other countries who are seeking refuge and asylum. The desperate efforts to reach a safer land involve fatalities on a weekly basis. Since the start of the Russian–Ukrainian war, around 210,000 Ukrainians have moved to the UK under the Ukraine Family Scheme and Ukraine Sponsorship Scheme, as of July 2024. Of those, the highest number had initially arrived in Scotland (18 per cent) and in London (17 per cent). The lowest number was in Northern Ireland at 1 per cent. The UK was fourth highest in terms of Ukrainian arrivals into European countries.

Forced migration due to humanitarian crises, however, is only one aspect of immigration. There are many who move to the UK from countries that are not at war because they find their country of origin oppressive for a variety of reasons, from religious discrimination to a lack of educational opportunity. Immigration is a complex phenomenon that can benefit a host country and provide opportunities to enrich a population, as well as raise fears about security, economic stability and social cohesion.

> **Key quote**
>
> The story of humanity is a story of mobility: the creation and revision of borders, of communities, the rules governing who can move and who can't, the social and political practices that shape who is accepted within what kinds of spaces.
>
> (Centre of Migration, Policy and Society [COMPAS])

Christianity: a story of migration?

Christians involved in welcoming migrants to their country and their churches believe that many biblical passages support their work. The story of Israel's faith begins with the call to Abraham and Sarah to leave their land and make a journey to Canaan. Later, Jewish tribes suffered an oppressive regime in Egypt and then wandered for decades without a home. It was during this period that the Bible says they received a command to treat those from other places with equality: 'When a foreigner resides among you in your land, do not mistreat them ... Love them as yourself, for you were foreigners in Egypt' (Leviticus 19:33–34).

The Gospels relate that Mary and Joseph were uprooted from their community three times: from Nazareth to Bethlehem, from Bethlehem to Egypt and from Egypt to Nazareth. Jesus told the parable of the Good Samaritan. In the story, it was the Samaritan who was the person who acted with compassion, but who was from a group despised by many of Jesus' contemporaries (Luke 10:30–37).

These passages show that Christians should offer humanitarian aid to refugees and extend a welcome to those migrants who are looking for a church home, no matter their culture. The importance of Christian outreach to migrants is reflected, for example, by the Catholic Church celebrating annually the World Day of Migrants and Refugees.

The Good Samaritan by Rembrandt (1633)

The challenges of Christian migration to the UK

Christianity is the religion with the largest representation among immigrants to the UK who have a religious affiliation. This means that large numbers of 'new' Christians to the UK are seeking churches to join: some will join churches that have long been in Britain and that are also in their country of origin, such as Anglican, Catholic or Methodist Churches. Others will join new denominations or independent churches that already attract an immigrant population. This large influx of Christians has caused the more traditional Churches to reflect on how effectively they welcome and integrate newcomers into their communities. Possible challenges include:

- A large influx of worshippers who may just be learning English can make pastoral care a challenge – how can a vicar or priest respond in a situation of personal crisis when there is a language barrier?
- Language barriers can also hinder teaching the catechism, baptism and confirmation classes.
- There can be significant differences in worship styles, even when an immigrant is attending the same denomination in Britain as in their country of origin.

There are many examples of British congregations that once had a majority white-British membership that have become multi-ethnic, having assimilated new members from diverse cultures. However, many of the churches and denominations appearing in Britain have a majority immigrant membership.

Black Pentecostal congregation

There may be several reasons that more traditional British churches have not assimilated more foreign-born worshippers:

- **Worship differences:** There are clear differences between the experiential style of Pentecostal worship and the more literary and **liturgical** approaches of many traditional Churches. However, this need not necessarily lead to a lack of assimilation since:
  1. there are many churches from long-standing denominations that have embraced a Pentecostal style of worship (these are often called *charismatic churches* (see page 114)
  2. there are indigenous Pentecostal denominations in Britain.
- **Social support:** Migrant groups have their own needs, related to the pressures of establishing a new home, a source of income and a social

> **Key term**
>
> **liturgical:** the public ritual of formal worship prescribed by a Church body

T3 Significant social developments in religious thought

network. Churches that have a significant proportion of membership from migrant backgrounds can offer understanding and support for these challenges. In fact, many minority-ethnic churches offer counselling on legal aspects of the immigration process and classes on career development, educational issues and financial management.

- **The uneven spread of immigration:** The Office of National Statistics (2022) reports that London has the largest number of migrants among all regions of the UK, with 37 per cent of the UK's total foreign-born population. After London and the South East, the West Midlands has the highest proportion of immigrants, reflecting that there are strong social and economic reasons for immigrants to settle in cities. Therefore, large regions across the UK do not have a significant number of immigrants and so there is limited opportunity for some churches to assimilate those from different cultures.

- **Racism:** An article in *The Guardian* newspaper in 2020 reporting the murder of George Floyd, an African American man, by a white police officer in the USA quoted Dipo Oluyomi, CEO of the Kingsway International Christian Centre, one of the largest majority-black churches in the UK: 'Churches should be the first to set an example of intolerance for racism. However this is not always the case, honestly speaking. The 11am Sunday morning service is often the most divided hour in the church – if young black people find themselves in majority white-led churches, they are only good for music, not leadership.'

New Pentecostal denominations and congregations in the UK

Pentecostalism is a movement in Christianity that emphasises the experience of the worshipper. It references the powerful experiences of the early Church in Acts 2, when it is reported that the Spirit of God came upon the followers of Jesus, enabling them to speak in other languages and perform acts of healing. Pentecostal worship services do not follow a written liturgy and can have many of these components: exuberant singing, dancing, clapping, spontaneous prayer, sermons punctuated by impromptu responses ('Yes!', 'Amen!'), faith healing and speaking in tongues.

> **Key quote**
>
> Pentecostalism is revolutionary because it offers alternatives to 'literary' theology and defrosts the 'frozen' thinking within literary forms of worship and committee debate. It gives the same chance to all, including the 'oral' people.
>
> (W Hollenweger)

> **Key quote**
>
> The declining fortunes of Christianity in the public space in Britain have been assuaged by the proliferation of the Black Majority Churches (BMCs). The involvement and influence of BMCs in various cities seem to position them as a source of religious hope in Britain.
>
> (Daniel Akhazemea of the Redeemed Christian Church of God)

The Pentecostal/Charismatic Movement is one of the fastest-growing trends in World Christianity today. This movement grew from 58 million in 1970 to an estimated 656 million in 2021. The Global South is home to 86 per cent of all Pentecostals/charismatics in the world. The largest influx of Pentecostal Christians in Britain has come from the Caribbean and West Africa, where Pentecostal Christianity is pervasive. This has led to thousands of new churches in Britain and even to active outreach from migrant communities to what is viewed as secular, atheist Britain. The Redeemed Christian Church of God has over 800 places of worship in the UK, with its largest congregation of over 2000 people at Sunday services at Jesus House in North London.

In Wales, the Welsh Revival of 1904–5 ultimately led to the establishment of the Crosskeys Full Gospel Mission in South-East Wales, which soon became a centre for Pentecostal activity.

The reverse mission movement to the UK

In the past, the UK sent missionaries to spread the Christian message throughout the world. As a result, Anglican and Methodist churches can be found in almost every place that was once part of the British Empire. However, missionaries are now coming to the UK from some of these very countries. This is called *reverse mission*: countries that once sent missionaries become themselves the target of missionary work from the countries they once **evangelised**.

> **Key quote**
>
> ... the energy of Christians in particular coming to a wearied, Western secularised culture is giving it new hope ...
>
> (Archbishop VC Nichols)

Key terms

evangelise: share the Christian message in the hope of conversion

secular: not connected to religion

One reason for reverse mission is the global shift of Christianity to the southern hemisphere. Another reason for reverse mission is the dramatic church decline in the UK and the perception of those from majority Christian countries that Britain is increasingly atheistic and **secular** – a view supported by the 2021 census.

In the 2011 census of England and Wales, 63.1 per cent of the population identified as Christian. However, in the 2021 census, 27.5 million people identified their religion as 'Christian'. That represented 46.2 per cent of the population. This was the first time that less than 50 per cent of this population identified as Christian. In Wales, it was 43.6 per cent. There was also an increase in the 'No religion' response. In the 2011 census it was 25.2 per cent (14.1 million), but in the 2021 census it was 37.2 per cent (22.2 million). The 2022 Scottish census found that 51.1 per cent of the population identified as having no religion, which is the first time the majority of people in Scotland have said they are not religious. This is up from 36.7 per cent in 2011. In 2021, 17.4 per cent of people in Northern Ireland identified as non-religious, in 2011 it was 10.4 per cent. The 2021 census also showed that the average age of those who said they were Christian was 51, compared to 45 in the 2011 census. The proportion of those identifying as Christian who are aged 21 to 25 has fallen from 5.1 per cent (2011) to 3.9 per cent (2021).

There are many different activities that could be labelled 'reverse mission':

- Short-term visits of a group of non-British Christians, perhaps sponsored by a host church in the UK: for example, a church group from an African country comes to share music, drama and dance in churches and in public spaces, with the intention of spreading their religion.
- Church workers who come to the UK with the intention of 'evangelising' and bringing about conversions to Christianity of UK citizens: This may be in conjunction with the need to work or study; these individuals may be hosted by a church body (here or abroad) or may be wholly independent.
- Churches, church bodies or theological colleges intentionally appointing a leader from a migrant background as a pastor, priest, tutor or church leader as part of a plan to reinvigorate the British church.
- A church in Britain that has a significant migrant population and views outreach to white-British nationals as a part of its God-given mission.

These different activities are united by the perception of Britain as increasingly hostile to Christianity and the desire to see Christianity thrive here once again. However, many reverse missionaries report facing cultural challenges, including the resistance of secular British nationals to the Christian message. As a result, some reverse missionaries have shifted their focus to their fellow nationals, establishing churches that support the unique needs of migrant communities. Reverse mission has caused long-standing British Church bodies to reflect more intensely on the quality of their own outreach.

Does Christianity in the UK need the support of missionaries?

Many scholars of sociology and religion have supported the **secularisation thesis**; the view that modern societies such as Britain are becoming secular in at least one of three ways:

1. A decline in church attendance
2. A decreasing role for the Church in public life
3. A loss of personal belief in God and other Christian beliefs.

Advocates of this thesis predict that Britain faces a future of steady Christian decline.

Certainly, the 2021 census results seem to support this view. About 10 per cent of Church of England churches (approximately 2000 buildings) have closed since 1969. This is for a variety of reasons, including: declining numbers attending church services; buildings falling into disrepair, coupled with churches being unable to afford their upkeep; and fewer priests and ministers to serve the churches.

However, there are challenges to the secularisation thesis. Christianity continues to play a part in public life. For example, the monarch, King Charles III, is Head of the Church of England, and 26 bishops sit in the House of Lords. There are many well-established faith schools, both Roman Catholic and Protestant, in the UK, as well as evidence of a renewed interest in spirituality.

But not all Christians believe evangelism is a Christian duty, as they have a pluralistic approach to worshipping God. As a result, they would see no need for evangelism. Others would favour 'interfaith dialogue' rather than conversion, arguing that all religions offer an experience of the Ultimate Reality (see page 167 [John Hick section]).

Though it is difficult to make a prediction on what may happen in the future, it is probably true that much Church growth that has occurred in recent times in the UK has been a result of immigration.

> ### Key term
>
> **secularisation thesis:** the belief that as societies modernise, religion will decline

AO1 Activity

a Explain the differences between:
   i. migration and immigration
   ii. Pentecostals and Evangelicals
   iii. reverse mission and conversion.

   This helps you understand some key terms.

b Draw a mind map of the challenges of Christian migration to the UK.

   This helps you prioritise and select a core set of points to develop an answer and ensure that you are making accurate use of specialist language and vocabulary in context.

Summary

★ Both the Old Testament and the New Testament teach that Christians should offer humanitarian aid to refugees, and welcome those migrants who are looking for a church home, no matter their culture.

★ Possible challenges to integrating migrants include language barriers, worship differences and racism.

★ The huge increase in the number of Pentecostal Christians in Britain is due largely to Caribbean and West African migrants.

★ Most migrant churches in the UK see engaging in outreach as part of their mission.

★ Reverse mission has not stemmed the tide of Church decline. The 2021 Census shows declining church attendance and a shift in beliefs from a personal God to agnostic and atheist beliefs and attitudes.

Issues for analysis and evaluation
The extent to which the UK is a modern mission field

Possible line of argument	Critical analysis and evaluation
The UK is a Christian country and needs to send out missionaries to other countries. It does not need missionaries to the UK. Christianity is embedded in our culture.	The UK is no longer a Christian country. The latest census showed less than 50 per cent called themselves Christian. The UK is more of a secular country.
We have many churches in every part of the UK. There is no need for missionaries from outside the UK. We have local Christians in local churches spreading the message of Jesus.	In Matthew 28:19, Jesus commands his followers to go and make disciples of all nations. Where there are people who do not follow Jesus, then that is a mission field.
The UK has many evangelical Christians in traditional churches, such as Holy Trinity Brompton, which has developed the popular Alpha course.	A great influx of evangelicals have come from the Pentecostal Churches of the Caribbean and West Africa. An example is the independent Kingsway Christian Centre, which sees evangelism as a central activity.
The UK is multifaith, so countries that have now become predominantly Christian view the UK as a mission field.	Countries once targeted by British missionaries are now sending missionaries to the UK: 'reverse missions'.
Christians from abroad have tended to form their own churches rather than integrate into an already existing traditional church.	UK traditional churches do not fit the worship, music and culture of many immigrant communities.
For many Christians, mission is about humanitarian aid. Therefore, the question of the UK as a mission field is not relevant.	Jesus' command was to love your neighbour, but the first commandment was to love God.
Some Christians would argue that there are many paths to God – not just Christianity. Therefore, the idea of only one true faith – Christianity – is rejected, as are evangelical missions.	Interfaith dialogue and a joining together of different faiths to promote understanding is what mission should be about.
It is arrogant to think that people bring about conversion rather than it being a work of God. Therefore it is arrogant to treat any country as a mission field.	Jesus commands us to go and make disciples. It is a mystery as to what part human beings play in the process, but Paul prayed for people's conversion.

> This section covers AO2 content and skills

> **Specification content**
> The extent to which the UK is a modern mission field

> **AO2 Activity**
> a Evaluate three lines of argument from the critical analysis and evaluation of the extent to which the UK is a modern mission field. What are their strengths and weaknesses? Which line of argument is strongest?
> b Using the strongest line of argument, try to identify three key questions that could be asked – they could be critical questions, challenges, hypothetical or direct.

T3 Significant social developments in religious thought

This section covers AO2 content and skills

> **Specification content**
> The relative ease of assimilation of Christian migrants into Christian churches in the UK.

Exam practice

Sample question
Evaluate the relative ease of assimilation of Christian migrants into Christian churches in the UK.

Sample answer

The story of biblical faith has often involved a theme of migration, for example Abraham's call from Ur, the Israelites in the desert, and Mary and Joseph fleeing to Egypt. The parable of the Good Samaritan redefines who is classed as a 'neighbour'. In the UK, Christianity is the largest religion of all migrants coming to the UK.

[News reporter / Detective] — A good introduction that gives clear evidence from biblical texts that Christianity is involved with the theme of migration.

Probably the Roman Catholic Church has been the most successful in assimilating Christian migrants into their churches. The reason seems to be that they find many familiar features in their UK counterparts, such as liturgy, the role of the priest and the celebration of the sacraments. Clearly those not proficient in English would find it more difficult. However, many churches recruit leaders who speak the language, but it still requires a congregation to be willing to diversify its worship experience.

[Detective] — A clear, well-argued example of success in assimilation of Christian migrants into the Roman Catholic Church.

In contrast, it is the experience of many traditional churches that it is a struggle to assimilate migrants. Migrants have found it much easier to join a denomination or independent church that comes from outside the UK but has now started up churches in the UK and serve primarily migrant communities. It is these churches that are more able to meet the needs of migrants. For example, they offer classes on immigration, financial management and educational issues.

These new migrant churches are often Pentecostal, which is the majority form of religion that many migrants have come from, for example some of those from parts of Africa. These Christians may have an evangelical orientation and a worship style that focuses on the experience of the worshipper, including spontaneous expressions of prayer as well as faith healing and speaking in tongues. This form of 'oral liturgy' bears little resemblance to the highly formal literary forms of worship that take place in many churches across the UK. The growth of reverse missionaries may be evidence of the difference between the ageing and more 'routine' forms of worship found in many UK churches and the vibrant forms of Christianity that some migrants may have experienced in their home countries.

[Tennis player / Detective] — The answer now considers an alternative position, focusing on why assimilation has been mainly unsuccessful. It gives good examples supporting the position.

However, there are many charismatic churches in the UK from long-standing denominations, as well as indigenous Pentecostal denominations in the UK, that have failed to assimilate migrants. It may be that language is the key to assimilation. It can be a challenge to provide pastoral care and teaching to worshippers who are just starting to learn English.

If many immigrants settle in one place, the factors that hinder assimilation can be intensified, and so traditional churches can struggle to cope.

[Critical thinker / Detective] — A reflective question is raised concerning why some indigenous Pentecostal churches have failed to assimilate. This leads to the conclusion that language is the key to assimilation.

Racism was identified recently as another possible cause of lack of assimilation. The leader of one of the largest majority-black churches in the UK said that the Sunday morning service can be the most divided hour in the church: 'Churches should be the first to set an example of intolerance for racism. However this is not always the case [...] if young black people find themselves in majority white-led churches, they are only good for music, not leadership'.

[Tennis player / Explorer] — The answer then cites another possible reason for lack of assimilation. The view is supported and illustrated by a helpful quotation.

We should expect to see ethnically diverse and dynamic congregations in areas where a significant proportion of migrant worshippers have the same ethnic background and where there is economic opportunity and support for challenges that they face as migrants. In places where there is less economic and cultural dynamism and where there are gaps between the religious expression and theology of indigenous Christians and Christian migrants, we should not be surprised to find that churches are less ethnically diverse.

> **Judge**
> A good conclusion that is consistent with the discussion that runs through the essay. The answer has a clear line of argument throughout. The arguments are well supported.

Over to you

Below is an evaluation of the UK as a modern mission field. At present, it has no references at all to support the arguments it presents. Underneath the evaluation are two references to the works of scholars that could be used to improve the evaluation.

Your task is to rewrite the evaluation making use of the references. Such phrases as 'in his book, (scholar) argues that ...', '... (scholar) makes an interesting argument in support of this, suggesting that ...' or 'the work of (scholar) has made a major contribution to the debate by pointing out ...' may help.

Usually, a reference includes a footnote, but for an answer in an A Level essay under examination conditions this is not expected.

Evaluation

Does the UK need missionaries from outside it if Christianity is to grow? There are several reasons that this idea can be refuted – whether or not one is a Christian. It can be argued that nothing yet has significantly stemmed the tide of secularism.

Fewer people attend church, and even new churches are not making up for the emptying and closure of old churches. Religion is increasingly irrelevant to contemporary society. There have been 'reverse missionaries', but no one claims that these have made a significant impact on the UK. From a different point of view, yet still refuting the idea that Britain needs missionaries from the outside, it can also be argued that Christianity has an indigenous presence that is strong underneath the surface. That is, there is quite a bit of 'Christian life' and influence already present in Britain that has the potential to grow and spread. If this already strong Christian presence isn't enough for Christianity to grow, then nothing else will be.

Quotation 1

We may want to explain the secularity of some elite groups (such as professional scientists) by the impact of science and rationalism, but to understand the mass of the population it is not self-conscious irreligion that is important. It is indifference. [And] the primary cause of indifference is the lack of religious socialisation.

(Steve Bruce)

Quotation 2

A Christian nation can sound like a nation of committed believers, and we are not that. Equally, we are not a nation of dedicated secularists. I think we're a lot less secular than the most optimistic members of the British Humanist Association would think.

(Rowan Williams)

This section covers AO1 content and skills

Specification content
Feminist theology and the changing role of men and women; the contribution of Rosemary Radford Ruether to feminist theology

C: Feminist theology and the changing role of men and women

What is feminist theology?

Feminist theology is an examination of theology, religious history and religious communities that takes seriously the experience of women. At the heart of feminist theology is the recognition that religion has played a part in the historic and continuing oppression of women; an oppression that is pervasive and frequently violent.

Rosemary Radford Ruether (1936–2022), an American scholar and Roman Catholic theologian, and Mary Daly (1928–2010), an American philosopher and theologian, shared the view that sexism plays a large role in the Bible, in Christian theology and in the rituals and practices of the Christian Church.

Ruether believed that there is something more authentic in Christianity than sexism; she examined aspects of the Christian tradition, including marginalised forms of Christianity, which do not entail a male God, a male saviour and an exclusively male Church leadership. She called for the language, rituals and theology of Christianity to be reformed, which would include a greater commitment to the well-being of women.

By contrast, Mary Daly believed that sexism is far too embedded in Christianity for there to be such a reformation. She encouraged women to separate from the Church and to define 'God' in ways that are affirming to the journey of becoming a whole person.

The contribution of Rosemary Radford Ruether to feminist theology

Ruether argued that biblical and theological traditions have reflected the cultural view that men are more authentically human than women. This is called **androcentrism**, and she claimed it has been widespread not only in the Bible and Christian teaching, but also in the intellectual tradition of the West from the Greek philosophers to the present day.

The story of Adam and Eve has been interpreted to suggest that sin entered the world through Eve – and therefore women are more responsible than men for the 'fall'. Male pronouns have been used in relation to the term 'God', and the Bible has declared in both the Old and the New Testaments that women are to be 'subject' to men (Genesis 3:16 and Ephesians 5:24). Aquinas believed that the male–female hierarchy is not just a result of sin but is a part of the natural order created by God. So when the Bible implies that males are somehow closer to God than females, Ruether regarded this as the sin of idolatry.

Mary vs Eve

Ruether believed that the notions of masculinity and femininity come from culture and socialisation but are not a part of our inner nature. In the Church, however, women have been restricted to some characteristics (associated with cultural ideas of femininity) rather than others. For instance, they have been urged to follow the example of Mary, who exhibits qualities of passivity, gentleness, meekness and obedience. Mary has been extolled as a perpetual virgin (though Matthew seems to indicate that Mary did have children with Joseph). The implication is that for a woman to be truly spiritual she must not be 'sexual' – and even then she cannot attain to the rationalistic prowess of males. The only alternative is to be associated with Eve, who is viewed as the temptress and bringer of sin into the world!

Key term
androcentrism: focused or centred on men

> **Key quote**
>
> Both males and females, as human persons, have the capacity to do evil. Historically, however, women as well as subjugated men, have not had the same opportunities to do so.
>
> (R Radford Ruether)

Ruether was not surprised that women have been persecuted when they have manifested leadership tendencies or expressed views at odds with men. She suggested that the persecution and murder of women labelled as 'witches' stems from gender stereotyping, and she cited a fifteenth-century Dominican manual that states '... women are feebler both in mind and body ... For as regards intellect, or the understanding of spiritual things, they seem to be of a different nature from men ... But the natural reason is that she is more carnal than a man ...'

Given that gender stereotyping has long been a part of the Church, Ruether was not surprised that women had been excluded from ordination. She cited the 1976 Vatican declaration against women's ordination, which stated 'there must be a physical resemblance between priest and Christ'. In other words, possessing male genitalia is the essential prerequisite for representing Christ, who is the disclosure of the male God.

Marginalised forms of Christianity

Ruether pointed to several movements in Christianity that have not followed the dominant tradition in the role given to women in the Church. For example:

- **Montanism:** They believed in the continuing inspiration of the Holy Spirit in prophecy given to men and women. There is evidence that women were given equal status to men in the ministry of Montanist churches.
- **Gnosticism (see page 52):** Some Gnostic writings viewed women as Apostles and describe the nature of God as having female and male principles.
- **Quakers and some Baptist movements:** They included women in leadership.
- **The Shakers:** These promoted a view of God as bisexual or androgynous, based on the notion that since male and female humans were created in the image of God, then God must be, in some sense, both male and female.

Both Montanism and Gnosticism came to be viewed as heretical by the Church 'Fathers'. Ruether did not believe that these marginalised forms of Christianity were by any means perfect: these groups often had a negative view of sexual activity and marriage. Shakers were celibate and Gnostics advocated an unworldly asceticism. Ruether noted that none of these groups fought for women's rights outside of their gatherings. Yet, they are indications that not all Christians have seen sexism as a necessary part of Christianity.

The prophetic tradition

Ruether saw feminist theology as part of the prophetic tradition in the Bible. The prophets of Israel fought against the oppression of poor and dispossessed people by powerful individuals and groups – even when that oppression came from the religious establishment (see Isaiah 10:1–2 and Luke 4:18–19). Even though these prophets did not specifically fight against

> **Key terms**
>
> **Quakers:** members of a movement that believes in direct apprehension of God without the need for clergy, creeds or other ecclesiastical forms
>
> **Shakers:** members of an American religious sect dedicated to celibacy and belief in the imminent return of God

sexism, they displayed principles that extended to all forms of oppression. There are four themes in the prophetic-liberating traditions:
- God's defence and vindication of the oppressed
- a critique of dominant systems of power and their powerholders
- a vision of a new age where injustice ends under the reign of God
- a critique of the religious ideology maintaining injustice.

It is more accurate to see Jesus as a part of this prophetic tradition than it is to view him as the imperialistic Davidic Messiah-King and Son of God, as he became known in Christian theology. This is because the Jesus-movement had a counter-cultural character; like the prophets, he rejected the use of religion to establish oppressive hierarchy and stood up for poor and oppressed people. In fact, his movement appeared to place women on equal footing to men. His naming of God as 'Abba' (a familial and emotional term for a father) could be him distancing himself from patriarchal views of God, and it can be argued that he did not see himself as a patriarchal Messiah. Instead, he viewed himself as a servant determined to help liberate those who were suffering. Ruether says that feminist theology must reclaim this view of Jesus that his 'maleness' is of no importance.

Problems and solutions

The twentieth century, said Ruether, has seen several attempts to liberate women from sexism:

- **Romanticism**, a movement from the late eighteenth century, viewed emerging industrialism and the violence of war as stemming from male traits, and that social salvation would come through embracing female qualities: intuition, emotional sensitivity and moral purity. Because women have been forbidden from entire political realms, they retain more purity and goodness and are less prone to the sins of egoism. The weakness of this approach is that it leaves women trapped in romantic notions of what a female should be (cultural definitions of femininity), and can elevate the role of women in the home as the only way to maintain purity.

- **Liberalism** rejects traditional role models and attempts to fight for social reform – including the right to vote, to obtain divorce, to birth control and to equal pay. One of the main thrusts of liberalism is to give women the opportunity to enter into education so that they can develop the qualities needed to wield power in the spheres that have been dominated by men. In liberalism, the reform of Church structures is a part of a larger fight for women in society. Ruether noted, however, that liberalism is a largely middle- or upper-class phenomenon that has at least two weaknesses:
  1. In its concern to see women represented in traditionally male spheres, it does not critique the way power in those spheres functions.
  2. Middle- and upper-class women, after winning freedom for themselves, may hire lower-class women to take care of the work that they no longer do, thus perpetuating sexism in lower classes.

- **Marxism** asserts that both men and women should be viewed as equally able to contribute to society. Ruether noted two issues with the Marxist solution for women:
  1. Many women in communist countries are still expected to work more in the home than men.
  2. Women are viewed as subservient to their productivity on behalf of the communist state, rather than valued for themselves.

> ### Key terms
> **Romanticism:** an intellectual and artistic movement, critical of the enlightenment; instead focused on emotion and imagination
> **liberalism:** in politics, focused on the protection and freedom of the individual
> **Marxism:** the theories of Marx and Engels that developed into communism and aimed for a classless society

What does a liberating Church look like?

Ruether hoped that a reformed theology and Church could provide a setting that would be truly liberating for women. However, she was aware that many women would be required to find the support they need outside the Church in female **base communities**, since patriarchy and sexism continue in the Church. Her ideal was of the Church as a community that manifests the prophetic-liberation strand found in the Bible. This Church would become free of patriarchy, and institute changes in language used for God and be committed to fighting against the oppression of women (that is, sponsoring projects, such as a shelter for survivors of domestic abuse or a rape hotline). The Church would also have an inclusive approach to leadership. A new understanding of leadership accompanied by new rituals would be a part of making the Church a liberating community.

> **Key term**
>
> **base communities:** small, self-governing religious groups

The contribution of Mary Daly to feminist theology

The goal of human life, according to Mary Daly, is for all people to be free to engage in a journey of growth, becoming creative and fulfilled individuals, freely participating in communities that are healthy and liberating. But the opposite has been the case – especially for women. Instead of the freedom to be on a journey of growth, women have been trapped into oppressive roles. They have been told that their biology is their destiny, reduced to objects of men's desires and tools to accomplish male goals. Daly saw society as having created a 'sexual caste system'; a rigid hierarchy that places the female gender beneath the male gender. The Church has played a large role in helping culture maintain this caste system. It is time for women to overcome this system and the structures that force women into 'non-being'.

> **Specification content**
>
> The contribution of Mary Daly to feminist theology

> **" Key quote**
>
> Real liberation is not merely unrestricted genital activity (the 'sexual revolution'), but free and defiant thinking, willing, imagining, speaking, creating, acting.
>
> (M Daly)

God is not a noun

Daly's description of the goal of life uses verbs: *being, acting, changing, moving, actualising*, and so on. However, the problem is that women are treated as objects – as nouns. One of the themes in theology that has helped to turn women into objects is a static view of God. God has been defined as a noun rather than a verb. Traditional theology views God as a changeless, static being; a creator; and a ruler. Patriarchal images of God reinforce the notion of God as a noun: a white-bearded man in the sky. This God, said Daly, must be dethroned. There are three versions of this noun-God:

1. God as a stop-gap (God being used as an explanation of the unknown)
2. God as otherworldliness (God gives rewards and punishments after death)
3. God as a judge of sin (God insists on rules and establishes roles for men and women).

These images of God are static, doing nothing to inspire creativity, dynamism or growth.

The Church has also turned Jesus into a noun: the otherworldly God-Man who is the model for all Christians to follow. Women can and should follow

Mary Daly

T3 Significant social developments in religious thought

Jesus, though they can never hope to be as spiritual as men, since they are the 'wrong' gender. However, Daly asked, why should there be just one model for human living?

God is a verb

What we must do, said Daly, is to consider God as a verb; to see God in a process of becoming, with the universe as the force that helps us to become the people we are meant to be. Simply changing from male language to female language for God will not address the root issue but perpetuate the idea of God as a noun, now a female rather than a male noun. We must think of God as a transforming power – the power of being for all persons. When we do this, we come to see that:

- original sin is not disobedience, but turning women into objects who are forbidden to develop outside of their biological destiny
- salvation is not passive acceptance of doctrine or worship of a God-Man, but participating in being and becoming
- worshipping the God of patriarchy, which includes the God-Man Jesus, is a form of idolatry; Christians commit **Christolatry** and **Bibliolatry** when they insist that biblical forms of patriarchy are the final truth
- our goal is to struggle to be free human beings, staying open to the future
- if there is no fall, no frowning judge and no punishment, there is no need of a saviour
- to believe in the power of God is to believe in the power of being and becoming in all people.

> **Key terms**
>
> **Christolatry:** worship according to patriarchal categories rather than to a god who is beyond sex and gender
>
> **Bibliolatry:** worship of the Bible instead of God

A matter of life and death

Treating women as objects, said Daly, is at the heart of all human violence. She investigated the 'unholy trinity' of rape, genocide and war. Her argument is that violence becomes permissible in society when we no longer see human beings as on a valuable journey of being and becoming, but turn them into objects that are a means to increase our pleasure or decrease our pain.

- **Rape** involves just such an objectification of women. Furthermore, a patriarchal society has a vested interest in rape continuing, since rape reinforces the need for males to protect all women.
- **Genocide** is another form of objectification: the 'enemy' is viewed as an object or possession of a conquering army who can be dealt with in any way deemed satisfying in the moment – including wholesale murder. The link between rape and genocide can be seen in biblical commands to Israel to engage in both activities: 'Now therefore, kill every male among the little ones, and kill every woman who has known a man by sleeping with him. But all the young girls who have not known a man by sleeping with him, keep alive for yourselves' (Numbers 31:17–18). In other words, these humans are merely objects rather than human beings.
- **War** itself is about masculine dominance and the promotion of certain virtues that are associated with 'manliness'. Men are encouraged to be adventurous in violent ways, 'clobber the bad guy' and treat the enemy as an object.

> **Key quote**
>
> Obscene is not the picture of a naked woman who exposes her pubic hair but that of a fully clad general who exposes his medals rewarded in a war of aggression.
>
> (M Daly)

Society also contains different values, of passivity, gentleness, self-sacrifice, but it associates these with females – the very people who are treated as objects by men. Daly believed that this assigning of values by gender is a strategy to ensure that women do not change the social order; that they do not interrupt the work of this unholy trinity. In fact, women who have these 'feminine' qualities are rarely permitted into leadership positions because these are not the values that most influence society. This fact underscores the need for women to strive, not for feminine values, but for an androgynous form of life, where they make their own decisions and build their own ethics apart from gender.

The need for sisterhood

Daly believed that the Church is too bound to patriarchy ever to become a place where women can find the transformation they seek. She called herself a 'post-Christian', and called upon women to be 'antichurch' and leave this patriarchal structure. However, in a patriarchal world, nearly all organisations are to some degree patriarchal, so that women who want to enter into a journey of growth need to live on the boundaries of society. To do this, they need to seek the support of other women.

The term *sisterhood*, for Daly, speaks to finding relationships with other women to oppose the lovelessness of a sexually hierarchical society. She warned women that as they attempt to change their lives, men will criticise them, calling them names like 'castrating female', 'man-hater' and 'unfeminine'. Women also confront criticism from women who have not recognised the true oppression of a patriarchal culture. The sisterhood, however, will offer support.

It will have no hierarchy, no dogmas and will assist in bringing women out of patriarchal spaces and onto a path where they can develop into an androgynous form of living.

The ordination of women and the impact on Christianity

The issue of the ordination of women priests and bishops

Ordination is a rite that sets apart certain individuals for specific roles in the Church. The New Testament does not describe a rite of ordination, and considers all Christians to be *ministers* ('those who serve'). However, it is clear in the New Testament that there were some who were set apart for certain tasks and there are references to bishops, presbyters and deacons. Today, ordination services in many denominations involve the Church gathering together and praying, laying on of hands and invoking the Spirit in the lives of those it is setting aside for specific roles.

Historical scholars note that there were many women in leadership positions in the early Church. One female apostle is mentioned in the New Testament: Junia; Paul describes her as 'prominent among the apostles' (Romans 16:7). Other women in the New Testament were considered apostles by some

> **Specification content**
>
> The changing role of men and women with reference to the issue of the ordination of women priests and bishops; the impact on the lives of believers and communities within Christianity today

T3 Significant social developments in religious thought

traditions in the early Church and the early Middle Ages, including Mary Magdalen and the Samaritan woman at the well. In addition to this, there are stories told about holy women (such as Thecla and Nino) who are also described as apostles. Some descriptions of these figures maintain that their ministry was restricted to other women, but other traditions indicate they ministered to men as well. There are also possible references to female deacons (1 Timothy 3:11) and prophets (Acts 21:9).

In contrast, it was rare to find women in publicly recognised leadership positions in the Church until the last few decades. In fact, many early translations of the Bible altered the name Junia to the male form Junias, as it was supposed that a female apostle must have been a mistranslation of Paul's words! The concept of apostleship as described by Luke-Acts (later than Paul's letters) limited them to 12 – all men. Most theologians through the centuries have argued that women's ministry should be restricted in line with admonitions in the New Testament. Common arguments against women in ministry included:

- God chose to incarnate 'himself' in the form of a male.
- Christ appointed only men as the Apostles.
- Ordaining women would destroy the unity and **catholicity** of the Church that has, for centuries, ordained only men.
- Scripture forbids the leadership of women.

However, in the nineteenth century, when movements for the liberation of women began intensifying, counterarguments were raised:

- Jesus did not seem to restrict his message and teaching to men.
- Many passages in the Bible refer to ministry in inclusive terms.
- Women were ordained to the **diaconate** in the early Church.
- Not ordaining women has been a part of the historical suppression of women.

> **Key terms**
>
> **catholicity:** having a universal doctrine
> **diaconate:** an official body of deacons

The impact on the lives of believers and communities within Christianity today

On rare occasions, some women have been ordained or given public leadership positions in the Church since the time of the Reformation. However, it was not until the 1970s that women's ordination became standard practice in established denominations. In the Church of England, for instance, the vote to ordain women passed by a narrow margin in 1992. However, in 1993, the Church voted to allow individual congregations to opt out of accepting female priests. In 1994, nearly 1500 women were ordained in the Church of England, but over 470 male clergy protested by leaving the Church (many of these joined the Roman Catholic Church, which allowed them to function as married priests).

Current issues with the ordination of women

Most Christians in the world today belong to churches that do not ordain women. For example, women cannot be ordained as deacons, priests or bishops in the Roman Catholic Church. In 2022, Pope Francis made it unequivocally clear that the Church's doctrine on male-exclusive priesthood cannot be altered. In an article a year earlier, he argued that the Petrine principle is one of ministry that is reserved for men, but there is also a Marian principle in the Church that needs to be developed that gives women dignity in the Church. The Pope referred to Mary as the Church's model of holiness because of her total surrender in love to God, and said the Church is 'feminine from its origins'.

> **Key quote**
>
> The Marian principle guides the church next to Peter.
> (Pope Francis)

In 2023, Pope Francis held a month-long summit to discuss pressing issues facing the Church. While there was a consensus that women's roles need to be promoted, participants remained divided on how to achieve that goal.

Two earlier commissions had raised the issue of female diaconate, which would allow women to preach at Mass and perform marriages and baptisms, but not celebrate the Eucharist or hear confessions. However, many fear that this would open the door to women being ordained as priests.

It is only since the late 1960s that women were ordained as deacons and priests in parts of the worldwide Anglican Communion, and only since the 1990s that they have been ordained as bishops (2015, Church of England; 2017, Church in Wales) – though this is only in a minority of the member churches that compose the Anglican Church.

In Churches that ordain women, there are continuing issues that impact the freedom of women to become fully equal to their male counterparts:

- The proportion of unpaid women clergy has increased in many church bodies that ordain women.
- Ordained women have had to fight for maternity rights in some denominations.
- Interview committees have been challenged to produce guidelines on appropriate or inappropriate questions for female candidates (for example 'are you planning to have children?' is an inappropriate question).
- Many congregations who belong to church bodies that do ordain women are reluctant to accept a female minister.
- Women find it difficult to access 'senior pastorates' or the role of bishop, with lack of experience used as an excuse.

Summary

- Feminist theologians recognise that religion plays a part in the historic and continuing oppression of women.
- Rosemary Radford Ruether argued that:
  1. biblical traditions reflected a cultural bias that men are more authentically human than women
  2. Jesus should be seen as more of a prophet than a patriarchal 'King'
  3. reform requires inclusive language, and empowering women through female base communities.
- Mary Daly argued that:
  1. the Church was too bound up in patriarchy ever to achieve equality for women, since it reflected society's sexual caste system
  2. God is a verb about a transforming power, but the Church has changed it to a noun – a static object – and so stands in the way of growth and of 'becoming'

T3 Significant social developments in religious thought

3   treating women as objects is at the historical heart of all human violence
4   to grow, women need to reject patriarchal society and live on the boundaries of society supported by other women in a 'sisterhood'.

★ In 1992, the Church of England voted to ordain women, but allowed individual congregations to opt out of having a female minister. In 2015, Libby Lane became the first female bishop in the Church of England.

> **AO1 Activity**
>
> a   Explain what Mary Daly means when she says that God is not a noun but a verb.
>
> This helps you develop the ability to select and present the key, relevant features of the contribution of Mary Daly to feminist theology.
>
> b   Draw a line down the middle of a revision card. In the left-hand column, list all the common arguments against women in ministry, including at least two biblical texts that support the argument. In the right-hand column, list the counterarguments, including at least two biblical texts that support the counterargument.
>
> This helps you select and recall the key points on the different views of women in ministry.

Issues for analysis and evaluation
Whether men and women are equal in Christianity

Possible line of argument	Critical analysis and evaluation
The Bible makes clear that men and women are not equal. It reinforces a patriarchal society. God is male and sends a male saviour. The Twelve Apostles were men.	The New Testament gives full equality of men and women. Paul states in Galatians 3:28: '... there is neither male nor female, for you are all one in Christ Jesus'.
The presentation of women in the Bible shows inequality between men and women. Eve is depicted as a temptress responsible for the fall of Adam, and Mary is depicted as passive and subservient – an example of how Christian women should be.	Christianity has been influenced by religious and philosophical views of the time. However, Jesus had an inclusive ministry in which women appear to be treated more equally to men than they were in the wider culture.
The early Church did not treat men and women equally. Paul commanded women to keep silent in Church and asserts the headship of men over women.	There are many female leaders mentioned in the early Church, including deacons and prophetesses. Some argue that Romans 16:7 refers to a woman apostle called Junia. This was later changed in some manuscripts to the male form of the name: Junias.
The Roman Catholic Church still allows only men to become priests. This is because God chose to incarnate 'himself' in a man. Also Jesus chose only men to be his Apostles.	The Church of England ordains women as priests and bishops. As yet, there has been no woman archbishop. Some other denominations accept women as leaders.
Mary Daly views the presentation of women such as Eve and Mary as serving male interest for power. This makes it easier to view women as objects. The fall is about the dominance of one gender over another.	Daly says that women should leave the Church and find support in a 'sisterhood' that lives outside all patriarchal organisations.
Both Ruether and Daly argue that it is the Church that has distorted Christian beliefs about equality between men and women.	Ruether argues that Jesus reflects the prophetic spirit of justice – which does not pay attention to gender but to love and justice – in his inclusive ministry. However, Christian beliefs about Jesus quickly moved from a prophet fighting for justice to the God-Man who brings salvation.
The Christian Church has systematically disempowered women in the Church. Their experiences have been ignored and their contributions minimised.	Many women participate in the Church, including leading a church. The heart of Christianity is not inequality, but the Church may have continued patriarchal culture.

> **This section covers AO2 content and skills**
>
> **Specification content**
> Whether men and women are equal in Christianity
>
> **AO2 Activity**
> a Evaluate three lines of argument from the critical analysis and evaluation of whether men and women are equal in Christianity. What are their strengths and weaknesses? Which line of argument is strongest?
> b Using the strongest line of argument, try to identify three key questions that could be asked – they could be critical questions, challenges, hypothetical or direct.

This section covers AO2 content and skills

Specification content
The extent to which feminist theology impacts modern Christian practice

News reporter
Good introduction with reference to two main scholars.

Tennis player
Detective
Philosopher
The answer poses an opposite view, suggesting that feminist theology has made an impact but notes the limitations.

Explorer
Detective
The answer reconsiders the impact of feminist theology in the light of most Christian Churches not ordaining women. It gives the reasons why certain Churches remain opposed to women having an equal role with men in Church structures.

Tennis player
Explorer
This paragraph explores the views of two feminist theologians in relation to their impact on modern Christian practice.

Exam practice

Sample question
Evaluate the extent to which feminist theology impacts modern Christian practice.

Sample answer

The last few decades have seen a rise of feminist theology that has called for reform in the Church. In the past, Christianity has suppressed women. Vatican II promised equality in the life of the Church. But this was not realised in relation to women. So has feminist theology brought about any changes? Certainly the writings of Rosemary Radford Ruether, Mary Daly and other feminist theologians have had an impact. However, many feel that patriarchy and sexism are too deeply embedded in Christian traditions for things to change by much.

Nevertheless, feminist theology has led, in some Churches, to the Christian ordination of women. Since the 1970s, many Protestant denominations have ordained women. Most parts of the Anglican communion ordain women as priests; some parts of this communion also ordain women as bishops (England since 2015 and Wales since 2017). Despite this, the Church of England allows congregations to opt out of having a female priest. Feminist theologians have influenced women studying for the ministry as their textbooks are a part of the seminary curriculum. Even if there were equal numbers of men and women in leadership, the model of leadership is itself patriarchal and in need of reform.

However, most Christians today belong to Churches that do not ordain women. For example, women cannot be ordained as deacons, priests or bishops in the Roman Catholic Church. In 2022, Pope Francis made it unequivocally clear that the Church's doctrine on male-exclusive priesthood cannot be altered. The Catholic Church's justification of this position is related to God choosing a male (Jesus) in the incarnation.

Conservative and evangelical Protestant Churches take a literal approach to the Bible and so view feminist theology with suspicion. They believe that the Bible is the word of God, and so the patriarchal language and structures have been set by God through divine revelation, that is, reflect the will of God. This includes verses such as women being submissive to their husbands and, in 1 Timothy, Paul saying: 'I do not permit a woman to teach … she must be silent'.

Both Mary Daly and Rosemary Radford Ruether express frustration that feminist theology has not impacted the Church very deeply at all. Mary Daly actually urges her readers to be 'antichurch'; to leave the Church altogether and to support one another in a sisterhood that is non-hierarchical, inclusive and non-dogmatic. Ruether is more hopeful, but she too recognises that women need to find support in female 'base communities' as they struggle for a less patriarchal Church.

In judging whether feminist theology has impacted modern Christian practice, perhaps two areas need to be examined. The first is language. Do these Churches speak of God using terminology from both genders and do examples of the life of faith include women who are not conceived of as 'feminine' in a stereotypical way? There is evidence of change in this area, as many inclusive-language Bible versions are available.

The second area involves rituals. Does the Church have rituals that imagine women as well as men progressing on a path of growth and healing and do women as well as men lead these rituals? Again, there is evidence of some change, with women's ordination. However, it is debatable as to the extent of the impact throughout Christian Churches, suggesting the impact is still very limited.

The very good, well-developed conclusion is consistent with the arguments presented throughout the answer. It is a balanced conclusion that indicates that the impact of feminist theology has had only limited impact on modern Christian practice.

Over to you

Below is an evaluation of the continuing inequality of women in the Church. You must use this in an essay but, as it stands, it is a weak argument because it has no quotations or references as support in it at all. This time, you have to find your own quotations (about three) and use your own references (about three) to strengthen the evaluation. Remember: sometimes a quotation can follow from a reference, but they can also be used individually as separate points.

Evaluation

Although many denominations have now ordained women as priests for several decades, it is not true to say that women have achieved equality with men when considering the worldwide context of Christianity. The starkest fact is that most Christians continue to worship in churches where women are not ordained. Even many Churches that ordain women as priests do not ordain them as bishops. There are examples of churches in denominations that ordain women who avoid calling a woman 'priest'. Or, if they do call women 'priests', of not being fair in the way they ask interview questions. Though the Roman Catholic Church has very recently decided to study the issue of women as deacons, this is at the level of 'study' only; no decision has been reached. Furthermore, the Pope has made it clear that there are areas of ministry where women will not be permitted to go.

The result will be a fairly lengthy answer, and so you could check it against the band descriptors for A2 (WJEC) or A Level (Eduqas) and, in particular, look at the demands described in the higher band descriptors, which you should be aspiring towards. Ask yourself:

- Is my answer a confident critical analysis and perceptive evaluation of the issue?
- Is my answer a response that successfully identifies and thoroughly addresses the issues the question raises?
- Does my work show an excellent standard of coherence, clarity and organisation?
- Will my work, when developed, contain thorough, sustained and clear views that are supported by extensive, detailed reasoning and/or evidence?

T3 Significant historical developments in religious thought

This section covers AO1 content and skills

> **Specification content**
>
> The conflicting religious and non-religious views on Christianity in the UK (whether the UK can be called a 'Christian country')

D: Challenges from secularisation

Conflicting religious and non-religious views on Christianity in the UK

Whether the UK can be called a 'Christian country'

It is difficult to know quite what to take into account when trying to decide whether the UK is a 'Christian country'. On the surface, there appear to be lots of churches that reflect a wide spectrum of denominations, and there are a significant number of schools that have a Christian affiliation. Twenty-six bishops sit in the House of Lords, one of the main decision-making bodies in the UK, and TV and radio broadcast some programmes that have Christian content.

However, the 2021 Census showed that less than half the population of England and Wales (46.2 per cent) would call themselves Christian, and the number of people identifying as having 'no religion' was 37 per cent. In Scotland, the trend is even more pronounced. The 2022 Scottish census revealed that just over half of the population identified as having no religion, marking the first time non-religious individuals became the majority. Northern Ireland, while still more religious than other UK nations, also experienced a shift, with those identifying as non-religious rising from 10.4 per cent in 2011 to 17.4 per cent in 2021.

According to the Church of England's 2022 statistics, only 1.7 per cent of England's population were part of the Church of England's worshipping community. Recent surveys show a continued decline in those participating in rites such as baptism, marriage and funerals. Before the beginning of the twentieth century, it would have been normal to undergo each of these life passages in the Church; now it is increasingly rare. In 1957, 72 per cent of all marriages in England and Wales were conducted in churches; by the year 2019 this had dropped to 18.7 per cent. Every year since 1992, civil marriage ceremonies have outnumbered religious ones. While religious funerals remain quite common, many families now choose to have a 'celebration of life', perhaps conducted by a representative from the British Humanist Association.

There are additional points that we can explore and debate in relation to whether the UK is a Christian country.

> **"Key quote"**
>
> Britain ... exists somewhere in between – between Christian, multi-faith and 'none'.
>
> (L Woodhead)

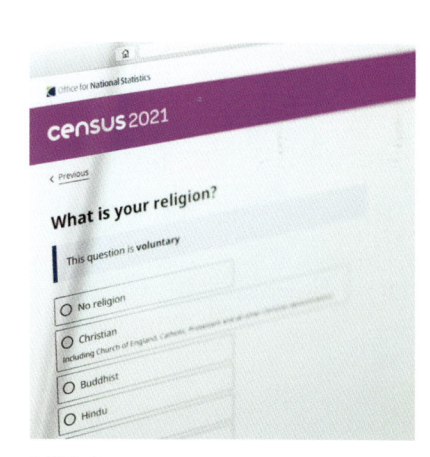

2021 Census question on religion

Seeming to support the notion of the UK as a Christian country
- Some studies have shown that numbers of worshippers, pilgrims, tourists and visitors are growing at cathedrals.
- The majority of people still have some form of religious funeral ceremony.
- Chaplains provide a Christian presence in many areas of our social life: health care, the prison service, the armed services and higher education.

- There are many popular Christian festivals, such as Word Alive, Spring Harvest, New Wine, Bible by the Beach, Keswick Convention and Big Church Day Out.
- The majority of British people believe that 'there are things in life we simply cannot explain through science or any other means'.

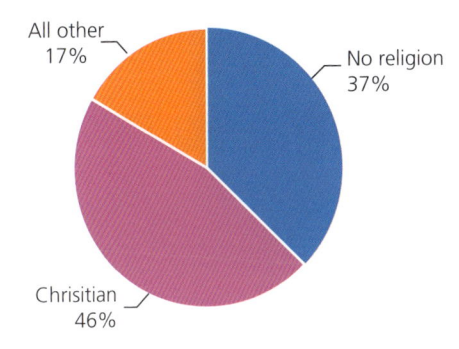

> **Key quote**
>
> We are a Christian country and we should not be afraid to say so.
>
> (D Cameron)

2021 Census results: No religion 37%, Christian 46%, All other 17%

Seeming to challenge the notion of the UK as a Christian country

- The census for England and Wales showed a decline from 59 per cent to 46 per cent between 2011 and 2021 of those saying they belong to Christianity, while those professing 'no religion' increased from 25 per cent to 37 per cent.

> **Key quote**
>
> … how can the Church of England remain in any meaningful sense the national legally established church, when it caters for such a small proportion of the population?
>
> (A Copson)

- There is a continuing shift away from those who believe in a personal God towards those who prefer a less specific formulation.
- Over the last several decades, there has been a dramatic shift from what is allowed on Sundays, with increasing participation in sports, shopping and work.
- Churches are being turned into commercial spaces, dwellings, temples and mosques. According to research from the Brierley research consultancy, 2000 churches in the UK closed over a ten-year period (2011–2021), with a possible additional 350 Church of England buildings closing in the next two to five years in England.
- Atheism and humanism are now presented more widely in British schools (including in this textbook).
- The average age of those who identified as Christian in 2021 was 51. In 2022, 36 per cent of those who were regular worshippers at a Church of England service were over the age of 70.

The decline in Church attendance has been accompanied by a decline in participation in Christian rites such as baptism and marriage

What does it mean to have 'no religion' in the UK?

One of the most striking results from the 2021 Census was the growth in the 'no religion' category. It showed a 12.0 percentage point increase to 37.2 per cent, which means that 22.2 million people in England and Wales identified

T3 Significant historical developments in religious thought

with 'no religion'. More people under 40 in England and Wales now declare 'no religion' than profess to be Christian – the first time the UK's dominant religion has been pushed into second place in any age group. The 2021 Census also shows that 50 per cent of those in their twenties are not religious.

> **Key quote**
>
> … there are still large sections of the population who expect their parish church, just like the NHS, to be there at the point of need for those who want it.
>
> (G Davie)

According to an article in *The Guardian* (30 January 2023), campaigners for non-religious people said that the figures 'make plain that the UK faces a non-religious future' and called on the government to adjust public policy and 'renegotiate the place of religion or belief in today's society'. The dramatic shift to 'no religion' may provide some insights into whether the UK can be called a Christian country.

But what are the beliefs and attitudes towards religion for those in the 'no religion' category? Research suggests that it is composed not just of atheists but also those who doubt the existence of God or think that 'maybe' God exists. Many in this category have a positive opinion of religious leaders such as the Dalai Lama and Pope Francis. Many of those in this category even report taking part in some sort of religious or spiritual practice at least monthly (such as praying). What binds this group together may not be hostility to Christianity or religion but, simply, not being a part of a religious community.

The value of Christian faith schools

The UK has many 'faith schools'; these are primary and secondary schools affiliated with a religious tradition. In England and Wales, these are called 'schools with a religious character'; and in Scotland and Northern Ireland, they are known as *denominational schools*. Most faith schools are affiliated with Christianity and, in some regions of the UK, account for over 30 per cent of all schools.

These schools receive some of their funding from a religious organisation, which may own the school buildings and the land. A certain number of the school's governors are appointed by the school to represent its religious ethos. Often it is the governors, rather than the Local Authority, who are responsible for the school's admission policy and appointing staff. This means that there can be a preference for hiring teachers and support staff who adhere to the school's religion.

In terms of admission, some Christian faith schools might prioritise students who are affiliated with the school's faith. They may ask for a baptismal certificate and/or a letter from a religious leader that certifies their family's attendance at worship to strengthen their application. This has led to some families attending church simply to get a place at the school, to the detriment of those who live nearer to the school but do not have a religious affiliation. However, many faith schools have removed any faith criteria from their admissions policy to avoid this issue. Faith schools must follow the National

Specification content

The conflicting religious and non-religious views on Christianity in the UK (the value of Christian faith schools)

A significant percentage of children in the UK attend faith schools

Curriculum in all subjects; however, in RE these schools can focus on their religious tradition, though many do present other religions. Faith schools are inspected regularly by Ofsted. Ofsted is the education regulator for England. Wales, Scotland and Northern Ireland have their own educational regulators.

Those who support faith schools point to several advantages:

- Parents who want their children to have a religious grounding in their education can have this need met.
- Faith schools tend to be among the best-performing state schools.
- They add an element of diversity and choice to the educational landscape.
- The values and ethics of the religious tradition these schools represent fosters inclusivity, tolerance, love and justice.

Objections to faith schools

The British Humanist Association (BHA), however, actively campaigns against faith schools; invites the public to petition the government against the creation of new faith schools; and urges that existing faith schools be made more inclusive. It believes that faith schools, by their very nature, contradict the principle of a fully inclusive and integrated education system that does not exclude staff, students or governors based on belief. In other words, it believes that faith schools create a segregated future, and that public funds should not be used to promote religion.

The BHA has raised the following objections to the curriculum at faith schools:

- The teaching of religious education in faith schools is not specifically inspected by Ofsted in England.
- Religious education aims to instruct children in the doctrine and practices of a particular religion, rather than taking a more objective approach.
- Religious education in faith schools does not have to cover other religions and 'almost certainly fails to give a fair account of non-religious views'.
- Ethical issues, such as abortion or assisted dying, might be approached from an explicitly religious perspective.
- Personal, Social, Health and Economic Education (PSHE) might teach the sex and relationship components in a way that is homophobic or gender discriminatory.
- Some faith schools have taught creationism and intelligent design as scientific theories.

It is not clear how important 'faith' is to those who send their children to a faith school. Many say that their main motivations in sending their children to these schools have little to do with the religious element. The reasons parents choose (or, hypothetically, would choose) a faith school include:

- academic standards
- location
- discipline
- ethical values
- prestige
- exposure to a faith tradition
- transmission of belief about God.

T3 Significant historical developments in religious thought

> **Specification content**
>
> Beliefs conflicting with laws of the country; perceived challenges to Christianity (decline of role and status of Christianity; reduced impact in public life; restricted religious liberty)

Beliefs conflicting with laws of the country and perceived challenges to Christianity

The declining role and impact of Christianity and restricted religious liberty

Ban on the Lord's Prayer at *Star Wars*

In 2015, the Church of England produced an advertisement to be shown in cinemas at the beginning of *Star Wars: The Force Awakens*. The advert shows several people in different settings saying the Lord's Prayer – including weightlifters at a gym, refugees, a sheep farmer, a Gospel choir and the Archbishop of Canterbury.

> **Key quote**
>
> This [The Lord's Prayer] is a prayer that is 2000 years old and informs our whole culture
>
> (Sadiq Khan, Mayor of London)

The company that administrates media adverts in cinemas, Digital Cinema Media, banned the advert because it transgressed its policy of not promoting adverts with political or religious messages. It was thought that the film could offend people of 'differing faiths or no faith'. This caused an outcry from several leaders and personalities, including Sadiq Khan, Stephen Fry and the prime minister at the time, David Cameron. The Equality and Human Rights Commission (EHRC) spoke in favour of the advert, saying 'There is nothing in law that prevents Christian organisations promoting their faith through adverts'. However, many commentators disagreed, saying that the public did not want religions 'preaching' to them: 'The C of E is perfectly entitled to make its views known, but it should do so from the pulpit. But of course, they can't get many people to go to church so they want to take their message to the cinemas' (John Hegarty, advertising executive). The advert was not shown in the cinemas but was released, instead, on YouTube. The decision to ban an advert of the established Church of England may reflect the decreasing influence of Christianity in Britain. Or, the outcry against its ban could be seen to show widespread support for Christianity.

Gender identity and same-sex marriage

In recent years, it is in the area of sexual ethics that Christianity is most likely to come into conflict with the laws of the country – it is where the law and public opinion can differ from traditional biblical teaching. However, the government website (gov.uk) refers to freedom of religion or belief, describing it as 'not just the freedom to hold personal thoughts and convictions, but also being able to express them individually or with others, publicly or in private'.

Case studies

In May 2018, the UK Supreme Court heard Ashers Baking Company's case. The family-run bakery was appealing against a ruling that said it broke the law by declining to decorate a cake with a pro-gay marriage campaign slogan. In October 2018, the judges unanimously ruled in favour of Ashers Baking Company.

In 2019, Cornerstone Fostering Service, an evangelical Christian charity, was downgraded from 'good' to 'requires improvement' by Ofsted, who accused it of unlawful discrimination because it recruited only evangelical Christian carers. After a legal challenge, the High Court ruled that Ofsted was wrong to try to force Cornerstone to work with non-evangelical Christian carers, citing the exemption in the 2010 Equality Act for religious organisations.

In 2022, 'Susan', a Christian parent governor of a Gateshead school, was dismissed for raising concerns with the trans-affirming sex education policy at her children's primary school. One of the lesson plans she had challenged was the claim that being a 'man' or a 'woman' was determined by personality, hobbies and clothes – not biology. The High Court ordered her reinstatement.

Churches and same-sex marriage

In July 2016, the United Reformed Church allowed same-sex marriage. The Scottish Episcopal Church voted to allow same-sex marriage in 2017. The Church in Wales approved a service of blessing for same-sex couples in 2021. In the same year, the Methodist Church's conference overwhelmingly voted to allow the marriage of same-sex couples in Methodist churches and by Methodist ministers. Methodists may affirm one of two parallel definitions of marriage: 'only between a man and a woman' or 'between any two people'. No minister shall be compelled to perform same-sex marriages.

In November 2023, the General Synod of the Church of England narrowly voted in favour of having special services of blessing for same-sex couples. The services, while not formal weddings, can include the wearing of rings, prayers, confetti and a blessing from the priest. Also, from Sunday 16 December 2023, they allowed a blessing for same-sex couples to be given in a regular Sunday morning service. Various groups within the Church of England regarded this as a move away from biblical teaching of marriage being between one man and one woman.

The General Synod

One of the prayers to be trialled is:

'God of grace, whose beauty, ever ancient, ever new, sings through all creation: enfold your servants N and N with your encouragement, hope, and love. Fill them with the grace to rejoice always in their love for one another, and to follow the Way of holiness and hope revealed in your Son Jesus Christ.'

Those who opposed the trialling of prayers for same-sex blessings pointed out that, once they had been tried, they would be hard to retract. The Bishop of Winchester, who co-chaired the Living in Love and Faith steering group, said 'The truth is ... the Church of England is not of one mind on questions of sexuality and marriage'

On 18 December 2023, Pope Francis announced that Catholic priests could bless same-sex couples as long as they are not part of regular Church rituals or liturgies, nor given in contexts related to civil unions or weddings.

Most Pentecostal churches and the vast majority of Baptist denominations around the world hold a conservative view on homosexuality and only support sexuality in marriage between a man and a woman.

Pope Francis

T3 Significant historical developments in religious thought

To be or not to be ... secular

The word *secular* means 'not to be connected to the Church or religion'. Secularisation is the process of a society once dominated by religious institutions becoming non-religious. Few people would deny that there has been a process of secularisation at work in the UK – this is shown, as we have seen, by decline in several areas: church attendance; the performance of rituals; and influence of the Church in government and society. However, there is disagreement as to whether secularisation is a good thing.

There are many who are committed to an ideology of secularism – the belief that religion is 'otherworldly', and that less of a religious focus entails a more humane society. Those who embrace **secularism** believe that it is both natural and good that society should become secular. They may associate Christianity and religion with superstition, violence, authority, monarchy, control, repression and intolerance. Science, on the other hand, may be associated with progress, peace, humanity, tolerance and democracy. The assumption that some secularists make is that the more modern society becomes, the less religious it will be. In other words, someone cannot be both religious and modern.

> **Key term**
>
> **secularism:** the belief that secularisation is a benefit to society

Is Christianity merely a relic from the past?

There are some reasons for questioning this viewpoint. First, many people are disillusioned with modern science: prosperity and health care have not been delivered for all; famine persists; and there is global warming and the threat of nuclear warfare.

Furthermore, there are not always strong boundaries between science and religion. For instance, the Occupy movement (protesting the excesses of global capitalism) moved from Fleet Street to the grounds of St Paul's Cathedral, hoping that the Church would be an ally with their cause. Some of the protesters asked, 'What would Jesus do?'. The Campaign for Nuclear Disarmament is just another example of a social cause that brings together both believers and those with no religion.

Some have suggested that, rather than the decline of the Church, what we are seeing is a movement from religion as duty and obligation to religion as a choice. Even though this may mean fewer numbers in church, it may also mean that those who believe and practise their faith may find it more meaningful.

> **"Key quote"**
>
> Britain emerges as religious and secular.
> **(L Woodhead)**

There are several Christian initiatives that might be seen as progressive, positive and modern, and yet as reflecting the time-honoured values of religion. One example is the Street Pastor movement, a Church response to urban needs. Volunteers are trained in providing a positive and helpful presence on the streets of UK cities on a Friday and Saturday night, offering a helping hand, a listening ear and practical help. Their mission is 'listening, caring and helping'. At present, Street Pastors work in over 300 towns and cities across the UK. Over 20,000 volunteers are associated with this initiative.

Of course, we could interpret these points as the last gasps of a dying religion. However, sociologists Elisabeth Arweck and James A Beckford name six factors that committed secularists may want to consider before they reach this conclusion:

1. **Religious vitality:** Religion continues to be popular for many in different forms. These include, but are not limited to, charismatic expressions, cathedral worship and various forms of spirituality.
2. **The nature of modernity:** There are different ways of being 'modern'; many 'modern' people see religion as a resource for modern living when science does not provide all the solutions.
3. **De-privatisation:** Rather than seeing religion as only a private personal belief, some observe that religion has helped to bring about positive social change.
4. **Globalisation:** There are transnational religious movements that focus on faith or human rights across the world. This can give Christianity a boost in some locations.
5. **Gender:** Christianity has a wide range of views on women's roles in leadership and the Christian community, which might explain the success or failure of various individual denominations and churches and forms of spirituality.
6. **Rational choice:** Some suggest that religion is a 'market' that thrives when state regulation (in the form of the established Church) is lower. This suggests that the decline of the state Church is not the same as the decline of Christianity.

Street Pastors work to strengthen community and create safer streets

> ### Summary
>
> - The 2021 Census showed that only 46.2 per cent of the population would call themselves Christian, while 37 per cent identified themselves as having 'no religion'.
> - Three areas to consider when deciding whether the UK is a Christian country are:
>   1. church attendance
>   2. personal belief
>   3. public life.
> - Faith schools are schools affiliated with a religious tradition and receive part of their funding from a religious organisation.
> - The main objections to faith schools are that they are not inclusive and that public funds should not be used to promote religion.
> - Sexual ethics is the most likely area where beliefs conflict with the laws of a country, as has been shown by court cases such as Cornerstone Fostering Service and Ashers Baking Company.
> - In December 2024, both the Church of England and the Roman Catholic Church allowed clergy to bless same-sex couples but only in very restricted circumstances.
> - Rather than the decline of the Church, what we may be seeing is a movement from religion as duty and obligation to religion as a choice.

AO1 Activity

a Explain the differences between:
   i   atheist and agnostic
   ii Church of England schools and faith schools
   iii secularisation and privatisation.

This helps ensure you make accurate use of specialist language and vocabulary in context.

b Draw a line down the middle of a revision card. In the left-hand column, write the heading 'A Christian country'. In the right-hand column, write the heading 'Not a Christian country'. Then give two arguments on each side based on church attendance, two based on personal belief and two based on public life.

This helps you select a core set of points to develop an answer of whether the UK is a Christian country using three areas of possible decline.

T3 Significant historical developments in religious thought

> This section covers AO2 content and skills

> **Specification content**
> The effectiveness of the Christian response to the challenge of secularism

Issues for analysis and evaluation

The effectiveness of the Christian response to the challenge of secularism

Possible line of argument	Critical analysis and evaluation
The Christian response to secularism is clearly ineffective since the Church has declined in terms of attendance, social influence and political power, as seen in the data from the 2021 Census.	The census data does not take into account the growth in charismatic churches and cathedral worship. In the past, people often said they were Christians but were not practising Christians.
Immigration has led to growth in charismatic churches and cathedral worship attracts pilgrims and tourists. In terms of percentage of population, the Church is in decline.	Christian involvement is not just about worship and church attendance. It can involve social initiatives such as foodbanks and supporting charities such as Christian Aid.
These social initiatives are simply a 'stop-gap' and will disappear as society introduces more changes. This will result in even greater decline of the Church.	There is evidence that large-scale social initiatives, such as the Street Pastor movement, are flourishing rather than diminishing.
Society is wanting to restrict religious influences as it moves towards secularism.	There have been several recent court cases about the freedom of Christians where the courts have judged in favour of religious freedom.
The role of Christianity in public life and rites of passage is declining. Humanist services are replacing religious weddings and funerals.	The Church is central in national ceremonies such as Remembrance Day. Services are provided in every town and village in the UK, from baptisms and marriages to funerals.
The Church is out of step with most people's views on sexual morality, which adds to the move towards secularism.	Christians who regard the Bible as the word of God argue that same-sex relationships and same-sex marriage are wrong, while other Christians embrace it. Both the Roman Catholic Church and the Church of England allow for same-sex blessings.
Secularist ideology argues that Christian decline is necessary for society to progress.	Secularism has not delivered solutions to global problems. What is needed are Christian values to bring about social change. A completely secular society is not a foregone conclusion.
Other movements, rather than Christianity, may be more effective in combating secularism. You don't have to be a Christian to be compassionate.	Christianity, along with other movements, may be best way of combating secularism and building a just society with Christian values.

AO2 Activity

a Evaluate three lines of argument from the critical analysis and evaluation of the effectiveness of the Christian response to the challenge of secularism. What are their strengths and weaknesses? Which line of argument is strongest?

b Using the strongest line of argument, try to identify three key questions that could be asked – they could be critical questions, challenges, hypothetical or direct.

This section covers AO2 content and skills

Specification content
The extent to which the UK can be called a Christian country

Exam practice

Sample question
Evaluate the extent to which the UK can be called a Christian country.

Sample answer

It seems hard to deny that Christianity has shaped UK culture, language, architecture and even the calendar that we live by. Christianity has an implicit presence in our culture. In the past, it has influenced our national life, as is shown in the prominent role of the Church in the monarchy and the division of all of Britain into administrative parishes based around churches. Prior to the twentieth century, it would have been normal for most people in Britain to have been baptised, married and buried by the Church.

News reporter / Detective: A good, strong opening paragraph citing the way the line of argument will go.

Christianity continues to permeate contemporary life in the UK. Twenty-six bishops of the Church of England sit in the House of Lords, one of the main decision-making bodies. The House of Commons starts with prayers each day, though they are private and not broadcast. Over 30 per cent of all schools are faith schools, most of which are linked to a Christian denomination and partly funded by the state. The UK has an 'established Church' that is highly visible during national events such as royal weddings, Remembrance Day ceremonies and celebrations of national Christian holidays such as Christmas and Easter. Chaplains provide a Christian presence in many areas of our social life, such as health care, the prison service, the armed services and higher education.

Detective: Lots of good examples further support the argument.

Despite the ongoing influence of Christianity in the UK, it is also clear that the influence is fast declining to the point that the UK can no longer be described as a Christian country. L Woodhead commented that 'Britain … exists somewhere in between … Christian, multi-faith and none'. Perhaps the best example to support this view is the recent census of 2021 for England and Wales. It showed a decline from 59 per cent in the 2011 Census to 46 per cent in 2021 of those saying they belong to Christianity. Those professing 'no religion' increased from 25 per cent to 37 per cent in the same period, which means that 22.2 million people in England and Wales identify with 'no religion'. More people under 40 in England and Wales now declare 'no religion' than identify as Christian. With such clear data as this, it is difficult to see how the UK can be called a Christian country.

Detective / Judge: Good evidence using quotations and recent census data to continue the case for the UK no longer being a Christian country.

T3 Significant historical developments in religious thought

Detective

A final paragraph of arguments concludes a one-sided argument. The evidence is wide ranging and thorough.

Perhaps a better description of the UK is to call it a *pluralist* country rather than a Christian one. Society recognises this change, firstly in that there has been a dramatic shift from what is allowed on Sundays, with increasing participation in sports, shopping and work; secondly in the curriculum of Religious Studies, which now involves world religions and non-religious points of view. Even those parents who send their children to faith schools say their main reason for doing so has to do with academic standards rather than religious faith.

The evidence for decline is further highlighted by the ages of those attending church. In 2022, 36 per cent of those who were regular worshippers at a Church of England service were over the age of 70. Young people turning away from Christianity suggests the future of the Church is in serious doubt.

Explorer · **Critical thinker** · **Philosopher** · **Judge**

This final section questions whether we are considering the right measure. It makes good use of a scholar. The earlier arguments all use the measure of 'belonging', but what if we examine the measure of believing? It may produce a different result.

A very good and thoughtful conclusion.

However, maybe we are applying the wrong measure. Grace Davie, Emeritus Professor of Sociology, has commented that while 'belonging' to Christianity is clearly declining in the UK, 'believing' may not be. Support for this view is that fewer than half of those who claim to be non-religious are comfortable with the label 'atheist'. In other words, they do not want to belong to a spiritual community but many of them have a positive opinion of religious leaders such as the Dalai Lama and Pope Francis. Some even report praying. This suggests they may not be hostile towards Christianity or religion, but they do not want to be part of a religious community. Though they may not attend church services, the number who say they believe in God or some higher power is quite high. However, such 'fuzzy' beliefs are a long way from traditional Christian beliefs. Perhaps the best conclusion, given the evidence, is that the UK is seeing the end of Christianity as a duty. In its place is a stronger focus on Christianity as a voluntary activity. It may also mean that this decrease in numbers is leading to a stronger 'core'. In other words, it means something to be a Christian in an environment where it is the norm to profess no religion. This might explain growth and vitality in some forms of Christianity. But even so, it would still be inaccurate to describe the UK as a 'Christian country'. Perhaps it would be better to describe the UK as a pluralistic or multifaith country.

Over to you

Below is a one-sided view concerning the UK as a secular nation. It is 160 words long. You need to include this view for an evaluation. However, just to present one side of an argument or one line of reasoning is not an evaluation. Using the paragraph below, add a counterargument or alternative line of reasoning to make the evaluation more balanced. Allow about 100 words for your counterargument or alternative line of reasoning.

Evaluation

There are many reasons to support the view that the UK is a secular nation. By *secular*, we mean that there is a marked decline in religious belief, in religious attendance and in the presence of Christianity in cultural and political 'spaces'.

We have solid statistics concerning the dramatic decrease in participation and interest in religion. It seems that the UK is less Christian than it ever was, and it is only a matter of time before even Christians who support a state Church admit that this has become a truly secular nation in all three senses of the word. Since all this is compelling evidence, we can agree with Steve Bruce, who writes: 'the voluntary association type of religion continues to engage perhaps 10–12 per cent of the population. With around 80 per cent of the population showing no interest in any form of religion, it seems entirely sensible to describe the UK as a largely secular country'.

Example of a counterargument

Theos Think Tank argue that, for all that formalised religious belief and institutionalised religious belonging have declined over recent decades, the British have not become a nation of atheists or materialists. On the contrary, a spiritual current runs as, if not more, powerfully through the nation than it once did.

Now think of another line of argument or reasoning that may support either argument, or even a completely different argument, and add this to your answer.

Then ask yourself: will my work, when developed, contain thorough, sustained and clear views that are supported by extensive, detailed reasoning and/or evidence?

This section covers AO1 content and skills

Specification content

Richard Dawkins' and Alister McGrath's contrasting views on the relationship between religion and science, and the nature of proof; the limits of science; the 'God of the gaps' argument

Key persons

Richard Dawkins (b. 1941): British evolutionary, zoologist, biologist and author of the book *The God Delusion*; a major figure in the New Atheism movement

Alister McGrath (b. 1953): Northern Irish scientist and theologian

William Paley, Anglican priest and writer on natural theology

Key person

William Paley (1743–1805): an English Anglican priest; his book on natural theology, where he presents the teleological argument for the existence of God, was very influential

E: Challenges from science

Contrasting view

At the heart of science is evidence: making observations, testing those observations and arriving at a theory – and then subjecting that theory to further tests. **Richard Dawkins**, the renowned scientist and proponent of atheism, declares that he is passionate about the scientific method and it is his science that leads him to his atheistic viewpoint. **Alister McGrath** and Joanna Collicutt McGrath say that they too are passionate about evidence, and maintain that their Christian faith is compatible with the discoveries of science.

Richard Dawkins, former Charles Simonyi Professor for the Public Understanding of Science at the University of Oxford (1995–2008)

Alister McGrath, current Andreas Idreos Professor of Science and Religion at the University of Oxford

Dawkins says evidence suggests that religion offers no real answers to the questions we ask. In fact, it is prone to anti-intellectualism and violence. Science, on the other hand, is actively unlocking the mysteries of life: 'I am thrilled to be alive at a time when humanity is pushing against the limits of understanding. We may eventually discover that there are no limits.' McGrath disagrees with Dawkins' description of religion and believes that there are questions that science simply cannot answer. In fact, he says, science and religion need each other.

The relationship between religion and science

One of the most interesting facts about life is the incredible complexity of the natural world. Just consider almost any element, for example an eye or a wing. Each of these is composed of a myriad of processes that work together to allow sight or flight. How did these come to be?

Dawkins says that, when faced with something that is incredibly complex, humans have tended to turn to a religious answer – God created these. The idea that an eye or a wing could have somehow come about by chance seems impossible. In the late eighteenth century, **William Paley** attempted to justify this kind of religious answer. He spoke about someone on a hike who finds a watch. To come across something in nature that is incredibly complicated and displays intricate design is surely different from coming across a rock or a blade of grass. We think, says Paley, that there must have been a designer. Dawkins refers to a contemporary example of this religious argument: to consider that a tornado could blow through a scrapyard and somehow randomly throw together a fully functioning Boeing 747 aircraft would be absurd according to this way of arguing.

WJEC/Eduqas Religious Studies for AS & A Level Christianity

Problems with religious answers

Dawkins says that there are two problems with the **God hypothesis** of design in the natural world:

1. We are not faced with a choice between chance and God. Natural selection actually explains how there can be the appearance of complex, seemingly improbable things from small and relatively simple causes. Natural selection is the process whereby an organism that is better adapted to the environment tends to survive and produce more offspring. Those traits that helped the organism survive are passed down to the next generations so that, over long periods of time, there can be huge and complex developments. In other words, natural selection breaks down the problem of improbability into small pieces. Looking at the development of the eye or wing doesn't seem that improbable from the evolutionary point of view.

> **Key quote**
>
> ... the designer himself, in order to be capable of designing, would have to be another complex entity of the kind that, in his turn, needs the same kind of explanation.
>
> (R Dawkins)

2. Saying that God designed complex things is no answer at all because God would have to be at least as complex as the thing he designed. Religious believers explain a highly improbable thing in terms of a more highly improbable thing. This means that God is the 'ultimate Boeing 747'! It does no good insisting, as some theologians do, that God is 'simple', because a god who could know everything that was happening, listen to everyone's prayers, sustain the world and design complex biological forms of life would have to be very complicated. To say that God designed the world just begs the question: Who designed God? Natural selection is the alternative we must embrace to avoid these religious dilemmas.

How did life originate?

Natural selection explains our complex world. It does not, says Dawkins, explain why there is life in the universe and how life came to be on planet Earth. Instead of turning to a God hypothesis (that is, we don't understand, so it must be God's doing), natural selection should inspire us to find an explanation that makes sense of the improbable existence of life.

> **Key quote**
>
> Darwin is a role model to inspire all who follow the logical and courageous compulsion to explain complex things in the only legitimate way, which is in terms of simpler things and their interactions.
>
> (R Dawkins)

Dawkins proposes the *anthropic approach*: Since we exist, Earth is the kind of place that is 'life-friendly'. When we consider that there are billions of billions of planets where life could have developed, is it unreasonable to think that the conditions friendly to life could occur on at least one of these? 'The anthropic principle states that, since we are alive, eukaryotic [having the kind of cells with features not present in bacteria], and conscious, our

> **Key term**
>
> **God hypothesis:** Richard Dawkins' phrase to describe the claim that there is an interventionist God in the universe; this should be treated like any other scientific hypothesis

planet has to be one of the intensely rare planets that has bridged all three gaps' (Richard Dawkins). Why is the universe able to support life? Instead of invoking God, we might consider *multiverse theory*; the idea that there is an endless number of universes each with different variations, and ours happens to be one with the variations to support life. Dawkins says that there is a 'Darwinian' feel to this kind of thinking – explaining life in terms of developments and variations, rather than just positing a god.

Religion does not offer reasonable answers to questions about life, says Dawkins, because it has been flawed from its very beginning. His theory is that religion (defined as belief in God) originated as a misfiring in the brain of an otherwise useful activity. There are many things that give creatures survival value – however, in some situations, those things can lead to destruction. Dawkins gives the example of the moth's navigation system, which is oriented to celestial bodies and guides it to warmth and light. However, it can also guide it to death in a flame. Religion (death in the flame) is a by-product of at least two qualities that often provide survival value:

1. **The human tendency to obey elders:** This is a very good trait that saves lives and increases our safety – except when the elders are mistaken.
2. **The biologically programmed tendency to assign meaning and purpose to animals and objects:** If a lion is snarling at you, it is a good idea to assign to that lion the purpose of wanting to eat you, says Dawkins. This activity of assigning purpose and value will save your life. However, humans assign value to all kinds of things: 'that rock exists to help that creature scratch its back' and 'the being that made this universe loves me'.

> **Key quote**
>
> The general theory of religion as an accidental by-product – a misfiring of something useful – is the one I wish to advocate.
> (R Dawkins)

These traits explain why people have a psychological disposition that can favour religious belief. In terms of how we came up with the actual details of religious belief, Dawkins uses the concept of *memes* – an element of culture that is passed on from one person to another by imitation or non-genetic means. There are many elements of culture (memes) that include God and have added appeal because they are associated with other memes. Religious leaders can manipulate these memes in ways that give rise to varieties of religious belief. Therefore, we culturally inherit all kinds of beliefs and values, which include belief in God.

The wall between religion and science

Because religion provides only unreasonable answers to our deepest questions, and science proceeds only on evidence, Dawkins finds it hard to imagine that any real scientist can be a religious believer. He thinks that many scientists who speak positively of Christianity aren't really Christians. Either they are afraid of sharing their real beliefs, or they confuse Christianity with cultural values about beauty and goodness. Dawkins, for example, does not believe that Einstein was a theist, and he accuses many contemporary scientists of accepting prizes from religiously based bodies by passing themselves off as 'faith-friendly', when they do not really believe in a being who creates and sustains life.

> **Key quote**
>
> Science without religion is lame. Religion without science is blind.
>
> (A Einstein)

Alister McGrath and Joanna Collicutt McGrath, authors of *The Dawkins Delusion*, couldn't disagree more. They note that there are a number of scientists who are quite clear about their Christian belief.

They cite Elaine Ecklund, who, with six colleagues, widened an earlier 2010 survey to include other countries than just the USA (*Secularity and Science: What Scientists Around the World Really Think About Religion*). It revealed the differences between scientists working in different cultures and societies. In the UK, 43 per cent of scientists questioned were atheists (with proportionally more biologists than physicists), and only 23 per cent identified themselves as theists, though the scientists surveyed seemed 'remarkably friendly to the value of religion'. In both Taiwan and Hong Kong, scientists are as religious, or more religious, than the general population.

> **Key quote**
>
> I do not believe in a personal God.
>
> (A Einstein)

One of the concluding claims of the research was that, across the world, 'there are more religious scientists than we might think'. In the first of the studies, which Elaine Ecklund and her colleagues carried out in 2018, they surveyed 14,000 scientists and could 'count on two hands the number of atheist scientists ... who have the same attitude to religious people as Richard Dawkins'. In a later book in 2021 (*Varieties of Atheism in Science*), the same authors found that the New Atheists' narrow view of atheism doesn't represent even the more extreme scientific atheists' view.

> **Key quote**
>
> I started out as an atheist, who went on to become a Christian – precisely the reverse of Dawkins' intellectual journey.
>
> (A McGrath)

Some arguments against Dawkins

It is significant, say the McGraths, that so many thoughtful human beings become Christians in their adult years. This is not what we would expect if belief in God were like belief in Santa Claus or the Tooth Fairy. They note the change of thinking of Antony Flew, who wrote *There Is A God: How the world's most notorious atheist changed his mind when he was in his 80s*. In fact, one of the greatest weaknesses of atheism is the 'persistence of belief in God, when there is supposedly no God in which to believe' (A McGrath and J Collicutt McGrath).

If religion really were a 'virus of the mind', with a biological foundation, then we would expect that there would be some scientific evidence to back up this theory. The McGraths note that Dawkins has provided no evidence. Furthermore, the idea that religious belief reflects a deficient psychology, which makes faulty assumptions about the natural world and tends to irrational and violent behaviour, is yet another assertion that Dawkins presents without evidence. This lack of evidence is an indication to the McGraths that *The God Delusion* is a work of **polemic** that is 'more designed to reassure atheists whose faith is faltering than to engage fairly or rigorously with religious believers and others seeking for truth'.

> **Key term**
>
> **polemic:** an aggressive verbal or written attack

The limits of science

The McGraths find evidence lacking for many of Dawkins' views in *The God Delusion*. Not only has Dawkins reinvented religious belief according to his own negative views, but he has artificially constructed a wall between religion and science when, for many scientists, there is no wall.

> **Key quote**
>
> Either half my colleagues are enormously stupid, or else the science of Darwinism is fully compatible with conventional religious belief – and equally compatible with atheism.
>
> (SJ Gould)

The McGraths point to the writings of the evolutionary biologist Stephen Jay Gould. Gould, himself a sceptic of religious belief, said that science and religion represent **non-overlapping magisteria (NOMA)**. The term *magisterium* means 'domain of competency'; Gould was referring to the domain of science as the empirical realm and the domain of religion as questions of ultimate meaning. These two realms do not overlap – they each focus on their separate realms of enquiry. The McGraths find this approach widespread among scientists. For instance, the astrophysicist Martin Rees says that ultimate questions lie beyond science and that there is never enough evidence to provide answers to these questions.

> **Key term**
>
> **non-overlapping magisteria (NOMA):** the view Stephen Jay Gould advocates, that science and religion are two different areas of inquiry

The biologist Sir Peter Medawar says that there are three questions that science cannot answer:

1. How did everything begin?
2. What are we here for?
3. What is the point of living?

The McGraths actually prefer the concept of *POMA* ('partially overlapping magisteria') to NOMA. This means that science and faith can interpenetrate each other, helping each other to become more informed.

When it comes to natural selection, the McGraths' view is that this is a fact that can be interpreted atheistically, theistically or in any number of other ways. We bring our worldviews to the facts. They accuse Dawkins of confusing the worldview of atheism with the fact of natural selection.

The 'God of the gaps' argument

As we have seen, Dawkins questions the God hypothesis – the idea that God can be invoked to explain a gap in our knowledge. He notes that theologians have often explained gaps by invoking God. One contemporary example he gives is of those who describe themselves as 'intelligent-design' theorists. These theorists point to complex features of biology that they think cannot be argued to be a part of the process of natural selection, for instance how an underdeveloped wing offers survival value to an organism. These theorists propose, as William Paley did, that the only answer is God. Yet Dawkins shows how each of their proposals has failed. For instance, half a wing can be of enormous survival value, increasing the height an animal can jump to escape death, or glide to find food. The intelligent-design theorists have to retreat to yet another complex aspect of life that does not yet have a natural explanation.

The problem with this strategy is that, as the gaps in our knowledge decrease, God becomes increasingly irrelevant, retreating further and further away from daily life. Dawkins notes that, since Darwinian evolution explains the complexity of the natural world, gap theologians now pin their remaining hopes on the origin of life. However, as soon as science discovers evidence that points to a theory, then God will disappear.

Another way to fill the gap

There is a gap in our lives in the sense that we need to find inspiration and meaning. Dawkins believes that science can fill that gap. In fact, science can fill the four main roles that religion has traditionally filled:

- **Explanation:** By understanding natural selection and scientific ideas that can explain the existence of life in the universe, we no longer need religion to explain life.
- **Exhortation:** Religion used to exhort us to live moral lives; so much so, that people think that religion is the only source of morality. However, it is easy to prove that religious people do not lead more moral lives than non-religious people – you can be good without God. In fact, religion leads, for Dawkins, to violence and segregation (as anecdotal evidence, he cites the violent hate mail he has received from Christians).
- **Consolation:** While it is true that religion offers consolation, this does not make it true. There are many examples of atheists who are consoled, not by religion, but by discovering new ways of thinking about the world.
- **Inspiration:** People do not need religion to be inspired. Gazing at the sheer grandeur and complexity of life all around us is an endless source of inspiration.

Interestingly, Dawkins notes that the theologian Dietrich Bonhoeffer rejected the 'God of the gaps' approach. The McGraths do as well, pointing out that this approach represents only a small portion of Christians, and stems from the eighteenth and nineteenth centuries. The majority of theologians, according to the McGraths, have viewed the reality of God as intimately and actively involved in all of life.

In fact, say the McGraths, it is not the gaps in our knowledge that require an explanation, but the notion that we live in an intelligible and explainable universe. Why do we take the idea that we live in such a universe for granted? They point to the philosopher Richard Swinburne, who argues that the best explanation for the intelligibility of the universe is that it has been created by an intelligent being.

> **Key quote**
>
> But could it be that God clutters up a gap that we'd be better off filling with something else? Science, perhaps? Art? Human friendship? Humanism?
>
> (R Dawkins)

T3 Significant historical developments in religious thought

> **Key quote**
>
> Christians do not worship gaps. What elicits our excitement, our sense of wonder, is the *big picture*.
> (A McGrath)

Is religion the axis of evil?

The McGraths share their surprise and disappointment that a fine scientist such as Dawkins could so easily mischaracterise religion as an evil and violent reality. They think that this must be because Dawkins cares more for the eradication of religion than he does about the truth. For the McGraths, there are several facts about religion that Dawkins ignores:

- **The prophetic critique of religion:** Religion is capable of self-critique. The prophets of Israel, who criticised religious practices, proved this when they condemned such practices that involved social oppression and transgressed the spirit of the law.

- **Jesus' inclusive ministry:** Dawkins characterises Jesus as having an in-group mentality, but ignores:
    - the admonition to love one's enemy
    - the anti-nationalistic tone of the parable of the Good Samaritan
    - the inclusion in his movement of tax collectors and prostitutes (who had been rejected by the religion of his day)
    - his open dialogue with Gentiles.

- **The capacity of religion to transcend and transform human conflicts:** Some of the biblical passages that Dawkins condemns appear alongside passages that encourage: compassion; welcoming strangers; hospitality; forgiving debt; prohibiting slavery; and forbidding infant sacrifice.

- **The danger of an absence of religion:** Without religion, society can turn ideas into idols and commit violence against people who reject those ideas. The McGraths cite the excessive violence that accompanied the French Revolution.

- **That religion is more than belief:** Dawkins reduces religion to dogmatic beliefs and ignores how religion has many dimensions. The faith of believers often goes beyond intellectual assent to the kinds of propositions that Dawkins attacks.

Why, ask the McGraths, does Dawkins ignore that institutionalised atheism can lead to incredible violence, such as the Soviet authorities practised from 1918 to 1941? Furthermore, millions were killed by Pol Pot in the name of socialism. Even when it seems that religion is directly behind violent acts, such as the destruction of the Twin Towers on 9/11, there are studies that show that religious belief alone is not sufficient to cause these acts. Social oppression, foreign occupation and other psychological and material factors hugely contribute. Perhaps, then, religion does not have a 'corner on the market' of violence, as Dawkins suggests. Furthermore, there are many studies that indicate that religious belief and commitment have a positive effect on human wellbeing and longevity. This does not mean that religion is true, but it does mean that assertions of the 'badness' of religion can be proven to be non-scientific in nature.

Scientism or science?

The McGraths accuse Dawkins of confusing scientism with science. *Scientism* is the faith that scientific knowledge and techniques will find answers to everything. This might even include areas that philosophy, the social sciences and the humanities are currently investigating. The McGraths base their accusation on the lack of evidence provided for key assertions in *The God Delusion*; the mischaracterisation of religion as violent; and the claim that science will provide answers to everything. Dawkins, however, is adamant that he is committed to the evidence – wherever it leads.

Thus far, it has led away, he says, from a religious point of view on the world. Even though there are questions that science cannot answer at the moment, there is no reason to declare that it has limits. Furthermore, if there is no metaphysical reality beyond the created world, it is quite right to focus on scientific rather than religious answers.

Summary

Two scientists who hold contrasting views about God:
- Richard Dawkins:
  - Religion is anti-intellectual and is the cause of much violence.
  - Natural selection explains the origin of life.
  - Misfiring in the brain explains a belief in God.
  - No real scientist can be a religious believer.
  - We invoke God to explain gaps in our knowledge.
- Alister McGrath:
  - Christian faith is compatible with the discoveries of science.
  - There is no scientific evidence to support the view that religion is 'a virus of the mind'.
  - Ultimate questions lie beyond science.
  - Natural selection can be interpreted atheistically or theistically.
  - Christians view God as intimately and actively involved in all of life, not as 'God of the gaps'.

AO1 Activity

a Explain each of the following terms:
   i   the God hypothesis
   ii   God of the gaps
   iii natural selection
   iv   theistic evolution.

   This helps ensure you make accurate use of specialist language and vocabulary in context.

b In your own words, describe how Dawkins believes science has filled – and will fill – the gaps in our knowledge of the world. Now describe why the McGraths reject the 'God of the gaps' approach.

   This helps you select a core set of points to develop an answer about the relationship between religion and science, and ensure that you make accurate use of specialist language and vocabulary in context.

T3 Significant historical developments in religious thought

This section covers AO2 content and skills

Specification content

Whether science has reduced the role of God in Christianity

Issues for analysis and evaluation

Whether science has reduced the role of God in Christianity

Possible line of argument	Critical analysis and evaluation
Science has already replaced the role of God in providing answers to the world we live in, e.g. Darwin and natural selection.	Science may have answered some mysteries but not all, e.g. why there is something rather than nothing; why there is life on our planet.
Science shows that we can find answers to the remaining mysteries without the need to resort to a god, e.g. multiverse theory.	Until there is evidence to support some of the proposed theories that attempt to explain mysteries, it is reasonable to posit God.
The 'God of the gaps' approach has forced God into retreat, such that he finally becomes irrelevant.	The 'God of the gaps' approach is wrong. We should view God as actively sustaining all of life. Evolution through natural selection is compatible with theistic belief.
We keep belief in God to give our lives meaning, purpose and direction. But science can provide us with meaning, purpose and direction.	Richard Swinburne argues that we live in an intelligible world that is best explained by the existence of an intelligent being behind all that we see and know.
The idea that science will one day explain everything is called *scientism*; a new kind of faith.	Belief in God among many scientists persists. We can give a theistic interpretation to scientific discoveries.

> **AO2 Activity**
>
> a   Analyse three possible conclusions that could be drawn from the critical analysis and evaluation of whether science has reduced the role of God in Christianity. What are their strengths? Which conclusion do you think is the weakest?
>
> b   Evaluate three lines of argument that persuade you that this is the weakest conclusion. What questions could you to raise in response to these arguments?

Exam practice

Sample question
Evaluate the extent to which a scientist must be an atheist.

Sample answer
Perhaps the most vocal and high-profile scientist who has argued that religion is a barrier to rational enquiry is the renowned scientist Richard Dawkins. He argues that religion is prone to anti-intellectualism and to violence. Science, on the other hand, is actively unlocking the mysteries of life and proceeds only from evidence. As a result, Dawkins finds it hard to imagine that any real scientist can be a religious believer.

But there are many scientists who claim they do have a religious belief, for instance John Polkinghorne and Francis Collins. So how does Dawkins explain this?

He argues that many scientists who speak positively of Christianity aren't really Christians. Either they are afraid of sharing their beliefs, or they confuse Christianity with cultural values about beauty and goodness. However, in 2018 Elaine Ecklund surveyed 14,000 scientists and could 'count on two hands the number of atheist scientists … who have the same attitude to religious people as Richard Dawkins'. In a later book (2021), the same author found that the New Atheists' narrow view of atheism doesn't represent even the more extreme scientific atheists' view.

However, Dawkins argues that science and religious belief are incompatible. He maintains that religious belief is a biological and psychological aberration and has no value in the quest for knowledge. In fact, he goes further, claiming that religious belief can even act to deter us from the quest for truth. He describes religion as a 'misfiring of the brain'.

So where is Dawkins' evidence? For Dawkins, the evidence is obvious: the events of 9/11, the extreme beliefs of terrorists, the long history of religiously motivated wars and the suppression of scientific truth by religious bodies. Not surprisingly, those with a religious belief challenge such a view of religion. But is such a conclusion correct?

The McGraths are two of the scientists who challenge Dawkins. They claim that the real problem is not religion but the sociological and psychological attitudes that sometimes lead to extreme beliefs. Dawkins does not take into account the many aspects of religion that have actually been a part of resolving conflicts, for example the Reconciliation Commission that drew upon the Christian values of compassion in the healing of South Africa after Apartheid. Indeed, in the Old Testament there are examples of the prophets challenging religion when it loses a humanitarian focus. In the New Testament, Jesus commands people to love their enemies.

When religion is eradicated or suppressed, does it lead to peace and scientific progress? The evidence suggests not. The McGraths point to the violence of institutionalised atheism in Soviet Russia from 1918 to 1941 and to the murder of millions in the name of socialism by Pol Pot in Cambodia.

It does seem that Dawkins fails to present a persuasive case. In fact, there are studies that show religious belief is related to a sense of wellbeing and longevity. This does not mean that religion is true, but that science might accomplish even more with these factors in place.

This section covers AO2 content and skills

Specification content
The extent to which a scientist must be an atheist

Tennis player / Detective / Critical thinker / Philosopher
The opening presents a number of arguments by Dawkins with detailed replies and arguments, and good knowledge of scholars.

Tennis player / Detective / Critical thinker / Philosopher
This is another strong section of 'for' and 'against' arguments supported by good knowledge and examples. The use of questions is a helpful structure that guides readers through the arguments.

Philosopher — Judge
The answer now starts to draw towards a conclusion that is consistent with the arguments throughout.

Explorer — **Judge**

A good last paragraph that raises a final possible objection to the previous conclusion but then clearly dismisses that objection. In the final sentence, there is a reference back to the actual essay question, drawing attention to the word *must* in the original question. A strong answer showing good knowledge and clear structure.

Perhaps we can make a case that religion can sometimes get in the way of science. This could be on a collective level when communities have hindered any progress in the name of religious truth, or on an individual level when individual scientists may resist thinking through their observations to an anti-religious conclusion. However, this is clearly countered by the sheer number of scientists who conduct research and push forward the frontiers of science while holding religious beliefs. Even if all scientists were atheists, this would not prove that a scientist must be an atheist!

Over to you

Below is an evaluation concerning religion as a destructive and violent force in the world, antithetical to science. It is 150 words long. After the first paragraph, there is an intermediate conclusion that is underlined. As a group, try to identify where you could add more intermediate conclusions to the rest of the passage.

Evaluation

Alister McGrath and Joanna Collicutt McGrath raise a number of arguments against Dawkins' portrayal of religion. First, where is the evidence for the assertion that religion is a misfiring of the brain? We would expect that an assertion involving biology would be backed up with observations. Furthermore, the assertion that religion is the dark side of the traits of obeying elders and attributing intention to the environment appears to be merely a suggestion. <u>It seems then, that the Dawkins' view of the origin of religion is based on opinion rather than fact.</u>

When we examine religion, we find many positive aspects. Studies indicate that it contributes positively to health and longevity. Furthermore, the ethics of the prophets and of Jesus seem to lead in an opposite direction to violence: critique of inhumanity among religious leaders, the admonition to love one's enemy, teaching on compassion, and so on. Furthermore, there are times in history when religion has acted as a force for healing and reconciliation. None of these observations mean that religion is true, of course, but they help to provide a more complete picture of religion.

When you have done this, you will see clearly that in AO2 it is helpful to include a brief summary of the arguments you have presented as you go through an answer, and not just leave it until the end to draw a final conclusion. This way, you are demonstrating that you are sustaining evaluation throughout an answer and not just repeating information you have learned.

F: Challenges from pluralism and diversity within a tradition

Difference between religious pluralism and tolerance of religious diversity

Make sure you have read and understood the set texts: Deuteronomy 6:5; Joshua 23:16; John 14:6; Acts 4:12.

The exclusivist and inclusivist views expressed in the Christian Bible

Broadly speaking, theologians have taken three views on the potential for salvation for those who are not Christians. The first of these is *exclusivism*: salvation exclusively belongs to Christianity – there are no other paths. Some exclusivists, though not all, have thought that everyone who is not a Christian will be damned. However, this position has been considered too harsh by many. This is because there are many people who have never known Christianity, will never know it or are in societies where it is unlikely that Christianity will ever be a serious option.

This has led to *inclusivism*; Christ's work somehow 'includes' all people – though the fullest expression of salvation is found in explicitly knowing Christ and belonging to his Church. More recently, a third option has appeared, though it is seen as too radical to be accepted by any major Christian denomination: *religious pluralism*. Religious pluralism views Christianity as the way to God for Christians only; other religions have equally valid paths to divine reality. In a broader sense, the term *pluralism* extends to the idea of different communities and cultures fostering tolerance and living side by side.

> **Key quote**
>
> God our saviour ... desires everyone to be saved and to come to the knowledge of the truth.
>
> (1 Timothy 2:4)

There are passages in the Bible that seem to reflect the exclusivist viewpoint. In the Hebrew scriptures, God called out a group of people to follow him and commanded that they dedicate themselves to exclusive worship: 'Love the LORD your God with all your heart and with all your soul and with all your strength' (Deuteronomy 6:5). Furthermore, to turn away from this exclusive worship of God had negative consequences: 'If you violate the covenant of the LORD your God, which he commanded you, and go and serve other gods and bow down to them, the LORD'S anger will burn against you, and you will quickly perish from the good land he has given to you' (Joshua 23:16).

In the New Testament, Jesus appears to echo these exclusivist views: 'Jesus answered, "I am the way and the truth and the life. No one comes to the Father except through me"' (John 14:6). The early Church is quite clear that salvation is to be found only in Jesus: 'Salvation is found in no one else, for there is no other name under heaven given to mankind by which we must be saved' (Acts 4:12). Clearly, the plain sense of these passages is that Christianity provides the only path to God.

These are far from the only exclusivist passages in the Bible – there are a number of verses that speak of condemnation for unbelief and eternal punishment.

This section covers AO1 content and skills

Specification content

Difference between religious pluralism and tolerance of religious diversity; the exclusivist and inclusivist views expressed in the Christian Bible (Deuteronomy 6:5; Joshua 23:16; John 14:6; Acts 4:12)

> ## " Key quote
>
> This is how it will be at the end of the age. The angels will come and separate the wicked from the righteous, and throw them into the fiery furnace, where there will be weeping and gnashing of teeth.
>
> (Matthew 13:49–50)

Theological statements developed that were exclusive in nature, such as the dogma *extra ecclesiam nulla salus* ('outside of the Church, no salvation'). This phrase comes from the third-century Christian theologian Cyprian of Carthage, and continues to be a part of Catholic teaching. Many Protestants have a similar approach but, because of a different view of the Church, express their exclusivism as 'no salvation outside of faith in Christ'. However, the message is essentially the same: to be saved, one must become a Christian.

The contribution of Karl Rahner to Christian inclusivism

Karl Rahner was one of the most important Roman Catholic theologians of the twentieth century. His views were a major influence on the documents produced by **Vatican II**, the assembly of Roman Catholic leaders who reconsidered Church practice and theology in the 1960s.

Specification content
The contribution of John Hick and Karl Rahner to Christian inclusivism (and the difference between their positions)

Key person
Karl Rahner (1904–84): a German Jesuit priest and theologian who coined the phrase 'anonymous Christians'

Key term
Vatican II: the council of Roman Catholic leaders that met in 1962–65 to consider the relationship between the Church and the modern world

Karl Rahner

A session of the second Vatican council in St Peter's Basilica, 1962

Rahner thought it was possible to make a positive use of modern philosophy while, at the same time, holding true to Catholic doctrine. One of his central ideas was that all human beings have an awareness of something beyond the finite realm. All things, persons and events are a part of a larger horizon, an infinite reality – God. When we think about particular, finite things, we are, whether we know it or not, reaching out beyond these things to an infinite reality, which is God. Thus, it is possible for people to have an implicit awareness of God without explicitly knowing that this is the case. Furthermore, Rahner believed that God is actively offering grace to all people, wherever they are, in whatever religion (or non-religion) they may be involved.

> **Key quote**
>
> Rahner's rather daring claim then, is that everyone is in some sense aware of God whether they realise it or not, and that all our pedestrian dealings with the world would in fact be impossible without this awareness.
>
> (K Kilby)

Anonymous Christianity

Because God is active everywhere in all experiences, offering grace and the opportunity to respond to his presence, Rahner felt that the Church should not view those outside it as merely 'non-Christians', but as anonymous Christians. An *anonymous Christian* is one who responds to God's presence but may not be explicitly aware of God, and is certainly not aware of God's full expression in Christ and the Church. In one of his most famous essays, 'Christianity and the Non-Christian Religions', Rahner develops this idea in four theses:

- **1st Thesis:** '... Christianity understands itself as the absolute religion, intended for all men, which cannot recognise any other religion beside itself as of equal right.' For Rahner, this thesis is necessary, since the Church believes that God has chosen to relate to the world though his incarnation as Christ. However, Christianity has a starting point in time and space and, prior to this, God did not demand explicit assent to Christianity – there were other ways to come to God, even though, from God's point of view, these ways were all through a single plan. The question that Rahner raises is whether there can be other ways to come to God in the present.

- **2nd Thesis:** 'a non-Christian religion can be recognised as a lawful religion (although only in different degrees) without thereby denying the error and depravity contained in it.' By 'lawful religion', Rahner means a religion that provides a way for people to find a right relationship with God. Christians normally associate 'lawful religion' with Christianity – but Rahner introduces the idea that there may be other lawful religions to a greater or lesser degree. For instance, in the Old Testament, there were people who pleased God but were outside of God's 'lawful religion' of Judaism. Also, Paul in Acts 17 refers positively to pagan religion.

  God wants to reach out to all human beings with salvation; this means that every single person must have the possibility of a genuine saving relationship to God. Therefore, we must be open, says Rahner, to the idea that God uses other religions to reach people. This does not mean that everything in these religions is true and right, but merely that God is using it as a part of his plan of salvation.

- **3rd Thesis:** 'If the second thesis is correct, then Christianity does not simply confront the member of an extra-Christian religion as a mere non-Christian but as someone who can and must already be regarded in this or that respect as an anonymous Christian.' Rahner wants the Church to recognise that, even before missionaries arrive to proclaim their message, God has already been at work. This does not mean, however, that Christianity is not needed; becoming a Christian is the final step of a process that begins with anonymous Christianity.

- **4th Thesis:** 'the Church will not so much regard herself today as the exclusive community of those who have a claim to salvation but rather as the historically tangible vanguard and the historically and socially constituted explicit expression of what the Christian hopes is present as a hidden reality even outside the visible Church.' Here, Rahner is trying to change the attitude of the Church. The Church should not see itself as the sole possessor of truth and goodness opposed to all who are outside of it. Instead, it should remember that God is greater than the Church, working beyond its walls through the reality of religious pluralism. At the same time, it should be thankful that it knows the full expression of God. Rahner ends his essay by urging the Church to have the attitude of St Paul when he said to the Greeks, 'What therefore you do now know and yet worship (and yet worship! [Rahner's emphasis]) that I proclaim to you' (Acts 17:23).

> **Key quote**
>
> If, however, man can always have a positive, saving relationship to God, and if he always had to have it, then he has always had it within that religion which in practice was at his disposal by being a factor in his sphere of existence.
>
> (K Rahner)

Key person

John Hick (1922–2012): an English-born philosopher of religion and theologian who taught for most of his career in the United States; he gradually moved away from his conservative evangelical beliefs and argued for religious pluralism

The contribution of John Hick to Christian inclusivism

John Hick notes that, for many centuries, we used to think that the Earth was the centre of the universe, as conceived by Ptolemy, the Greek mathematician and astronomer. However, as astronomers noticed more details about how the planets actually moved, it became difficult to maintain this theory. Rather than abandon the notion of the Earth at the centre of the universe, astronomers conceived that the planets moved in a series of smaller circles within their orbit, called *epicycles*. Thinking in this complicated way enabled these thinkers to maintain their belief that the Earth really was the centre of the universe.

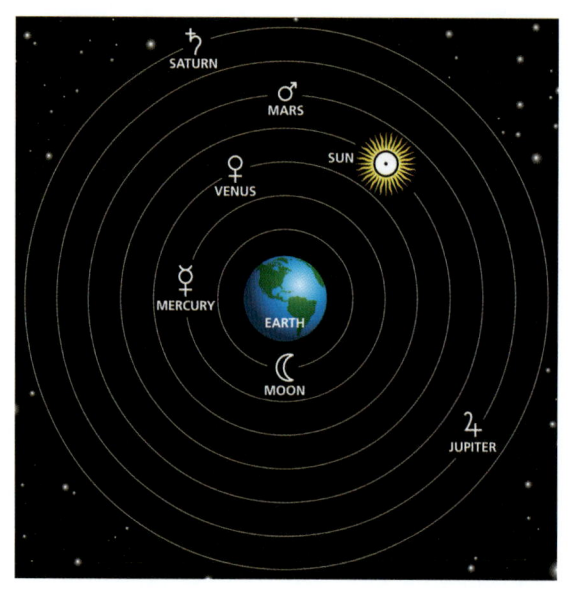

The Ptolemaic universe – note the Earth at the centre

Then came the Copernican revolution: It is the Sun and not the Earth that is the centre of the universe. The Earth is just one of several planets that circle the Sun.

Suddenly, the complicated theory of epicycles was no longer needed, and the science of astronomy took a large leap forward.

> **Key quote**
>
> the Copernican revolution ... involves a shift from the dogma that Christianity is at the centre to the realisation that it is God who is at the centre, and that all the religions of mankind, including our own, serve and revolve around him.
>
> (J Hick)

Hick believed that a Copernican revolution is needed today in theology. For centuries, Christian theologians have believed that Christ was the centre of the religious universe, that all the world's religions, whether they knew it or not, were circling Christianity. However, this was, according to Hick, a 'Ptolemaic' way of thinking. What is needed is the realisation that Christianity is, like other religions, circling something else, which Hick calls **Ultimate Reality**. We need to move from a Christocentric or ecclesio-centric universe (the Church or Christianity at the centre) to a theocentric one (God/Ultimate Reality at the centre).

> **Key term**
>
> **Ultimate Reality:** John Hick's term to describe the object of religious belief for the world's religions

Hick: Inclusivism is an awkward epicycle

Theologians through the centuries realised that there were spiritual people and profound truths to be found outside of Christianity – how could they account for these while holding to the Church or Christ as the centre of the theological universe? Like astronomers of old, they created their own version of 'epicycles' – adjustments to the theory so it could still work. This entailed viewing God as forgiving to those in other religions who did not have a chance to know Christ. Furthermore, those outside of Christianity could be viewed as having 'implicit faith' – they would accept Christ if they had the opportunity. Without this opportunity, they could be seen as possessing the 'baptism of desire' (that is, their desire to live in a right way could be counted as baptism). Hick sees Rahner's theory of anonymous Christians, as well as Vatican II statements about truth in other religions, as further epicycles.

In fact, Hick attacks inclusivist theology for failing to recognise one central fact: That Ptolemaic theology often depends on where a believer happens to be born. We now know enough about the world to say that most people born in India, who study within certain traditions, will form a Hindu inclusivism. Other people elsewhere in the world might form a Muslim, Buddhist, Sikh or Jewish inclusivism – seeing their religion as the centre of the universe, with the other religions as distant planets, perhaps having some truth but always less than the planet at the centre. Hick sees this thinking as an outdated and perhaps imperialistic way of looking at the world.

> **Key quotes**
>
> Can we then accept the conclusion that the God of love who seeks to save all mankind has nevertheless ordained that men must be saved in such a way that only a small minority can in fact receive this salvation?
>
> (J Hick)
>
> Can we be so entirely confident that to have been born in our particular part of the world carries with it the privilege of knowing the full religious truth?
>
> (J Hick)

Further criticisms of inclusivism

1. An inclusive approach also has an exclusivist message. However, if the inclusive approach argues that people can live spiritually rich lives and obtain salvation without having any conscious connection with Christ, without the Christian Church and without even hearing the Christian message, then what remains of the exclusivist message that they cannot be saved outside the Church (exclusivist Catholic Christianity) or outside of Christ (exclusivist Protestant Christianity)? Hick argues that it would be better to move to a position that affirms that all people can potentially be on different paths leading to one Ultimate Reality.

2. The inclusivism approach claims that, though all people can come to a partial truth in their own religion, the full truth is only to be found in Christianity. If that is correct, then we would expect to find more 'saintliness' in Christianity compared to other religions, since someone could reach greater spiritual heights by being a Christian. This does not appear to be the case, says Hick, though it is hard to tell how this could ever be measured!

Pluralistic universalism

John Hick argues for a philosophy of *religious pluralism*; the belief that there is a common experiential basis underlying all the major world religions. This common basis moves us from self-centredness to 'reality-centredness'. In developing this idea, Hick was influenced by both his philosophical reflections as well as his experience of attending worship services of different religious communities.

> **Key quote**
>
> There is not merely one way but a plurality of ways of salvation or liberation.
> (J Hick)

In the field of philosophy, Hick, following Kant, came to the view that, though there is a reality that is beyond our sense perceptions (the 'noumenal' realm), we are strongly empirical creatures. That is, we interpret reality through our senses in our historical, social and cultural contexts. This means that we never have direct access to the noumenal realm; we can know something only through our interpretation of it. The *noumenon* (that which is beyond the senses) is always a phenomenon (something we grasp through our interpretation).

Even statements about religion and God are 'phenomenal' – coloured by our own unique language, history, culture, geography, and so on. However, when you study many religions in all their differences, there appears, for Hick, to be a common core – a *noumenal* reality behind them. The analogy that Hick uses to explain this is the refracted light from the Sun. The Earth's atmosphere refracts the light from the Sun into different colours of the rainbow: 'Perhaps the ultimate light of the universal divine presence is refracted by our different human religious cultures into the spectrum of the different world faiths. Or, in the words of the medieval Sufi thinker, Jalaluldin Rumi, "The lamps are different but the Light is the same: it comes from Beyond"' (John Hick).

In 1967, when Hick arrived in Birmingham to teach theology, he became interested in the ethnic diversity of the city and wanted to play a part in reducing inter-racial tensions through an appreciation of the many religions

---

Specification content

The differences between Christian universalism and pluralistic universalism

represented. So, he began visiting the many religious communities and attending religious services. When he did this, he noticed many differences between them in the concepts, the scriptures and the many ways of worship. However, he also noticed one element common to them all: When people came together in their religious place of worship, their hearts and minds could be opened to a higher reality that called them to live an ethical life. Hick saw this as reflecting his views of the phenomenal and noumenal realms: These religions had many different human phenomena, but seemed to bear witness to one noumenal reality.

Hick's theory of religious experience

These philosophical insights and observations about religious communities led Hick to form a theory of religious experience. At the heart of religion is an experience of the divine world that raises us beyond our mundane life in the material world. In this experience, we are called away from a self-centred life and opened up to a new world. When we attempt to communicate these experiences, we have to use culturally conditioned language, and express our experience through stories or myths that make use of cultural concepts.

Over time, religious traditions harden this language into doctrine. These doctrines develop and are viewed as absolute by believers in that religious tradition. This absolutism, in turn, breeds intolerance and feeds into violence, war and inhumanity.

However, the problem isn't religion itself, but the turning away from religious experience. Hick believes strongly that the heart of religion is not scripture or tradition, but experience. In fact, religious experience is a force for good in the world, and an antidote for religion that becomes harsh and inhuman through the tendency to cling absolutely and exclusively to one's own doctrine, creeds, scriptures and traditions.

If one experience, why so many religions?

Hick uses the parable, attributed to the Buddha, of the blind men and the elephant. In this story, an elephant is brought to a group of blind men who have never encountered the animal before. Each of the men feels a different part of the elephant and mistakes their experience for the entire creature: One man feels the leg and concludes that the elephant is a giant pillar; another feels the trunk and reports that the elephant is a great snake, and so on.

The parable of the blind men and the elephant

Hick compares this to different accounts of God or the Ultimate Reality. Every major religion, he says, believes that the divine is beyond its grasp, so we can witness only to the partial understanding that we have. However, Hick says that there are two qualifications to using the story in this way:

1. **Not all religious experience is equally valid.** Religion is a human phenomenon and can be motivated by fear or attempts to control the spiritual world for personal gain. Here, Hick is speaking of what he calls the 'great revelatory experiences' of the main world religions. However, these experiences have been tested through a long tradition of worship and have sustained and inspired millions of lives over many centuries.

2. **The parable should not be used to make the point that there are different 'parts' of the divine.** There is, says Hick, one Ultimate Reality. The differences arise as we come to religious experience with different historical and cultural viewpoints.

The biggest roadblock to Christian pluralism

Hick says that the most difficult part of the pluralistic hypothesis for Christians is the doctrine of the incarnation. This is traditionally expressed in the Chalcedonian creed (451 CE) that Jesus was fully God and fully man. This means that Christians have viewed Jesus as God incarnate; the second member of the Trinity living a human life. This uniqueness would seem to demand exclusivism. Christians would be correct in holding that all people must come to Christ if there was only one unique incarnation of God in the world.

However, Hick notes that there are some issues with viewing Jesus in the traditional way:

- No one has ever satisfactorily explained how the two natures ascribed to Jesus work together.
- Hick accepts contemporary research that questions the historicity of supernatural reports of the Bible. He sees the infancy narratives as a reflection of the importance of Jesus to the disciples, rather than as historical fact, and the resurrection as having been a spiritual rather than a physical event.

What is crucial for Hick is that there is another way of having a Christology than that prescribed by Chalcedon. Instead of viewing Jesus as 'God-Man', he can be seen as a human being on a spiritual journey, where he reached a high 'degree' of God-consciousness. Hick calls this a *degree Christology*, and it enables Christians to see Jesus as an example they can follow; one who opens the reality of God for them – but also to be open to other figures in other religions who also reached a high degree of God (or 'reality') consciousness.

Pluralism on exclusive claims in the Bible

We've already seen that the Bible contains many passages that seem clearly to promote an exclusive view of salvation. How does a Christian pluralist explain these? The Catholic theologian and pluralist thinker Paul Knitter believes there are several factors that we should keep in mind when reading these passages:

1. **Absolutist language is a result of historical factors.** The disciples had a lack of historical consciousness of other religions, other teachings and other ways. Furthermore, they represented a minority under threat of religious persecution – when this happens, hard and absolute positions develop to maintain a sense of identity. They also had an 'apocalyptic

mentality'; their beliefs in the coming end of the world enabled 'all-or-nothing' thinking. Without these factors, the disciples might have said 'God really acted in Jesus'. What they ended up saying was 'God only acted in Jesus'.

2   **Titles given to Jesus are not propositional truths but literary or symbolic expressions of experience.** In other words, the disciples had experiences of Jesus that led them to have their own experiences of God. They expressed their admiration and awe for Jesus' role in this – but these expressions were never meant to be 'hardened' into absolute dogma.

3   **'Christ' is more than 'Jesus'.** John 1 talks about a divine 'logos' that permeates the universe, which reveals God. It is therefore possible to say that God is in the 'revealing business' and that Jesus is but one of many expressions of this 'logos' or 'Christ'.

> **Key quote**
>
> In the beginning was the Word [logos], and the Word [logos] was with God and the Word [logos] was God. He was with God in the beginning.
>
> (John 1:1–2)

Knitter believes that there is a strong biblical reason to accept pluralism: Jesus' teaching to 'love your neighbour as yourself'. To love someone includes seriously considering their views, not assuming – before you have even spoken to them – that they have less wisdom than you. They might even have more wisdom.

Universalistic pluralism and Christian universalism

Hick's pluralism is 'universal' in the sense that it sees salvation and liberation as offered in all the major world religions. It makes the radical step of declaring that the universe contains many religions that can each be a path to salvation in their own right without one of them being 'more true' than another. Hick, however, is quick to say that this is not relativistic, because religions can be judged by how effectively they help people to become less self-centred and more reality-centred.

Hick's pluralism is different from Christian universalism. Christian universalism is simply the belief that God, through Christ, will save everyone – in the end. This position is founded on scriptural principles:

- God wills that everyone be saved (1 Timothy 2:4)
- Jesus died for the sins of the entire world (1 John 2:2)
- the Bible speaks of a universal restoration (Acts 3:21; 1 Corinthians 15:22)
- God's love is incompatible with eternally damning people to hell (Ezekiel 18:23).

Universalism appeals to the simple logic that God cannot fail. If God wills that everyone be saved and has enabled this through the sacrifice of Jesus, then, surely, God will accomplish this. Many early theologians raised this possibility, including Clement of Alexandria, Origen and Gregory of Nyssa. Origen even taught that the devil, after a time of punishment, would be purified for heaven.

Universalism was condemned in 543 CE at Constantinople; however, it has emerged in the writings of many mystics and theologians through the centuries. Near the end of the eighteenth century, the Universalist

Church was founded in the United States. It distinguished itself from other denominations with its denial of the final reality of hell and its declaration of salvation for all. Opponents of universalism say that it denies free will and contradicts clear biblical teaching about eternal punishment.

> ### Summary
> - The status of the truth and salvation in other religions from various Christian viewpoints:
>   - **Exclusivism:** Christianity is the only way to salvation or liberation.
>   - **Inclusivism:** Other religions may contain partial truth, but Christianity is the 'final' way to salvation or liberation.
>   - **Pluralism:** All religions, in different ways, reflect divine truth, or Ultimate Reality.
>   - **Christian Universalism:** God, through Christ, saves everyone.
> - The views of Karl Rahner:
>   - It is possible for all people to have implicit awareness of God.
>   - People outside of the Church may respond to God's grace without knowing Christ.
>   - God may use other religions to help people find the truth, but Christianity is the fullest truth.
> - The views of John Hick:
>   - Inclusivism fails to recognise that where you are born determines your religion.
>   - There are different paths that lead to the same Ultimate Reality.
>   - There is a common experiential basis underlying all the major world religions.

AO1 Activity

a Explain:
  i why Rahner is not an exclusivist
  ii why Hick is not an inclusivist.

This helps you understand the difference between exclusivist and inclusivist, and ensures you make accurate use of specialist language and vocabulary in context.

b Give yourself 15 minutes to re-read the views of Christian pluralism in this unit. Now try to write a list of all the items that an exclusivist would object to. See whether you can identify more than five points.

This helps you prioritise and select a core set of points to develop an answer about Christian pluralism and exclusivism.

Issues for analysis and evaluation
The extent to which the Christian Bible promotes exclusivism

Possible line of argument	Critical analysis and evaluation
Both the Old Testament and the New Testament support the view that there is only one way to eternal truth and salvation.	Both the Old Testament and the New Testament support the view that there are individuals outside of Israel who were recognised as being righteous.
Biblical support for exclusivism includes Deuteronomy 6:5; Joshua 23:16; John 14:6; Acts 4:12.	Karl Rahner refers to passages that mention people who are 'God-pleasing pagans', and Paul indicates in Acts 17 that God is at work throughout the world. John 1:1 shows that the 'word' is beyond Jesus.
Exclusivists can appeal to a number of Bible passages to support their view.	Pluralists have far fewer passages that they can reference to support their view. They tend to view the Bible more as a human document than a revelation from God.
Karl Rahner believes that the fullest expression of truth is found in the life of Jesus and the community of the Church.	Rahner notes as well that the Bible also indicates that the expression of truth is not found only in Christianity. God works through other religions.
Many biblical passages emphasise punishment and damnation if a person does not believe in Jesus (John 3:18).	The exclusivist passages in the Bible are addressed only to those who already know the truth, so can make a choice for Jesus. But there are many places where the message of Christianity is never heard. God is greater than the Church.
'Love God' is the first commandment and 'love your neighbour as yourself' is the second. Loving your neighbour includes warning them of judgement if they do not know Christ.	The only way to love our neighbour is to be open to the possibility that they have truth or wisdom that you do not have. This is the deeper meaning of the Bible's teaching about love.
The Bible is the inspired word of God and so is true.	The Bible expresses some of its teaching in exclusivist ways to strengthen Christians' identity as they were under threat as a minority group.

> **This section covers AO2 content and skills**
>
> **Specification content**
> The extent to which the Christian Bible promotes exclusivism

AO2 Activity
a Evaluate three lines of argument from the critical analysis and evaluation of the extent to which the Christian Bible promotes exclusivism. What are their strengths and weaknesses? Which line of argument is strongest?

b Using the strongest line of argument, try to identify three key questions that could be asked – they could be critical questions, challenges, hypothetical or direct.

This section covers AO2 content and skills

Specification content
The extent to which it is possible to be both a committed Christian and a religious pluralist

News reporter
The opening sets out a clear case to support the view that it is not possible to be a committed Christian and a religious pluralist.

Philosopher
Tennis player
Detective
The answer now questions whether the case is quite as straightforward as the first paragraph implies. The views of John Hick are given to support this challenge.

Detective
Hick's arguments are now further developed, centring on the view that experience is at the heart of Christianity. The idea of absolute doctrine can lead to hatred and segregation. Instead, we should recognise that other religions can have equally valid religious experiences.

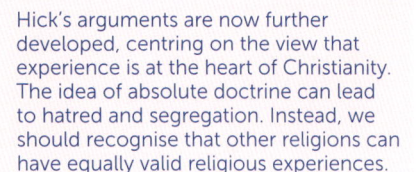

Exam practice

Sample question
Evaluate the extent to which it is possible to be both a committed Christian and a religious pluralist.

Sample answer

If you are a committed Christian then you would agree that Christ is unique among all human beings and all religions, since he is the incarnation of God; one person with two natures, human and divine, who came to offer salvation for all human beings through his death on the cross. This means that other religions who offer a path to salvation must deny Jesus' universal status and so deny the most important doctrine of Christianity. Therefore, it is contradictory to claim to be both a committed Christian and a religious pluralist. This is why the Roman Catholic Church, as well as the majority of Protestant Church bodies, have condemned pluralism.

However, the argument may not be quite as clear cut as that. This position rests on a particular assertion about the person of Jesus. But the statement about the two natures did not become Church doctrine until 451 CE at the Council of Chalcedon. Therefore, it may be wrong to make this doctrine the standard for all Christians to believe. John Hick has said that there is an alternative way to think of Jesus than the two-natures approach. Jesus could be considered someone who achieved a very high degree of God-consciousness; so much so that he became an example and inspiration for others. This means that a Christian can be led to God through Jesus without having to believe the creeds. This allows for the idea that figures in other religions could achieve God/reality consciousness. What makes a person Christian rather than, for example, Buddhist, isn't about doctrine, but that they came to a deeper understanding of life through Jesus rather than through the Buddha.

Hick was a Christian pluralist who saw Jesus as someone who opened up to his disciples an experience of reality that was new; a less self-centred way of life that utterly changed them and gave them the mission of sharing the love of God. He was adamant that experience is at the heart of Christianity. So Christianity is about having an authentic experience rather than believing in the 'right things'. Therefore, being a committed Christian is compatible with being a religious pluralist.

The danger is that experience gets hardened into teaching that in turn gets hardened into absolute doctrine – and then labels such as 'right' and 'wrong' get applied, which leads to hatred and segregation. Instead, Hick favoured the idea that those in other religions can have equally valid experiences that can also lead to less self-centred lives.

In reply, some people argue that this pluralistic approach is wrong because it means that believing anything could potentially lead a person to 'Ultimate Reality'. However, others disagree and say it is to misunderstand religious pluralism. While doctrines are relativistic, experiences can be judged on how well (or not) they lead to a less egoistic and more loving way of life. If Christianity is thought of as a 'loving path', then religious pluralists can be thought of as committed Christians. But if the incarnation is true and Jesus is God come to save human beings by means of his sacrifice on the cross, then it seems difficult to see how committed Christians can be religious pluralists. The debate is more about whether the incarnation is true as that is the crucial point, and it is hard to believe that God would sacrifice his son on the cross if there were other ways to salvation.

Tennis player · **Explorer** · **Judge**

This final section raises a challenge about the pluralistic approach and then answers it. It draws a conclusion consistent with the arguments about religious experience. But then the answer goes back to the beginning of the essay, where it identifies the doctrine of the incarnation as the key to the cause of incompatibility, and concludes that that is really the issue that needs to be decided upon to determine whether a committed Christian can be a religious pluralist.

Over to you

Below are listed three basic conclusions drawn from an evaluation of Christian exclusivism. Your task is to develop each of these conclusions by identifying the strengths (referring briefly to some reasons underlying it) but also the challenges made to it (these may be weaknesses, depending on your view).

Conclusions

1. Christian exclusivism has the strength of not being overly complicated; the Bible makes it clear in many places that there is only one way to salvation.
2. Christian exclusivism takes seriously beliefs about Christ that the Church has held for hundreds of years.
3. Christian exclusivism avoids relativism: there is a clear path to find salvation and clear ways to go wrong (other religions).

The result should be three very competent paragraphs that could form a final conclusion of any evaluation.

When you have completed the task, refer to the band descriptors for A2 (WJEC) or A Level (Eduqas) and, in particular, look at the demands described in the higher band descriptors, which you should be aspiring towards. Ask yourself:

- Is my answer a confident critical analysis and perceptive evaluation of the issue?
- Is my answer a response that successfully identifies and thoroughly addresses the issues the question raises?

T3 Significant historical developments in religious thought

T4 Religious practices that shape religious identity (1)

This section covers AO1 content and skills

Specification content
The case for infant baptism by Augustine and Zwingli (the role of baptism in salvation; the role and importance of Christian parents)

Key term
sacrament: an outward and visible sign of an inward and invisible grace

A: Religious identity through diversity in baptism

Baptism in early Judaism

The use of symbolic purification by water was, and is, part of Jewish tradition. The immersion or baptism would take place in a ritual bath called a *mikveh*. Gentile converts were immersed when they converted to Judaism, as were Jewish people after any time of impurity and before religious holidays. This meant that Jewish people were ritually immersed in water on many occasions. Therefore, John the Baptist baptising people would not seem unusual to Jewish people. However, what did draw the attention of the crowds was that John baptised in a river, not a ritual bath; that he performed the baptism rather than people immersing themselves; that he linked it to repentance; and that he taught that there was someone coming who would baptise with the Holy Spirit.

In Christianity, baptism is seen as a **sacrament**, begun by Jesus who was baptised by John the Baptist (Mark 1:9–11) and who instructed the apostles to baptise in the name of the Father, the Son and the Holy Spirit (Matthew 28:19).

> **Key quote**
>
> At that time Jesus came from Nazareth in Galilee and was baptised by John in the Jordan.
> (Mark 1:9)

The controversy is whether baptism should include infants, or whether it is for adults on profession of faith.

The case for infant baptism

Augustine wrote that baptism was a 'tradition received from the apostles' as a means of removing original sin. The Council of Carthage in 418 CE declared that 'even babies, who are yet unable to commit any sin personally, are truly baptised for the forgiveness of sins, for the purpose of cleansing by rebirth what they have received by birth'.

There is biblical support for the practice:

- Under the Abrahamic covenant, those who were born within the covenant community received the sign of the covenant as infants, which means all males were to be circumcised as eight-day-old infants (Genesis 17:12–13). **Circumcision** marked a boy's entrance into the covenant community. Baptism in the New Testament represents the new sign of the covenant: 'a spiritual circumcision' (Colossians 2:11–12). It is a sign that all people, whether Jewish or Gentile, male or female, could receive.

Key term
circumcision: the removal of the foreskin from the penis

> **Key quote**
>
> Every male among you shall be circumcised. You are to undergo circumcision, and it will be a sign of the covenant between me and you.
>
> (Genesis 17:10–11)

> **Key quote**
>
> In him you were also circumcised, in the putting off of the old nature, not with a circumcision done by the hands of men but with the circumcision done by Christ, having been buried with him in baptism and raised with him through your faith in the power of God, who raised him from the dead.
>
> (Colossians 2:11–12)

- Circumcision under the Abrahamic covenant was applied to infants on the basis of parental faith. In the same way, water baptism is applied to infants on the basis of parental faith.
- In his **Great Commission** (Matthew 28:19), Jesus commands his disciples to 'go and make disciples of all nations, baptising them in the name of the Father and of the Son and of the Holy Spirit'. Baptism begins the discipling process, but is not a statement by the person being baptised. It is about the infant of believing parents entering into the Church community.
- Jesus' blessing of babies is illustrated in Luke 18:15–16: 'People were also bringing babies to Jesus for him to place his hands on them. When the disciples saw this, they rebuked them. But Jesus called the children to him and said, "Let the little children come to me, and do not hinder them, for the Kingdom of God belongs to such as these."'
- In John 3:5, Jesus tells Nicodemus: 'Very truly I tell you, no one can enter the Kingdom of God unless they are born of water and the Spirit'. His words include infants.
- There are examples of whole households being baptised (Acts 16:33; 1 Corinthians 1:16). The term indicates a family as a unit, including children and infants.

Church history supports the practice:

- All the Church Fathers, such as Irenaeus, Origen and Augustine, supported infant baptism.

> **Key term**
>
> **Great Commission:** Jesus' instruction to make disciples worldwide

> **Key quote**
>
> The custom of Mother Church in baptising infants is certainly not to be scorned, nor is it to be regarded in any way as superfluous, nor is it to be believed that its tradition is anything except apostolic.
>
> (Augustine)

T4 Religious practices that shape religious identity (1)

Infant baptism

- Augustine wrote that infant baptism was something that the universal Church had 'always held', and was 'most correctly believed to have been handed down by apostolic authority'.
- That infants are not able to profess personal faith was not seen as preventing baptism. Augustine argued that infants who are baptised believe not on their own account, but 'through the Church's faith communicated to them'. It is 'the whole company of saints and faithful Christians ... it is done by the whole of Mother Church'.
- For Augustine, baptism is a *sacrament* – a religious rite that imparts spiritual grace. He asserted 'that without baptism and participation at the table of our Lord, it is impossible for anyone to attain either to the Kingdom of God or to salvation and life eternal'.
- In 416 CE, the Council of Mileum II endorsed this teaching, and it was constantly reaffirmed during the Middle Ages.
- Even the early reformers, such as **Huldrych Zwingli**, did not dispute this teaching, except that he did not agree that baptism contributed to the washing away of sins. He saw infant baptism as divinely instituted, and efficacious to aid and strengthen faith and to confer spiritual blessing, based on their parents' pledge to bring them up in the Christian faith. It is a sign of belonging to the new covenant, just as circumcision was a sign of belonging to the old.

Key person

Huldrych Zwingli (1484–1531): a leader of the Reformation in Switzerland

Huldrych Zwingli

Key quotes

In this matter of baptism ... I can only conclude that all the doctors have been in error from the time of the Apostles ... All the doctors have ascribed to the water a power it does not have and the holy Apostles did not teach.

(H Zwingli)

Circumcision was given to the children of the Hebrews. Therefore, baptism ought not be refused to the children of the Christians.

(H Zwingli)

The case for believer's baptism

Supporters of this view point out that in the Old Testament, God entered into a covenant with an entire nation, and infants were part of the nation God was covenanting with. However, in the New Testament, God's covenant is with believers, and infants can't believe.

Jesus was baptised as an adult, and it is unlikely John baptised any infants, since he demanded that people repent as a condition for baptising them.

Jesus' Great Commission makes clear that baptism was linked to discipleship, and every example of someone being baptised in the New Testament was a person old enough to decide to follow Christ. For example:

- **Acts 8:12:** The Samaritans are baptised after they believe the good news Philip preaches.
- **Acts 8:35–36:** The Ethiopian eunuch is baptised after he believes.
- **Acts 9:18:** The Apostle Paul is baptised after he encounters Jesus in a vision on the road to Damascus.
- **Acts 10:44–48:** Peter baptises Cornelius and his household after they show evidence of their faith.
- **Acts 16:14–15:** Lydia and her household are baptised after she believes.
- **Acts 19:5–6:** The disciples of John the Baptist are baptised after they accept Paul's teaching about Jesus.

Baptism invariably follows faith and is the first act of discipleship made by people of responsible age who have professed their faith in Christ. However, no Christian objections to the practice of infant baptism were ever voiced until the Reformation.

> **Key quote**
>
> But the right baptism, which is preceded by teaching and oral confession of faith, I teach, and say that infant baptism is a robbery of the right baptism of Christ.
>
> (B Hubmaier)

Karl Barth: Baptism as union with Christ

Karl Barth (1886–1968), one of the twentieth century's most influential theologians, endorsed believer's baptism. In his book *The Teaching of the Church regarding Baptism* (1948), Barth wrote that baptism does not bring about human salvation, but points to salvation by symbolically representing renewal in Christ.

Barth argues that baptism:

- with water marks the first step of a life lived in Christ
- is a human response to God's saving grace
- is not a sacrament; it is an image of salvation history
- shows a person's faith in Jesus by following Jesus' command to be baptised
- 'seals' the reality of God's grace, but does not generate that reality
- is a free act in response to God's grace.

Barth also argues that only an adult can have faith and show it by following Jesus' commands, and that infant baptism is a 'clouded baptism' since an infant is unable to take that first step that the baptism marks. However, Barth never said that infant baptism is invalid.

Specification content

The case for believer's baptism with reference to Karl Barth (the example of Christ; importance of consent)

> **Key quote**
>
> A man ... has no right to be baptised until he is saved.
>
> (C Spurgeon)

Believer's baptism

T4 Religious practices that shape religious identity (1)

> ## Key quotes
>
> In the sphere of the New Testament, one is not brought to baptism, one comes to baptism.
>
> **(K Barth)**
>
> Baptism without the willingness and readiness of the baptised is true, effectual and effective baptism, but it is not correct; it is not done in obedience, it is not administered according to proper order … we have in mind here the custom of the baptism of children.
>
> **(K Barth)**

Barth was aware that his views would cause controversy. Later, in 1967, he wrote in a foreword to his final book that was on baptism: 'this book … will leave me in … theological and ecclesiastical isolation …'.

The majority of Christian Churches accept infant baptism, while Christian denominations such as Baptists, Pentecostals and Assemblies of God oppose it.

Summary

- Almost all Christians believe that baptism is commanded by Christ and related to sin and redemption.
- There is disagreement over whether baptism:
    - should be for infants or (adult) believers
    - has saving power, or whether it is just a symbol.
- Augustine argued for infant baptism:
    - It is a tradition from the Apostles and practised by the early Church.
    - It is effective at bringing salvation since it cleanses infants from original sin.
- Zwingli also argued for infant baptism, but disagreed that an external act could save anyone.
- Those in favour of believer's baptism argue that, in the New Testament, baptism followed from faith.
- Believer's baptism is often performed by full immersion of the body under water.
- Karl Barth argued that baptism is a human rather than a divine act, and therefore does not bring salvation.
- Barth supported believer's baptism, but did not regard it as a sacrament.

AO1 Activity

a Explain Karl Barth's reasons for supporting believer's baptism.

This helps you understand and present the key features of Barth's views on baptism.

b Draw two columns on a sheet of paper. Label the columns 'Infant baptism' and 'Believer's baptism'. List the key points for each of the two baptisms. Then write a report on the comparisons and contrasts between the two models of baptism.

This helps you recall the key points of each of the two models of baptism and the differences between them.

Issues for analysis and evaluation

The criteria for expressing the commitment to be baptised

Possible line of argument	Critical analysis and evaluation
The person who receives the gift of baptism should consciously accept it. This means that infant baptism is not valid.	Infant baptism is a sacrament of God's grace to remove original sin. It does not require a conscious acceptance of it by the person who receives it.
Infant baptism does require parents to make promises to raise their children in the Christian faith. It also requires a commitment from godparents or sponsors, as well as the entire church congregation.	Given the infant has no choice, it locks the child into a way of life that they have not chosen themselves, since parents give assurances that the child will receive a Christian upbringing.
Infant baptism involves a public confession of faith by parents and godparents or sponsors.	Believer's baptism involves a public confession of faith by the person being baptised.
Infant baptism is never administered without faith: the faith of the parents and that of the whole church.	What should be important is the faith of the person being baptised, not their parents.
Jesus was baptised as an adult and John the Baptist baptised adults, not infants.	The New Testament refers to whole households being baptised, which included children. If baptism is seen as replacing circumcision of Old Testament covenant inclusion, then it includes infants.
Baptism is a sacrament performed by a priest.	Baptism is symbolic and a form of obedience to Jesus' command to be baptised. It does not require an ordained person to do a baptism.
In the New Testament, baptism follows conversion (Acts 8:35–36), never precedes it, and it is a conscious voluntary decision to follow Jesus.	The emphasis on personal decision takes away from God's act of salvation. It puts the individual rather than God in the centre of the baptismal act.

This section covers AO2 content and skills

Specification content
The criteria for expressing the commitment to be baptised

> ### AO2 Activity
> a Select three lines of argument from the critical analysis and evaluation of the criteria for expressing the commitment to be baptised. Find three references from scholars, schools of thought or religious and philosophical texts that would support those arguments.
> b Using the strongest line of argument, identify three more quotations that could be used to support this argument – they could be from scholars, religious texts or schools of thought.

This section covers AO2 content and skills

Specification content
The extent to which both infant and adult baptism are just symbolic acts

News reporter
Tennis player
Detective

The answer has a good opening sentence that identifies the key issue. It then presents the argument that baptism is a symbolic act and gives strong examples with good biblical text support.

Tennis player
Detective

Again, a clear statement of the issue with good arguments supported by illustrations from Bible texts. The paragraphs use technical language well.

Critical thinker
Philosopher *Judge*

Having considered the arguments for symbolic and sacramental understanding of baptism, the answer now raises questions about the sacramental view. It then acknowledges that both views seem to have biblical support, so concludes that perhaps it is best to view baptism as a mystery. The conclusion is consistent with the evidence given throughout the answer.

Exam practice

Sample question

Evaluate the extent to which both infant and adult baptism are just symbolic acts.

Sample answer

One of the key questions that this issue poses is whether baptism is an essential part of salvation. In other words, is the act of baptism essential to the person being baptised? Many would argue that both infant and adult baptism are just symbolic acts. They are still important and significant, but not mandatory for salvation. Certainly, the New Testament has examples that support this view. For instance, both the thief on the cross and Saul (Paul) were saved before being baptised.

This suggests that baptism is a secondary and subsequent action to salvation. That does not diminish its rich symbolism of the forgiveness that has already been received. It is not the means of spiritual regeneration, but merely its sign and seal.

Another aspect of its symbolism is that the recipient has been accepted into the Christian Church. It can also be seen as a symbol of belonging to the new covenant – just as circumcision was a symbol of belonging to the old covenant. Some see a symbolism relating to the waters of the Flood, which divided between the lost and the saved. The most important symbolism that many Christians appeal to is the symbol of the recipient's participation in the death, burial and resurrection of Jesus. The recipient passes through a watery 'death' to a resurrected 'life'.

However, there is another possible approach to this issue. This puts the emphasis on what God does rather than on what the recipient does. Such a focus is associated most with the Orthodox Church and the Roman Catholic Church. It is sacramental theology, whereby the application of water to the baptised is the means that God uses to cause an ontological change. An ontological change is a change in the nature of someone's existence. This change is the removal of original sin – a change that cannot be explained away through symbolic interpretation alone.

We can find support for this view in the New Testament. The baptised person is 'a new creation' according to Paul in 2 Corinthians 5. In addition, baptism unites the recipient with Jesus. Paul writes that 'in the one Spirit we were all baptised into one body … the body of Christ'. Paul also identifies Christ's body with Christ's Church, so the recipient of baptism is united with the Church.

Needless to say, this sacramental view has been challenged on the grounds that it seems to put the power of salvation into the hands of the Church. Surely, salvation belongs with the Spirit, not the Church. However, both views seem to have biblical support. The account of the jailer's conversion when Paul was imprisoned at Philippi seems to link belief, salvation and baptism. 'The jailer asked "What must I do to be saved?" Paul replied "Believe in the Lord Jesus" … then immediately he and all his family were baptised.'

Perhaps the best conclusion is that baptism is a mystery.

182　　WJEC/Eduqas Religious Studies for AS & A Level Christianity

Over to you

Below is a list of indicative content that could be used in response to a question requiring an evaluation of whether the baptism most mainstream churches administer today is biblical. The problem is that it is not a very full list and needs completing! It will be useful, as a group, to consider what is missing from the list. You need to add at least six points (three in support and three against) that you would use to improve the list, and/or give more detail to each point that is already in the list. Remember: It is how you use the points that is the most important factor.

Apply the principles of evaluation by making sure that you:
- identify issues clearly
- present accurate views of others, making sure that you comment on the views presented
- reach an overall personal judgement.

You may add more of your own suggestions, but try to negotiate as a group and prioritise the most important things to add (additional points or detail to existing points).

Then, as a group, agree on your final list and write out your new list of indicative content, remembering the principles of explaining with evidence and/or examples. Put this list in order of how you would present the information in an essay, then you will have your own plan for an ideal answer.

List of indicative content

In support:
- In Luke, Jesus says: 'Let the little children come to me, and do not stop them'. The only way that the Bible gives of bringing anyone to Jesus is through baptism.
- In his Great Commission (Matthew 28:19), Jesus commands his disciples to go 'and make disciples of all nations, baptising them in the name of the Father and of the Son and of the Holy Spirit'. Infants are not excluded.
- The apostles baptised whole 'households', including children and infants.
- Your added content

Against:
- The New Testament has no record of infants being baptised.
- The Apostle Paul is baptised after he encounters Jesus in a vision on the road to Damascus.
- Lydia and her household are baptised after she believes.
- Your added content

B: Religious identity through diversity in Eucharist

The importance of the Eucharist in contemporary Christian communities

The **Eucharist** is the Christian Church's most important sacrament. The word *Eucharist* is the Greek word for 'thanksgiving'. Other names for the 'Eucharist' are *Holy Communion*, *Mass* and the *Lord's Supper*.

Aware of his approaching death on the cross, Jesus shared a farewell meal with his disciples (Matthew 26:26–30 and parallels). He took ordinary bread and wine and shared them, saying of the bread, 'This is my body', and of the wine, 'This is my blood'. According to Paul (1 Corinthians 11:26), he then added, 'For as often as you eat this bread and drink the cup, you proclaim the Lord's death until he comes'.

Similarities in Eucharistic practice in Christian traditions

At a celebration of the Eucharist, the Church community gathers, asks God's forgiveness for their sins and listens to readings from the Bible, including a reading from one of the Gospels. A sermon may be preached, hymns sung and the congregation prays together. Bread and wine are brought to the altar (table), the priest prays the Eucharistic Prayer and the congregation joins together to say the Lord's Prayer. The priest **consecrates** the elements of bread and wine, and the congregation share in the bread (and in most churches, the wine as well).

All Christians would agree that the Eucharist is a memorial action where the Church recalls what Jesus said and did at the Last Supper. They would also agree that participating in the Eucharist enhances and deepens the communion of believers with Christ and with one another.

Most Christian traditions teach that Jesus is present in the Eucharist in some special way. However, there is disagreement about the exact nature, location and time of that presence, while other traditions see the Eucharist as symbolic or commemorative. These disagreements have led to disunity.

> **Key quote**
>
> A tiny bit of bread is something useless; consecrated in the Eucharist it becomes supremely valuable.
>
> (A Hastings)

Roman Catholic understanding of the Eucharist

Transubstantiation

When the priest at the Eucharist (Mass) speaks the words of consecration, a change takes place: the bread and the wine are transformed into the body and blood of Christ. Medieval theologians used the terms *accidents* and *substance* to explain this change. *Accidents* have to do with the outward appearance, while *substance* refers to the invisible and eternal quality of a thing.

Though the appearance of the bread and the wine remain the same, the substance of the bread and wine change. They become Christ's **real presence**; that is, his body and blood.

Specification content
The importance of the Eucharist in the life of contemporary Christian communities; the similarities in Eucharistic practice in Christian traditions

Key term
Eucharist: one of the names referring to the service commemorating the Last Supper

Key term
consecrate: set apart as holy; make or declare sacred for religious use

Specification content
Selected Roman Catholic theories (transubstantiation, transignification and transfinalisation)

Key term
real presence: the actual presence of Christ's body and blood in the Eucharistic elements

The Orthodox Church is similar, and considers the change a 'divine mystery'.

Since the eleventh century, the Roman Catholic Church has used the term *transubstantiation* to describe this change.

The Council of Trent (1545–63) reaffirmed this view, as did Pope Paul VI's encyclical *Mysterium Fidei* ('The Mystery of the Faith') in 1965. This was a letter to all Catholic bishops written in response to two new terms that two contemporary Catholic theologians had proposed: *transignification* and *transfinalisation*.

Transignification

Transignification is a theory Edward Schillebeeckx (1914–2009), a Belgian Catholic theologian, put forward. It has to do with psychological reality.

He accepts the idea of a *real presence*, but states that there are two kinds of presence: local and personal. Students may be *locally present* in a class, but if their thoughts are far away then they are not *personally* present. In the Eucharist, Jesus is *personally* present but not *locally* present.

> **Key quote**
>
> Something can be essentially changed without its physical or biological make-up changing.
>
> (E Schillebeeckx)

Therefore, the theory proposes that, when the priest consecrates the bread and the wine of the Eucharist, they are not chemically changed. However, as soon as they signify the body and blood of Christ, they reveal Christ's presence in a way that is experienceably real. When the meaning of the elements change, their reality changes for those who have faith in Christ and who accept the new meaning that Jesus gave them. To those without faith, they remain bread and wine.

Transfinalisation

Transfinalisation is a theory the German Jesuit theologian Karl Rahner (1904–84) put forward.

It proposes that when the priest consecrates the bread and wine of the Eucharist, their purpose and finality are changed, but not their substance. They do not become Christ's body and blood, but serve a new function, which is to stir up faith in the mystery of Christ's redemptive love.

Pope Paul VI condemned both theories in the encyclical *Mysterium Fidei* (1965) because they may deny transubstantiation.

> **Key quote**
>
> It cannot be tolerated that any individual ... take something away from the formulas which were used by the Council of Trent.
>
> (Pope Paul VI)

Protestant understandings of the Eucharist

Consubstantiation

The Protestant reformers rejected the idea of transubstantiation, since it implied that Christ's sacrifice on the cross was continually re-presented and made present every time Eucharist is celebrated. However, they believed that Christ died once and for all was sufficient, and so his sacrifice cannot be repeated.

Specification content

Selected Protestant approaches (consubstantiation and memorialism)

T4 Religious practices that shape religious identity (1)

Nevertheless, Martin Luther (1483–1546) did think the statement 'This is my body' had to be taken in some literal sense. He argued that the physical body of Christ is co-existent with the bread and wine. Some commentators use the illustration of a sponge filled with water. The water is not part of the sponge but is present in it. Luther taught that it was a means for Christ to communicate grace to believers. The bread and wine remain bread and wine, but Christ is spiritually present within them.

Although consubstantiation was different from transubstantiation, since the bread and wine did not change, it was still susceptible to similar objections as transubstantiation. Luther never used the term *consubstantiation*. He used the term *sacramental union*.

Martin Luther

Memorialism

Memorialism is a term used to describe Huldrych Zwingli's view of the Eucharist. Zwingli (1484–1531) denied the real presence of Christ in the Eucharist and taught that the bread and the wine symbolically represented his body and blood. In Luke 22:19, Jesus commands his followers to 'Do this in remembrance of me'. The Eucharist is therefore a commemorative ceremony where participants remember Jesus' sacrifice for them on the cross. Jesus is present only to the degree that each individual brings him and his work to mind.

> **Key quote**
>
> There are innumerable passages in scripture where the word is means 'signifies'.
>
> (H Zwingli)

Summary

- The words *Eucharist*, *Mass* and *Holy Communion* all refer to the service commemorating the Last Supper.
- Most Christian traditions teach that Jesus is present in this service in some special way. However, there is disagreement about the exact nature, location and time of that presence.
- The Roman Catholic understanding:
  - **Transubstantiation:** The outward appearance of the bread and wine remain the same, but the inner reality is changed to the body and blood of Christ.
  - **Transignification:** The bread and wine do not change, but their significance for the believer changes.
  - **Transfinalisation:** The bread and wine stir up faith in the mystery of Christ's redemptive love.
- The Protestant understanding:
  - **Consubstantiation:** Jesus is mysteriously present without any changes in the bread and wine.
  - **Memorialism:** Jesus is present only to the degree that each individual brings Jesus and his work to mind.

AO1 Activity

a This unit is full of new terms. In revising, instead of just drawing up a glossary of key terms, try changing it into a flowchart that links each to an understanding of the Eucharist.

This helps you develop an ability to present the terms' inter-relatedness and demonstrate extensive depth and/or breadth.

b Prepare a case to defend the doctrine of consubstantiation against that of transubstantiation. The defendant must outline how the doctrine of consubstantiation fits in with Christian theology. In response, the case for the prosecution must outline how the defendant holds dangerous and heretical views that challenge the sacredness of the Eucharist.

This helps you select the key, relevant information for an answer to a question on Catholic and Protestant understandings of the Eucharist.

> **This section covers AO2 content and skills**

> **Specification content**
> The extent to which theoretical beliefs about the Eucharist affect the practice of different denominations

Issues for analysis and evaluation

The extent to which theoretical beliefs about the Eucharist affect the practice of different denominations

Possible line of argument	Critical analysis and evaluation
The Eucharist is similar in all traditions. The atmosphere is prayerful and reverent.	All traditions re-enact the last supper, and Jesus' body and blood as bread and wine. All traditions that celebrate the Eucharist recite the words of Jesus and have similar liturgies.
Orthodox and Roman Catholic Churches believe in transubstantiation and the service is more dignified than in those denominations that do not hold that belief.	Those traditions holding a memorialist view of the Eucharist may lack ceremony and a formal liturgy and structure, but conduct the service in a prayerful, dignified manner.
Those that believe in transubstantiation treat the consecrated bread and wine with pomp and ceremony, e.g. ornate vessels, colourful vestments, liturgy, procession and incense.	In contrast, the traditions that believe in transubstantiation argue that it requires proper priestly consecration of the bread and wine. For traditions that hold a symbolic view of the Eucharist, an ordained priest is not required to lead the Eucharist.
In Orthodox and Roman Catholic traditions, the Eucharist is the central point of worship. It is celebrated every Sunday and on feast days.	In other traditions that have a memorialist view of the Eucharist, it is often celebrated less frequently. They regard the preaching of the 'word' as equally important.
In Roman Catholic churches, the altar is central in the worship space and the unused consecrated host is placed in a locked box since it reflects the belief that the consecrated host is a transformed substance.	Those with a memorialist view do not have this.
In many churches, people kneel before an altar to receive the bread and wine, reflecting on the power of the consecrated elements.	In some churches, such as 'house churches', people may sit in a circle with each church member serving the other, reflecting on the power of God's Spirit in a community.

> **AO2 Activity**
> a   Select three lines of argument from the critical analysis and evaluation of the extent to which theoretical beliefs about the Eucharist affect the practice of different denominations. Find three references from scholars, schools of thought or religious and philosophical texts that would support those arguments.
> b   Using the strongest line of argument, try to identify three key questions that could be asked – they could be critical questions, challenges, hypothetical or direct.

Exam practice

Sample question
Evaluate the extent to which there is any common ground within contemporary understandings of the Eucharist.

Sample answer
Nearly all Christians participate in the Eucharist and would agree on how it functions.

They would all agree that the Eucharist was instituted by Jesus as a re-enactment of his Last Supper with his disciples. It is a meal in which the bread and the wine signify the body and blood of Jesus. It is a time when they remember Jesus' sacrifice, look forward to the future coming of Jesus, reaffirm individual faith and unite the Christian community in a common act.

One difference is in the frequency the Eucharist is celebrated. Some Roman Catholic churches may celebrate the Eucharist several times a day. Other churches, such as Anglican or Lutheran, may celebrate it less frequently, partly because these churches hold the preaching of the 'word' as equally important as the sacraments. Where the Eucharist is seen as a memorial only, churches may celebrate once a month or even less frequently.

However, the largest divide between Christians centres on the words 'This is my body … this is my blood'. The Roman Catholic Church insists that they be taken as literal. When the bread and the wine are consecrated, they are changed into the actual body and blood of Christ (*transubstantiation*). The Orthodox position is similar (*divine mystery*). The official position of the Lutheran Church is that the substance of the bread and wine do not change, but that Christ is spiritually present 'with them, in them and under them'. This is traditionally known as *consubstantiation*.

Other Reformed churches follow Zwingli's teaching that Christ is present in the bread and the wine only to the extent that the recipient brings him and his work to mind (*memorialism*). Some contemporary Roman Catholic theologians have proposed other theories, for example Schillebeeckx proposed that the significance of the elements changes at consecration (*transignification*) and Rahner proposed that the purpose of the elements changes at consecration (*transfinalisation*). However, the Roman Catholic Church, which views these interpretations as replacements for the doctrine of transubstantiation, have condemned them.

So, there is significant disagreement on the interpretation of the words 'This is my body … this is my blood'. However, there is certainly some common ground: all Christian denominations take bread and wine to remember Jesus and to give thanks for his sacrifice on the cross; all believe that the bread and the wine represent the body and blood of Jesus; and all conduct the Eucharist in a prayerful and dignified manner, with self-examination, confession and Bible readings.

It does seem that the common elements are more significant than, and override, any differences in understanding of how to interpret Jesus' words about his body and blood.

This section covers AO2 content and skills

Specification content
The extent to which there is any common ground within contemporary understandings of the Eucharist

Tennis player
News reporter
Detective

A good introductory paragraph, drawing out some common ground within understandings of the Eucharist.

Tennis player
News reporter
Detective

This paragraph examines the question of the frequency of celebrating the Eucharist as an example of the difference in understanding of the Eucharist.

Tennis player
News reporter
Detective

This section of the answer deals in depth with the heart of the differences in understanding; namely the words 'This is my body … this is my blood'. There is good knowledge of the diverse positions that the different Churches hold, and the appropriate technical language to describe those various understandings.

Philosopher
Critical thinker
Judge

A good, thoughtful, reflective consideration of the evidence has been set out. The conclusion is consistent with the arguments that have been given. There is a good weighing up of the importance or otherwise of those differences of understandings identified.

Over to you

For this task, you have only instructions with no examples. However, using the skills you have developed by completing the earlier tasks, you should be able to apply what you have learned and complete this successfully.

Your new task is to write a response, under timed conditions, to the question, 'Evaluate the view that there is no single correct way of celebrating the Eucharist.'

You need to focus for this and apply the skills that you have developed so far:

1. Begin with a list of indicative content. Perhaps discuss this as a group. It does not need to be in any particular order. Remember: This is evaluation, so you need different lines of argument. The easiest way is to use the 'In support' and 'Against' headings.
2. Develop the list using examples.
3. Now consider the order you would like to explain the information.
4. Then write out your response, under timed conditions, remembering to apply the principles of evaluation by making sure that you:
   - identify issues clearly
   - present accurate views of others, making sure that you comment on the views presented
   - reach an overall personal judgement.

Use this technique as revision for each of the topic areas that you have studied. The basic technique of planning answers helps even when time is short and you cannot complete every essay.

C: Religious identity through diversity in festivals

Christmas

The English word *Christmas* is derived from the words 'Christ's Mass'. It is the celebration of the birth of Jesus.

> **Key quote**
>
> No one knows when Jesus was born, either the year or even the time of year …
>
> (WO Cole and P Morgan)

Advent in the Western Church

No one knows the exact date of Jesus' birth. The Church in Rome first celebrated Christmas on 25 December in 336 CE, during the reign of the emperor Constantine. It has been suggested that this date was chosen to replace the Roman winter Saturnalia, a pagan festival, in honour of the god, Saturn, that lasted from 17 to 23 December. It had many of the traditions now associated with Christmas, such as wreaths, candles, feasting and gift-giving.

In the Western Church, Christmas is preceded by four weeks of preparation known as the season of *Advent*. **Advent** is the beginning of the Western Church year. It allows Christians to anticipate two events:

- the celebration of Jesus' First Coming to Earth as a baby boy
- Jesus' Second Coming at the end of time (the *parousia*); the theme of the biblical readings and hymns during Advent is often preparation for the parousia.

The Third Sunday of Advent is known as *Gaudete Sunday* (from the Latin for 'rejoice'). The theme of the day expresses the joy of anticipation at the approach of the Christmas celebration.

The **liturgical** colour (the colour used for church hangings and clergy vestments) during Advent is traditionally violet or purple.

Advent customs include:

- **An advent wreath:** It has four candles (three purple and one rose coloured), one for each of the four Sundays of Advent, and one white candle in the middle. Advent wreaths are circular, representing God's infinite love. They are usually made of evergreen leaves, which represent the hope of eternal life Jesus Christ brings. The individual candles, one lit on each of the four Sundays, represent hope, peace, joy and love, and the middle fifth candle lit on Christmas Eve or Christmas Day is known as the *Christ Candle*.

    Alternatively, some churches symbolise the first candle as the *Prophets' Candle* (the prophets of the Old Testament who waited in hope for the Messiah's arrival); the second as the *Bethlehem Candle* (Micah had foretold that the Messiah would be born in Bethlehem); the third candle as the *Shepherds' Candle* (the shepherds' joy as the angels announced Jesus' birth); and the fourth candle as the *Angels' Candle* (the angels announced that Jesus came to bring peace).

> **Specification content**
>
> Christmas: The similarities (with reference to the focus on incarnation of Christ) and differences (date of celebration; focus of Advent season; Christmas services) between the Eastern Orthodox and the Western Churches' celebration of Christmas

> ● **Key terms**
>
> **Advent:** a season before Christmas when Christians anticipate both the nativity of Christ and his Second Coming
>
> **liturgical:** the public ritual of formal worship prescribed by a Church body

Advent wreath

> **Key quote**
>
> Jesus' coming is the final and unanswerable proof that God cares.
> (W Barclay)

- **An advent calendar:** First used by German Lutherans in the nineteenth and twentieth centuries but now widely popular, it is a special calendar for each day of December up to and including Christmas Eve. The calendar window for each day opens to reveal an item relevant to the preparation for Christmas – a biblical verse, a prayer or a small gift, such as a chocolate or a toy.
- **Christmas decorations:** These are often set up in homes at the beginning of Advent.
- **Fasting:** This has now been relaxed in the Western Church, but the season is still kept as a season of penitence.

Christmas in the Western Church

During the period leading up to Christmas, churches hold carol services that relate the Christmas story in words and music. Often, they have a nativity crib depicting the stable in Bethlehem where Jesus was born. Nativity plays are also popular.

> **Key quote**
>
> Christmas is joy, religious joy, an inner joy of light and peace.
> (Pope Francis)

Nativity play

An old tradition in Wales is that of the Plygain. The word *plygain* comes from Latin, meaning 'cockcrow'. The Plygain was originally a carol service held in church between 3 a.m. and 6 a.m. on Christmas morning, when groups of men sang carols to await the Eucharist at daybreak. Modern Plygain services are held on any weekday evening from the Feast of St Thomas (21 December) to Old New Year's Day (13 January), and women now participate.

Christingle services have become popular in recent years. *Christingle* is a Scandinavian word meaning 'the light of Christ'. The christingle is an orange, with fruit or sweets attached using cocktail sticks. There is a red ribbon around the orange and a small candle on top, which is lit during the service. The orange represents the world; the four cocktail sticks represent the four corners of the Earth or the four seasons; the sweets and fruit represent the fruits of the Earth; the light of the candle represents Jesus, the Light of the World; and the red ribbon represents his saving blood.

Christingle

At Christmas itself, there are traditionally three Eucharists: the first at midnight on Christmas Eve, the second at dawn on Christmas morning and the third during Christmas Day.

Western Christians spend the rest of Christmas Day feasting and exchanging gifts with family and friends. The rampant consumerism that now characterises the festival is a fairly recent development, but threatens its religious observance.

Advent in the Eastern Orthodox Church

Many Orthodox Christians celebrate Jesus' birth not on 25 December, but on 7 January. The date corresponds to the old Julian calendar, which pre-dates the Gregorian calendar used in the West. The Armenian Orthodox Church uniquely celebrates Christmas on 6 January.

As in the Western Church, the equivalent of Advent is observed, but it is known in the Eastern Orthodox Church as the *Nativity Fast*. The Nativity Fast, which traditionally lasts for 40 days up to the eve of the Nativity (6 January), consists of abstaining from red meat, poultry, eggs and dairy products, fish, oil and wine. The eve of the Nativity is a strict fast day, known as *Paramony* ('preparation'), when no solid food should be eaten until the first star appears in the evening sky.

The Nativity Fast does not begin the Church year, as Advent does in the West, and there is no emphasis on the parousia. The liturgical colour red is used, with gold as an alternative. During the course of the Nativity Fast, a number of feast days celebrate Old Testament prophets who prophesied the incarnation. There are two other significant events:

- Two Sundays before the Nativity, the *Sunday of the Forefathers* commemorates the Church's ancestors.
- The Sunday before the Nativity, known as the *Sunday of the Holy Fathers*, commemorates all the righteous men and women who pleased God, from the creation of the world up to Saint Joseph, husband of Jesus' mother, Mary.

Christmas in the Eastern Orthodox Church

The following services, which last all night, are held on the eve of the Nativity. They are intentionally parallel to those held on Good Friday, to illustrate the theological point that the purpose of the incarnation was to make possible the crucifixion and the resurrection.

- **The Hours:** Special Psalms, hymns and biblical readings prescribed for each hour proclaim the joy and power of Christ's birth.
- **Vespers:** Eight biblical readings celebrate the incarnation and show that Christ is the fulfilment of all prophecies.
- **The Liturgy of St Basil the Great:** In the past, those who had been receiving instruction for baptism were baptised and integrated into the body of Christ at this baptismal liturgy.
- **The Vigil:** This begins with the service of Great Compline, which is the reading and chanting of some Psalms.
- **Matins:** For the first time at Christmas, the words 'Christ is born' are sung while the congregation venerates an icon of the Nativity.

Christmas crib

T4 Religious practices that shape religious identity (1)

Christmas Day is a day of feasting and enjoying the company of family and friends. Candles may be lit to represent the light of Christ, while the festive Christmas meal represents the end of fasting. White linen on dinner tables symbolises the cloth that wrapped the baby Jesus, and straw may be placed on the linen to symbolise the stable where he was born.

There is little emphasis on sharing gifts, and little of the consumerism that characterises the Western Christmas.

Easter

Easter is the most important of all Christian festivals. It is the celebration of the resurrection of Jesus. Jesus' death and resurrection took place at the Jewish Passover, which was celebrated on the first full moon after the vernal equinox. However, in most years, it is celebrated on different dates in Western and Eastern Orthodox Churches. This is because the Churches disagree on how the calculation of the date of Easter is interpreted:

> **Key quote**
>
> We are an Easter people, and alleluia is our song.
> (Augustine)

- While both Churches agree on Easter being the first Sunday after the first full moon on or after the vernal equinox, they base the dates (as with Christmas) on different calendars. The Western Church uses the Gregorian calendar, while the Orthodox Church uses the old Julian calendar.
- They differ on the definition of the **vernal equinox**. The Eastern Orthodox Church uses the actual, astronomical full moon and the actual equinox as observed along the meridian of Jerusalem. The Western Church has a fixed date for the vernal equinox as 21 March.
- The Eastern Orthodox Church also applies the formula so that Easter falls after the Jewish Passover, while in the Western Church Easter sometimes precedes Passover by weeks.

Lent in the Western Church

Easter is always preceded by a solemn season of religious observance known as *Lent*. It lasts for 40 days in commemoration of the 40 days Jesus spent fasting in the desert before he began his public ministry (Matthew 4:1–11 and parallels).

In the Western Church, Lent begins on Ash Wednesday, named from the custom of placing ashes made from palm branches blessed on the previous Palm Sunday on the heads of recipients while exhorting them to repent of their sins.

Specification content

Easter: The similarities (with reference to the doctrine of the resurrection of Christ) and differences (date; liturgical practice at Easter; the diversity within each stream of tradition) between the Eastern Orthodox and the Western Churches' celebration of Easter

Key term

vernal equinox: the time at which the Sun crosses the plane of the Equator, making day and night of equal length

> **Key quote**
>
> Lent comes providentially to reawaken us, to shake us from our lethargy.
> (Pope Francis)

Station of the Cross: Jesus carries the cross

Many Christians commit to fasting or giving up certain luxuries as a form of penitence and self-denial, and may read a daily devotional for spiritual discipline. Churches often remove flowers from their altars and cover religious symbols. The service of the **Stations of the Cross** is often observed. The liturgical colour for Lent is purple.

The season includes several significant dates:

- The fourth Sunday (halfway point between Ash Wednesday and Easter Sunday) is known as *Laetare* (Latin for 'rejoice') Sunday. It is an opportunity for one day to look forward, with hope, to Easter.
- The fourth Sunday is also known as *Mothering Sunday*. It has recently become an occasion for honouring mothers of children, but has its origin in a sixteenth-century celebration where people would return to the church they were baptised in for a special service.
- The sixth Sunday is known as *Palm Sunday*, which marks the beginning of Holy Week and commemorates Jesus' triumphal entry into Jerusalem (Mark 11:1–11 and parallels).
- Thursday of Holy Week is known as *Maundy Thursday*, and is a day Christians commemorate the Last Supper. As part of the celebration, the priest may wash the feet of 12 members of the congregation to remember Jesus washing the disciples' feet (John 13:1–20). In Malta, people visit seven different churches and say special prayers at each. This tradition is very popular and is said to date back to the Romans.
- The next day is *Good Friday*, the day of atonement, when Christians remember Jesus' crucifixion, death and burial. The Roman Catholic Church treats Good Friday as a fast day. There is no celebration of the Eucharist, but Holy Communion is distributed from the reserved sacrament. The only sacraments celebrated are baptism (for those in danger of death), penance and anointing the sick. The celebration of the **Passion** of Christ takes place usually at 3 p.m., and the vestments used are black or red. The Stations of the Cross are often prayed, either in church or outside.

In some southern Mediterranean countries, the Roman Catholic Church holds processions carrying statues representing particular episodes in the Passion of Christ story. The re-enactments involve hundreds of people dressed as biblical characters. Often these processions include a number of penitents dressed in white robes and hoods, walking barefoot, carrying crosses or with chains tied to their ankles. These are all acts of penance or in fulfilment of a vow.

The **Anglican** Church does not observe a particular rite on Good Friday, but a popular service is the three-hour Meditation on the Cross that begins at midday.

Easter in the Western Church

A Vigil may be held after nightfall on Holy Saturday or before dawn on Easter Sunday when a Paschal candle, symbolising the resurrection of Jesus, is lit. Statues and images that may have been veiled during Lent are uncovered.

Easter Day in the Western Church is a joyous celebration of Christ's resurrection. In stark contrast to the solemnity of Lent, the liturgical colour is white, often with gold, and churches are brightly decorated with white and yellow flowers. The music is joyful and the church bells are rung.

> **Key term**
>
> **Stations of the Cross:** pictures or carvings representing 14 key moments in Jesus' trial, crucifixion and burial

> **Key terms**
>
> **Passion:** sufferings
> **Anglican:** the Church of England or any Church in communion with it

Passion of Christ procession in Malta

An ornate bier

Lent in the Eastern Orthodox Church

In the Eastern Orthodox Church, Easter is preceded by the Great Lent or Great Fast – the most important fasting season in the Church year. The first week of Great Lent starts not on Ash Wednesday, but on Clean Monday. The name *Clean Week* refers to the spiritual cleansing of the faithful. There is strict fasting throughout the week. The second week commemorates St Gregory Palamas, one of the great saints of the Orthodox Church.

The midpoint of the Great Fast is the Sunday of the third week, when there is Veneration of the Cross. During an all-night Vigil, the priest brings a cross out into the centre of the church, where it is venerated by all. The fourth week is an extension of the Veneration of the Cross. Saturday of the fifth week is dedicated to the Mother of God. Great Lent ends with Vespers on the Friday of the sixth week, and is followed by Lazarus Saturday, which celebrates the resuscitation of Lazarus as a foreshadowing of Jesus' resurrection.

Holy Week services begin on the night of Palm Sunday when there is the blessing of palms on the Sunday morning. During Holy Week, each day has its own theme based on particular stories in the Gospels.

For instance, Great Tuesday has the theme of the Parable of the Ten Virgins; Great Wednesday has the theme of the anointing of Jesus at Bethany; and Great Thursday celebrates the institution of the Eucharist.

Great Friday is a strict fast day and the theme is Jesus' Passion. The evening service reflects Mary's lament for her son. A cloth icon bearing an image of the dead body, known as the *epitaphios*, representing the sheet in which Jesus was wrapped, is placed on an ornate bier representing Jesus' tomb. The priest then sprinkles rose water and fresh rose petals.

The theme of Great Saturday is Jesus' burial and his Descent into hell. This is another day of strict fasting. Services combine elements of sorrow and joy. At the beginning of the morning service, the liturgical colour is black but, just before the Gospel reading, it is changed to white and the atmosphere of the service turns from sorrow to joy. The priest sprinkles the church with fresh bay leaves to symbolise Jesus' victory over death and the work of salvation accomplished. The good news of his resurrection, however, will only be proclaimed during the Paschal Vigil.

Easter in the Eastern Orthodox Church

The last liturgical service in the Eastern Lent is the Midnight Office, which forms the first part of the Paschal Vigil. During this service, the priest places the *epitaphios* on the altar, where it remains until the feast of the Ascension. At the end of the Office, all church lights and candles are extinguished, and all wait in silence and darkness for the stroke of midnight, when the resurrection of Christ is proclaimed.

At midnight, the priest lights a candle. He then lights candles held by assistants, who in turn light candles held by the congregation. They all then process around the church, chanting 'At thy resurrection O Christ our Saviour, the angels in Heaven sing, enable us who are on earth, to glorify thee in purity of heart'.

Easter Vigil in a Ukrainian Orthodox church

The procession halts in front of the closed doors of the church, where the priest makes the sign of the cross, and all the church bells and percussion instruments are sounded. Then, Easter Matins begin, followed by the Easter Hours and the Easter Divine Liturgy.

Following the Liturgy, the priest may bless Paschal eggs and baskets containing foods forbidden during the Great Fast, and the congregation may share an agapé meal. It is also customary to crack open hard-boiled eggs, dyed red to symbolise the blood of Christ, to celebrate the opening of Jesus' tomb.

On Easter Sunday afternoon, Agapé Vespers are sung. During this service, a portion of John's Gospel may be read in several languages to demonstrate the universality of the resurrection.

The customary Easter greeting is: 'Christ is risen', and the response is: 'He is risen indeed'.

Summary

* Western Church festivals:
  * **Advent:** anticipates Jesus' First Coming and Jesus' Second Coming; it begins the Church year
  * **Christmas:** includes carol services, Christingle, midnight Mass, feasting and exchanging gifts
  * **Lent:** fasting; includes Palm Sunday, Maundy Thursday and Good Friday; some Roman Catholic countries have processions
  * **Easter:** Joyous celebration of Christ's resurrection; churches brightly decorated; any veiled statues/images are uncovered.
* Eastern Orthodox Church festivals:
  * **Advent:** anticipates Jesus' First Coming only, and does not begin the Church year
  * **Christmas:** celebrated on 7 January; services are parallel to those held on Good Friday; there is less emphasis on consumerism
  * **Lent:** period of fasting; the Special Good Friday service reflects Mary's lament for her son Jesus
  * **Easter:** lighting of candles, which are processed around the church.

AO1 Activity

a Explain:
  i the rituals and observances
  ii their significance for Christians

of the Christmas festival as celebrated in the Western Church.

This helps you develop the ability to select and prioritise appropriate material.

b Draw a mind map of the similarities and differences of the Easter festival as celebrated in the Western Church and the Eastern Orthodox Church.

This helps you recall the key points of the Easter festival of each of the two Church traditions, highlighting their similarities and differences.

This section covers AO2 content and skills

Specification content
Whether the different emphases and practices mean that Easter is a different celebration in the Eastern Orthodox and Western Churches

Issues for analysis and evaluation

Whether the different emphases and practices mean that Easter is a different celebration in the Eastern Orthodox and Western Churches

Possible line of argument	Critical analysis and evaluation
Both Eastern and Western Churches consider Easter to be the most important festival in the Christian calendar.	Easter celebrates the fundamental Christian belief in the resurrection.
Western and Eastern Orthodox Churches celebrate Easter on different dates.	They use different calendars and have different interpretations of what is meant by the vernal equinox and the full moon.
Lent begins on Clean Monday in the Eastern Orthodox Church. In the Western Church, it begins on Ash Wednesday.	In the Eastern Orthodox Church, there is more emphasis on strict fasting.
The Eastern Church has a different theme for each day of Holy Week.	The Western Church celebrates only Maundy Thursday, Good Friday, Holy Saturday and Easter Sunday.
For the Eastern Church, the main Easter celebration is an all-night service ending with Easter Divine Liturgy. Following the Liturgy, the priest may bless hard-boiled eggs, dyed red to symbolise the blood of Christ, to celebrate the opening of Jesus' tomb.	In the Western Church, statues and images that may have been veiled during Lent are unveiled. Some Roman Catholic countries have processions.
In some Eastern Churches, in the church at midnight all light is extinguished and then a new flame is struck at the altar. Everyone holds a candle and the light spreads outwards. Jesus, as Light of the World, returns from the darkness of death.	Some Western Churches hold a vigil after nightfall on Holy Saturday or before dawn on Easter Sunday. The main celebration is on Easter Day.
There are clear differences in the way the Eastern and Western Churches celebrate Easter.	However, both traditions hold the elements of death and resurrection equally central.
The emphases and practices are different in the two traditions, but the celebration and theology are the same.	The main differences within Christianity would be with the Christian groups that do not celebrate it at all.

AO2 Activity

a Select three lines of argument from the critical analysis and evaluation of whether the different emphases and practices mean that Easter is a different celebration in the Eastern Orthodox and Western Churches. Research and select three references from scholars, schools of thought or religious and philosophical texts that would support those arguments.

b Using the strongest line of argument, try to identify three key quotations that could be used – they could be from scholars, religious texts or schools of thought.

Exam practice

Sample question
Evaluate the relative importance of Easter and Christmas.

Sample answer

It seems quite clear that in the West, Christmas is a much more celebrated and popular festival than Easter. Whereas most people would be hard pressed to recite the line of an Easter hymn, many could recite the words of several Christmas carols. Nativity plays and carol services, including Christingle services, often see increased church attendance. The problem is that the popularity of Christmas often has little to do with Christian belief. Christmas is based on the ancient Roman Saturnalia, which it replaced in the West. The festival in recent years has become heavily secularised and commercialised. While most people of all faiths and none may have some idea what the Christmas celebration is about, and may often share in carol singing and charity fundraising at this time, belief in the incarnation may well be confined to a minority. However, being a popular festival is not the same thing as being an important festival, even if the festival's popularity is itself an opportunity for evangelism.

Easter, like Christmas, is a Christian festival that originally replaced an ancient festival. In the case of Easter, it was a spring festival that heralded the rebirth of nature with the return of the Sun at the solstice. In fact, the name 'Easter' derives from the name of the Anglo-Saxon spring goddess Eostre. However, unlike the Christmas festival, there is less scope to reinterpret Easter, even though there has been in recent years a relentless attempt to secularise and commercialise Easter, with an emphasis on non-Christian imagery such as Easter bunnies. Again, while most people of all faiths and none may be willing to share Easter eggs, few may know that they are intended as symbols of the resurrection. Fewer still may believe in the resurrection itself or be able to recite the first line of an Easter hymn. However, like Christmas, the Easter festival can provide an opportunity for evangelism. But the importance is cultural rather than ecclesiastical.

So how important are Christmas and Easter for the Church and for Christians? Traditionally, the most important Christian festival is Easter because it celebrates the fundamental belief in the resurrection of Jesus Christ, by which God set his seal of approval on his work. Without the resurrection, there is no hope of forgiveness and eternal life. In 1 Corinthians 15, Paul writes 'If Christ has not been raised, your faith is futile; you are still in your sins … If only for this life we have hope in Christ, we are to be pitied more than all men'.

However, Christmas celebrates the birth of Christ; the incarnation (God becoming flesh). This surely is an important celebration. Christmas heralds the life, work and death of Jesus. Without the incarnation, there could have been no resurrection. So Christmas and Easter are inextricably linked at the theological level. Therefore, perhaps for Christians, both festivals are important. They show God breaking into this world first as an innocent infant in the person of Jesus (the incarnation) and then as a mighty power raising the dead Jesus to life (the resurrection). The resurrection guarantees that God has accepted Jesus' death as atonement for human sin, thus making eternal life possible for human beings.

This section covers AO2 content and skills

Specification content
The relative importance of Easter and Christmas

A good introduction that raises the issue of popularity versus importance. It examines the Christmas festival in terms of its popularity. Good examples are cited to demonstrate its secular nature, and whether the festival reflects belief in the theological significance of the incarnation is questioned.

The essay now examines Easter using good examples. The Easter festival is less reinterpreted, but the question is raised again as to whether the importance is cultural rather than ecclesiastical.

This paragraph starts with a good question that returns the debate back to the relative importance of the festivals for Christians. It makes an argument that Easter is the most important theologically, and it shows good knowledge of biblical text.

The answer questions whether Christmas is the most important festival rather than Easter and concludes that perhaps both are important.

T4 Religious practices that shape religious identity (1)

Philosopher

Critical thinker

Detective **Judge**

The final paragraph, after some reflective thinking, argues for Easter as the most important festival. It is well argued and supported with clearly expressed reasons to justify this concluding view. It shows reflective thinking that traces a clear path to the conclusion.

However, surely Easter is more important because it is about Jesus' ultimate mission rather than just his birth. Without Easter, Christmas would be insignificant since it would just be about a birth of a good teacher, if the death and resurrection of Jesus are not true. Also Christmas is a late addition to Church celebrations. Easter is not. Easter is more focused, sombre and religious, while Christmas, though more popular, is the one that has somewhat lost its real religious significance and meaning. Even Christmas cards are rarely religious in their content. Finally, the birth of Jesus is referenced only in two Gospels, whereas the resurrection is in all four Gospels, which is clearly the event that created Christian faith.

Over to you

This task has only instructions with no examples. However, using the skills you have developed completing the earlier tasks, you should be able to apply what you have learned and complete this successfully.

Your new task is to write another response under timed conditions to a question requiring an evaluation of whether or not Christmas is a more important Christian festival than Easter. You need to do the same as your last AO2 developing-skills task, but with some further development. This time, there is a fifth point to help you improve the quality of your answer:

1. Begin with a list of indicative content. Perhaps discuss this as a group. It does not need to be in any order. Remember: This is evaluation, so you need different lines of argument. The easiest way is to use 'In support' and 'Against' headings.
2. Develop the list using examples.
3. Now consider the order in which you would like to explain the information.
4. Then write out your plan, under timed conditions, remembering to apply the principles of evaluation by making sure that you
    - identify issues clearly
    - present accurate views of others, making sure that you comment on the views presented
    - reach an overall personal judgement.
5. Use the band descriptors to mark your own answer, carefully considering the descriptors. Then ask someone else to read your answer and see if they can help you improve it in any way.

    Use this technique as revision for each of the topic areas that you have studied.

    Swap and compare answers to improve your own.

Religious practices that shape religious identity (2)

D: Religious identity through unification

The development of the Ecumenical Movement since 1910

World Missionary Conference

One of the sad facts of Christianity is the many divisions and conflicts that have persisted from the early centuries of the movement to the present day. There are many Christians who feel the force of this criticism, and want to see Christianity known more for what Christians share with one another than by what divides them. The Ecumenical Movement is this quest for unity. The term *ecumenical* comes from the Greek word *oikumene*, meaning the 'entire, inhabited world'.

Those involved in the Ecumenical Movement consider several passages in the Bible to be especially important. The most cited of these is the prayer of Jesus in John 17:20–21: 'My prayer is not for them alone. I pray also for those who will believe in me through their message, that all of them may be one, Father, just as you are in me and I am in you. May they also be in us so that the world may believe that you have sent me.'

In this prayer, Jesus recognises that the success of the mission of the Church is tied to Christian unity. The Apostle Paul lamented the arguments and division in the early Church, and urged that Christians be united (see 1 Corinthians 1:10 and 2 Corinthians 5:19). From the very beginning, the Church came together to overcome differences (Acts 15) and to feel the spiritual power of being united in worship (Matthew 18:19–20). Underlying these passages is the conviction that all Christians are called to a deep fellowship with God, and therefore can and should live in deep fellowship with one another.

> **Key quotes**
>
> I appeal to you, brothers, in the name of our Lord Jesus Christ, that all of you agree with one another so that there may be no division among you and that you may be perfectly united in mind and thought.
>
> **(1 Corinthians 1:10)**
>
> And he has committed to us the message of reconciliation.
>
> **(2 Corinthians 5:19)**

Does unity mean uniformity? The Church has always valued different perspectives, cultures and languages. There are, after all, four Gospels, each with different perspectives on the life and teaching of Jesus. However, the question of what Churches need to agree on and what they can surrender as 'non-essential' is perhaps the most important challenge that faces the Ecumenical Movement.

This section covers AO1 content and skills

Specification content

The development of the Ecumenical Movement since 1910 (World Missionary Conference); the World Council of Churches, its rationale, its mission and its work in three main areas: Unity, Mission, and Ecumenical Relations; Public Witness and Diakonia; and Ecumenical Formation

The Edinburgh Missionary Conference

Many scholars trace the beginning of the modern Ecumenical Movement to the Edinburgh World Missionary Conference of 1910. However, Christians had been gathering formally and informally over the centuries for common worship and common causes. In fact, the first use of the term *ecumenical* in Christian discussions was in 381 CE, when the Council of Constantinople applied this to the Council of Nicea of 325 CE. The Nicene creed is known as an *ecumenical creed*, one to which the entire Christian world at the time gave assent.

World Missionary Conference, Edinburgh, 1910

What makes the Edinburgh Missionary Conference so outstanding is that it brought together an unprecedented number of Christian groups and, in its wake, led to the formation of Church organisations that have evolved into today's World Council of Churches.

Over 1200 missionaries from about 160 missionary boards gathered for ten days in 1910 to consider reports on various aspects of missionary work. The goal that united these missionaries was to bring into being a self-governing, self-supporting Church in 'each non-Christian nation' that would reflect the undivided Church of Christ. However, the reality on the ground was often different: The divisions and arguments that marked the Churches in the West were manifesting themselves in new Churches in Africa and Asia. This is why the conference adopted the slogan 'Doctrine Divides but Service Unites'. It was felt that the way to make progress was not to engage in disputed theological questions, but to focus on the need all Churches felt to spread the Christian message.

Key quote

Ecumenism is the quest for unity among Christians now divided by denomination.

(S Harmon)

The only resolution of the Conference – which passed unanimously – was that a committee should carry on co-ordinating missionary activity. Nevertheless, this event was a breakthrough for the cause of ecumenism since: there was an acceptance of one another despite different denominational labels; a willingness to work together; and a commitment to further gatherings. However, this was solely an evangelical Protestant gathering attended by mostly Anglo-American missionaries. Neither the Roman Catholic Church nor the Orthodox Churches were invited – though some Anglican speakers at the conference urged that they be included in future gatherings. Furthermore, some at the conference viewed avoiding Church doctrine as a limitation. Surely, if there was to be greater unity between the Churches, they would need to explore differences in beliefs and reach agreement?

After the conference

There were several developments after the Edinburgh Conference that furthered the cause of ecumenism:

- In 1920, the Orthodox Patriarch of Constantinople, inspired by the proposal of a 'League of Nations', proposed a 'league' of Churches as a response to God's desire for Church unity.
- The International Missionary Conference was founded in 1921. This Conference extended the work of 1910 by bringing together Church leaders from around the world to consider issues such as the Christian message in a secular world and the relevance of the Gospel in response to issues such as war and slavery.
- The Life and Work Movement met in 1925 and focused on the responsibility of Christians to the social and economic problems in the aftermath of the First World War.
- The Faith and Order Movement met in 1927 to consider matters of doctrinal divisions between Churches.
- There were also a number of dialogues and mergers; the most comprehensive was the formation of the Church of South India in 1947, which brought together Anglican, Methodist, Presbyterian, Congregational, Lutheran and Reformed Churches into one denomination. (In 1971, the Church of North India formed as a merger between Anglican, Congregational, Presbyterian, Methodist, Baptist and Disciples of Christ.)
- In 1937, leaders from the Life and Work Movement and the Faith and Order Movement met together and proposed that they merge into a 'World Council of Churches'. The Second World War delayed their plans.

The World Council of Churches: rationale and mission

The first assembly of the World Council of Churches (WCC) was held in Amsterdam in 1948, with Willem A Visser 't Hooft as its first General Secretary: 351 delegates gathered, representing 147 Church bodies. The WCC now has 352 member Churches, and held its eleventh assembly in 2022 at Karlsruhe in Germany under the theme 'Christ's love moves the world to reconciliation and unity'. Over 4500 people attended, including 659 official delegates.

> **Specification content**
> The World Council of Churches: its rationale and its mission

T4 Religious practices that shape religious identity (2)

The logo of the World Council of Churches

At the 1948 assembly, the WCC defined itself as 'a fellowship of churches which accept our Lord Jesus Christ as God and Saviour'. The 1950 Toronto Statement made clear that 'the member churches seek to learn from each other and to give help to each other in order that the body of Christ may be built up and that the life of the churches may be renewed'.

The Toronto Statement also made clear that the WCC was not a superchurch or a negotiator for unions between Churches. It was not based on any one particular conception of the Church, and it did not imply the acceptance of a specific doctrine concerning the nature of Church unity.

The WCC has a General Assembly about every eight years. Between these assemblies, a central committee meets regularly and programmes run continuously. In 1961, there was a particularly significant assembly in the history of the WCC:

- The WCC revised and expanded its definition to include a reference to the Christian scriptures and to the Trinity: 'The World Council of Churches is a fellowship of Churches which confess the Lord Jesus Christ as God and Saviour according to the scriptures and therefore seek to fulfil together their common calling to the glory of the one God; Father, Son and Holy Spirit.'
- The International Missionary Council, which had been associated with the WCC since 1948, became fully integrated.

Key quote

The lives of churches in relationship to other churches and the lives of individual believers in relationship to other believers ought to be as inseparably intertwined as the three interlocking circles that symbolise the Trinity.

(S Harmon)

- The first Roman Catholics attended as official observers.
- The Russian Orthodox Church and other Eastern Orthodox Churches became members (the Ecumenical Patriarchate of the Eastern Orthodox Church was one of the founding members).
- The first Pentecostal Christian Church bodies joined the WCC; these were from South America.

The WCC describes its intentions in this way: 'The aim of the WCC is to pursue the goal of the visible unity of the Church. This involves a process of renewal and change in which member Churches pray, worship, discuss and work together.' This visible unity of the Church includes these elements:

- a common confession of the apostolic faith
- a common sacramental life
- mutual recognition of all members and their ministries
- a common mission in spreading the Gospel
- participation of all Churches locally and internationally in agreed structures
- common service to the world so that all might believe.

Of course, these elements are a final destination at which the WCC has not arrived; it is on a journey towards this goal through its various programmes.

The work of the World Council of Churches in three areas

There are three programme areas of the WCC, each of which includes specific projects, activities, conferences, networks and thinktanks that aim to advocate issues within the member Churches and wider society.

1 Unity, Mission and Ecumenical Relations

Unity, Mission and Ecumenical Relations is devoted to the pursuit of visible Christian unity. That the term *unity* comes first reflects Jesus' prayer in John for believers to be united so that the world might believe. Thus, this area also includes *mission* – the reaching out of the Christian message; as well as *ecumenical relations* – the strengthening of relationships between Christian Churches. There are at least two main challenges that the WCC faces in these areas:

1. The WCC defines *mission* as witnessing to the Christian Gospel, but it also says that mission is 'increasingly seen too as fostering solidarity and respect for people's dignity'. Thus, the WCC is involved in a number of projects aimed at social justice, such as advocating for those with disabilities, indigenous people and migrants. This has sometimes drawn criticism from member Churches that it is 'watering down' the focus on evangelism. That the WCC also engages in interfaith relations has added to these tensions.

> **Key quote**
>
> A purely inward or spiritual unity among Christians is not enough.
> (J Magina)

2. Not all Churches are members of the WCC; most notably, the Roman Catholic Church and a number of evangelical and Pentecostal Churches. This is why there are special working groups at the WCC tasked with building relationships with these Churches.

Finally, this programme area includes the Commission of Faith and Order, one of the two main movements that merged to form the WCC. This commission is responsible for producing perhaps the most widely studied ecumenical document of recent history, 'Baptism, Eucharist & Ministry' (1982), which explores the growing agreement and remaining disagreements between Christian Churches in these areas.

2 Public Witness and Diakonia

Public Witness and Diakonia recognises that Christians share many areas of social responsibility. This area is the legacy of the Life and Work Movement that formed the WCC in 1948 and was dissolved into the various programmes that now make up this area. The programmes in this area have two main goals:

1. To offer a highly public 'prophetic voice' that calls awareness to areas where Churches and the world need to pay special attention. This includes peace building in 'priority countries': the Korean Peninsula, Syria, South Sudan, Democratic Republic of Congo and Nigeria, as well as supporting Churches who find themselves in situations of conflict. This area includes sending observers to Israel and Palestine and seeking to influence key activities at the United Nations

---

Specification content

The World Council of Churches and its work in three main areas: Unity, Mission, and Ecumenical Relations; Public Witness and Diakonia; and Ecumenical Formation

2. To bring Christians together tirelessly and persistently to live out Christian values of social responsibility. The WCC uses the Greek term *diakonia*, which means 'service' and refers to the care of poor and oppressed people. This area includes activities around climate change, global health, water rights, a just economy, women's rights, stateless people and HIV and AIDS work.

3 Ecumenical Formation

Ecumenical Formation is the area of study, training and education so that the knowledge and convictions of ecumenism can take shape in the lives of individuals and Churches. The WCC has its own institute at Bossey, near Geneva, Switzerland.

The Ecumenical Institute at Bossey has its own teaching faculty and facilities for residential study, and grants diplomas through the University of Geneva. But the WCC also provides training and education opportunities throughout the world, through member churches in co-operation with the WCC.

The Ecumenical Institute of the World Council of Churches at Bossey

Tensions in the Ecumenical Movement

There are currently 352 Church bodies in the World Council of Churches; they do not always agree! In fact, there have been some serious disagreements in the last few decades. One of these concerns the Orthodox Churches. The Orthodox see themselves as identified with the universal Church. Their belief is that other Churches need to find consensus with the Orthodox Church if unity is to be achieved. This position conflicts with the tendency in the WCC to seek consensus between Churches, rather than to favour one Church. Even though there are only about 20 Orthodox Church bodies in the WCC, the baptised Orthodox members worldwide number nearly half of all Church members represented by the WCC. This had led to the Orthodox representatives feeling a tension about being treated as a small minority within the WCC, when they represent nearly a majority in terms of their overall size.

Other sources of tension include:

- The fall of communism has resulted in a strengthening of the Orthodox Church.
- One side of this development has been a rise in nationalism and xenophobia in countries where the Orthodox Church is strong. This, in turn, has led to suspicions about the Ecumenical Movement.
- Some Orthodox members of the WCC feel uncomfortable with the worship style adopted at WCC gatherings.
- There are difficulties with what is perceived by the Orthodox as a 'liberal' attitude to other religions and issues of social justice such as gay rights.

Evangelical and Pentecostal Church bodies, both inside and outside the WCC, have raised similar concerns about the growing liberal attitude to other religions and issues of social justice. Given that traditional Protestant bodies are declining in membership and that Pentecostalism is the fastest-growing movement in Christianity, this has meant further tensions in the WCC in the areas of understanding interfaith dialogue, and the role of sexuality and gender in ministry and social justice. In addition, the war in Ukraine has raised tensions due to the Russian Orthodox Church being a member of the WCC.

Relationship of the Catholic Church with the WCC

The Catholic Church did not react positively to the growing Ecumenical Movement of the 1920s. In 1928, Pope Pius XI published a letter in which he declared that the only way to realise the will of Christ for Church unity was for all Christians simply to return to the Church of Rome. The 'Apostolic See has never allowed its subjects to take part in the assemblies of non-Catholics: for the union of Christians can only be promoted by promoting the return to the one true Church of Christ of those who are separated from it'. Pius XI feared that agreements between Churches would lead to watered-down doctrine and, eventually, to irreligion. Not only did the Roman Catholic Church refuse to join the WCC in 1948, but it also forbade its members from even attending as observers.

With the election of Pope John XXIII in 1958, a new approach to ecumenism was taken. In 1960, the Pope met with the Archbishop of Canterbury, Geoffrey Fisher – the first time in 600 years an Archbishop of Canterbury had visited the Vatican! That same year, the Pope appointed a 'Secretariat for Promoting Christian Unity', with the purpose of developing an ecumenical spirit in the Catholic Church and developing dialogues and collaborations with other Churches. Shortly after, the Vatican approved Catholic observers for the WCC's assembly in Delhi in 1961, and also invited non-Catholics to be observers at Vatican II.

This new approach to ecumenism found expression in 1964 in the Vatican II document *Unitatis Redintegratio* ('Restoration of Unity').

The text of this document is significant for many reasons:

- It describes Christians outside of the Roman Catholic Church as 'separated brethren', rather than as 'heretics' or 'dissidents'.
- It accepts that both sides share a responsibility for divisions in the Church.
- It demonstrates an appreciation of the contributions non-Catholic Christians make to the spirituality and practice of Christianity.
- It moves away from the simple identification of the one true Church with the current form of the Roman Catholic Church.

Pope Pius XI

" Key quote "

There are also many true Christians and much that is truly Christian outside the Church.

(Pope Benedict XVI)

This last point is very significant. Instead of saying, simply, that the true Church of Christ is the Roman Catholic Church, this document states that the true Church subsists in the Catholic Church. The exact meaning of the term *subsist* in this document has been debated. However, as Pope Benedict XVI has said, 'the Council Fathers meant to say that the being of the Church as such is a broader entity than the Roman Catholic Church, but within the latter it acquires, in an incomparable way, the character of a true and proper subject'. In other words, the positive message to the Ecumenical Movement is that the Catholic Church recognises that there are Christian activities outside of it, but at the same time it insists that the Church of Christ is in the Roman Catholic Church in a way that is incomparable to other Churches.

T4 Religious practices that shape religious identity (2)

Unitatis Redintegratio also says 'For it is only through Christ's Catholic Church, which is "the all-embracing means of salvation", that they can benefit fully from the means of salvation. We believe that Our Lord entrusted all the blessings of the New Covenant to the apostolic college alone, of which Peter is the head, in order to establish the one body of Christ on Earth to which all should be fully incorporated who belong in any way to the people of God.'

The positive attitude to the Ecumenical Movement continued with the Catholic Church becoming full members of the Faith and Order Commission of the WCC (1968; though not full members of the WCC itself). In 1965, Pope John Paul VI and the Patriarch of Constantinople Athenagoras issued a joint statement that retracted the mutual excommunications and condemnations between their two Churches of 1054. The Pope famously gave the Archbishop of Canterbury, Michael Ramsey, an episcopal ring in 1966 and, the following year, they established the Anglican–Roman Catholic International Commission (ARCIC), dedicated to the ecumenical progress between these two Churches. Over the years, there have also been numerous dialogues between the Church of Rome and other Churches throughout the world.

Anglican–Roman Catholic tensions

In 1981, the ARCIC released a report that noted many areas of agreement, especially in understandings of the Eucharist and ordained ministry. It offered the view that the only really significant difference between the Anglican Church and the Roman Catholic Church was that the former was not in visible unity with the latter. The report even suggested that Anglicans might welcome a merging with the Catholic Church if the Papacy were seen more as a practical route to Church unity rather than a theological necessity. This would also deal with the criticisms many Anglicans have about Catholic doctrines of Mary (Immaculate Conception and the Assumption of Mary), which originated as pronouncements by 'infallible' papal teachings.

The Catholic Church, however, was quick to respond, noting that the Papal office is indeed a theological necessity, rooted in scripture; it 'belongs to the divine structure of the Church'. It is therefore not willing to surrender any doctrines that have been introduced by Papal authority. Thus, at the heart of division between these two Churches is the nature of authority.

The ARCIC has been threatened by several events:

- The ordination of women as priests and bishops by Churches in the Anglican Communion.
- The ordination of an openly gay man (Gene Robinson) as an episcopal bishop in the United States, which caused Pope John Paul II in 2003 to suspend participation in the ARCIC.

> **Key quote**
>
> Given the practical difficulties posed by issues of gender and sexuality, it is hard to see what unity between Catholics and Anglicans might look like – certainly not uniformity ... but emotionally the two Churches are closer than at any time since the reign of Henry VIII.
>
> (P Vallely)

Anglican tensions were deepened in 2009 when the Catholic Church facilitated for any Anglican clergy who disagreed with the ordination of women, to become ordained in the Catholic Church.

Despite these tensions, the ARCIC continues to meet and to encourage unity between Anglicans and Catholics. In 2023, the commission met in Cyprus in the third phase (2019–25) to discuss how the two communions discern their ethical teaching.

Alongside the ARCIC, another commission was set up in 2000 called IARCCUM (International Anglican–Roman Catholic Commission for Unity and Mission). One of its aims is to encourage Anglican and Roman Catholic bishops to develop projects and programmes of joint witness and mission in the world.

Summary

- The Ecumenical Movement exists to promote Christian unity.
- One reason that Christians seek unity is Jesus' prayer in John 17:21.
- The World Missionary Conference in 1910 brought together 1200 missionaries from 160 missionary boards. Neither the Roman Catholic nor the Orthodox Churches were invited.
- In 1937, a World Council of Churches (WCC) was planned, but because of the Second World War it did not meet until 1948.
- Today, the WCC represents 352 Church bodies, and the General Assembly of the WCC is held every seven years.
- The Roman Catholic Church is not a member, though it participates in the WCC's Commission on Faith and Order, and Commission on World Mission and Evangelism.
- Anglican–Roman Catholic relationships have developed through the work of ARCIC and IARCCUM, though tensions still remain.

AO1 Activity

a Explain what the Faith and Order Movement was before 1948, and what happened to it after 1948.

This helps you develop the ability to select and present the key, relevant features of the Faith and Order Movement.

b Write a simple flowchart of the main movements that merged into the World Council of Churches. Include dates and brief descriptions of each of the movements on your chart.

This helps you prioritise key, relevant material to show how the World Council of Churches developed.

This section covers AO2 content and skills

Issues for analysis and evaluation

Whether the work of the World Council of Churches can be viewed as a success or a failure

> **Specification content**
> Whether the work of the World Council of Churches can be viewed as a success or a failure.

Possible line of argument	Critical analysis and evaluation
The World Council of Churches (WCC) has 352 Church bodies represented.	However, half of the half a billion members come from just 22 member Churches (Orthodox). Any tensions from within the Orthodox Churches could have wide-ranging effects on the success of the WCC.
The fastest-growing movements in Christianity are Pentecostal and Evangelical.	However, very few of these groups are represented within the WCC.
The WCC has come a long way since it came into being in 1948, when it had 351 delegates representing 147 Church bodies.	The largest Christian Church – the Roman Catholic Church – is not a member, though it has become involved in several WCC programme areas.
The ecumenical experience that the WCC provides has aided various Church mergers. In January 2024, Pope Francis commissioned Anglican and Roman Catholic bishops for joint mission.	Despite the work of ARCIC and IARCCUM, tensions still remain in Anglican–Roman Catholic relationships.
The WCC has brought together most Orthodox Church bodies with hundreds of Protestant denominations.	There are growing tensions, with a perceived shift of the WCC to interfaith dialogue and social causes, including issues of sexuality and gender in leadership.
Most Christian denominations consider themselves to be the most authentic expression of the Church. Yet the WCC has shown that Churches can work together.	The Eastern Orthodox Churches identify themselves with the Universal Church, so see unity in terms of other Churches moving towards them rather than they towards other Churches.
Ecumenism is a journey not a destination.	The present growing tensions may suggest the journey is about to end.
Christian unity is a value that should be striven for regardless of how difficult or impossible it is to achieve.	It is God's business whether the WCC is a success or a failure (John 17:20–22). Christians are called to faithfulness not success.

> **AO2 Activity**
> a Select three lines of argument from the critical analysis and evaluation of whether the work of the World Council of Churches can be viewed as a success or a failure. Research and select three references from scholars, schools of thought or religious and philosophical texts that would support those arguments.
> b Using the strongest line of argument, try to identify three key quotations that could be used – they could be from scholars, religious texts or schools of thought.

Exam practice

Sample question
Evaluate the extent to which the non-membership of the Roman Catholic Church affects the aims of the World Council of Churches.

Sample answer
Christian unity has always been an issue for the Roman Catholic Church. It sees itself as the tradition that has been ordained by God to be the universal Church through a divinely appointed Papacy. In 1928, Pope Pius XI published a letter in which he declared that the only way to realise the will of Christ for Church unity was for all Christians simply to return to the Church of Rome. The Pope feared that agreements between Churches would lead to watered-down doctrine and, eventually, to irreligion. Hence it is not surprising that the Roman Catholic Church refused to join the World Council of Churches in 1948. In the light of the WCC's aim to encourage spiritual sharing between Churches so that the Church can be strengthened and renewed, it seems that the non-participation of the Roman Catholic Church has affected its aims.

However, if the aim of visible unity is considered more of a journey than a destination, then perhaps there are signs that the Roman Catholic Church is on that journey. A change occurred with the election of Pope John XXIII, who had a meeting in 1960 with the Archbishop of Canterbury. It was the first time in 600 years that an archbishop of Canterbury had visited the Vatican. That same year, the Pope appointed a Secretariat for Promoting Christian Unity with the purpose of developing dialogues with other Churches. In 1961, there were Catholic observers at the Assembly of the WCC, and non-Catholic observers were invited to attend Vatican II. Perhaps most significant of all was the 1964 document from Vatican II that described Christians outside as 'separated brethren' rather than as 'heretics'. It also acknowledged the contribution non-Catholic Christians make to the spirituality and practice of Christianity. Perhaps the most significant point in the document was the move away from the simple identification of the one true Church with the current form of the Roman Catholic Church. In 1968, the Catholic Church became a full member of the Commission of Faith and Order of the WCC, though not a full member of the WCC itself. This journey towards unity has continued. ARCIC continues to meet and, in 2024, Pope Francis commissioned Anglican and Roman Catholic bishops for joint mission.

Nevertheless, the journey ahead looks difficult and tension filled. The problem is over the issues of gender and sexuality. The ordination of women as priests and bishops, the ordination of an openly gay man as an episcopal bishop in the United States and the whole debate about same-sex marriage make unity look difficult, if not an unbridgeable gulf, between Anglicans and Catholics.

This section covers AO2 content and skills

Specification content
The extent to which the non-membership of the Roman Catholic Church affects the aims of the World Council of Churches

News reporter
Detective

The opening paragraph sets out clearly how the non-membership of the Roman Catholic Church affects the aims of the WCC.

Explorer
Tennis player
Detective

The answer now raises doubts about how to judge the progress and traces historical events of a journey towards unity.

Critical thinker
Detective

Although the journey has begun, difficulties are highlighted that cast doubt on whether unity is possible.

Philosopher — **Explorer** — **Judge**

This final paragraph gives a strong, reflective conclusion that is a consistent with the clear line of argument throughout the answer. It shows good understanding of the issues and is well supported by evidence and examples.

So, in one sense, the non-membership of the Roman Catholic Church has affected the aims of the WCC. But, as has been argued, it depends on expectations about the 'timing' of a 'visible union'. Before 1960s, there was little or no relationship between the Roman Catholic Church and the Church bodies that make up the WCC. Now, there is not only participation, but active dialogues. Agreed, these relationships may not always operate smoothly, but after centuries of Church division they could be viewed as a movement towards the aim of the WCC for visible unity.

Over to you

Your task is to write a response, under timed conditions, to a question requiring an evaluation of the degree to which tensions in the World Council of Churches threaten to tear it apart. This exercise is best done as a small group at first.

1. Begin with a list of indicative arguments or lines of reasoning, as you may have done previously. It does not need to be in any particular order at first, although as you practise this you will see more order in your lists, in particular by way of links and connections between arguments.
2. Develop the list by using one or two relevant quotations. Now add some references to scholars and/or religious writings.
3. Then write out your plan, under timed conditions, remembering the principles of evaluating with support from extensive, detailed reasoning and/or evidence.

When you have completed the task, refer to the band descriptors for A2 (WJEC) or A Level (Eduqas) and, in particular, look at the demands described in the higher band descriptors, which you should be aspiring towards. Ask yourself:

- Is my answer a confident critical analysis and perceptive evaluation of the issue?
- Is my answer a response that successfully identifies and thoroughly addresses the issues the question raises?
- Does my work show an excellent standard of coherence, clarity and organisation?
- Will my work, when developed, contain thorough, sustained and clear views that are supported by extensive, detailed reasoning and/or evidence?
- Have I used the views of scholars/schools of thought extensively, appropriately and in context?
- Does my answer convey a confident and perceptive analysis of the nature of any possible connections with other elements of my course?
- Is specialist language and vocabulary both thorough and accurate?

E: Religious identity through religious experience

This section covers AO1 content and skills

Introduction to the Charismatic Movement

A traditional service at an Anglican or Catholic church would most likely be very formal in nature, with robed processions, organ music and a set liturgy of singing hymns and reading prayers.

In contrast, a charismatic church service would be very spontaneous, with people lifting their hands in the air, a worship band, people speaking in tongues (an utterance of words or speech-like sounds believers think to be a language unknown by the speaker). During the Eucharist, the pastor or priest might encourage people who want healing to go forward for 'laying on of hands', asking the Holy Spirit to bring healing to the person. This focus on the gifts of the Spirit in churches other than Pentecostal denominations is called the Charismatic Movement.

Specification content
The Charismatic Movement

What does *charismatic* mean?

Charismatic comes from the Greek word *charismata*, meaning 'gifts of grace'. This is the word the Apostle Paul uses to refer to special qualities that Christians receive through the Holy Spirit. There are several lists of these 'spiritual gifts' in the New Testament. The lists don't agree with each other; it does not seem that Paul and others were trying to present a standardised list. Instead, they were drawing attention to the many different ways that Christian believers could express God's grace.

We do not know the reason, but in the early centuries of the Church there was the development of formal leadership and very little evidence of the more miraculous gifts in regular practice in Christian worship services.

The most extensive discussion of spiritual gifts is in 1 Corinthians 12–14. Paul is concerned that the Church should become aware of the true purpose of spiritual gifts: To strengthen the body of Christ. The gifts are not for attaining an individualistic spiritual 'high'; they are for sharing with others, so that everyone in the Church can have a deeper relationship with God. For this reason, Paul discouraged a chaotic practice of the gifts where there were multiple and simultaneous displays of tongues or prophecies so that all an observer would hear is a confusing babble of noise. Paul argued that tongues were more fitting for one's private worship, unless the experience was interpreted in an orderly fashion so that everyone could understand what was being communicated.

Charismatic worship in a church congregation

" Key quotes "

There are different kinds of gifts, but the same Spirit.

(1 Corinthians 12:4)

For anyone who speaks in a tongue does not speak to men but to God. Indeed, no-one understands him; he utters mysteries with his spirit.

(1 Corinthians 14:2)

Pentecostalism

Pentecostalism is the early twentieth-century movement that believed the miraculous events in the Book of Acts – with its outpouring of the Spirit on the Apostles, mass conversions and miracles of healing – should not be seen as part of a past age, but should be a present reality for the Christian Church. Many scholars trace the beginnings of this movement to a temporary Bible school that preacher Charles Fox Parham set up in Topeka, Kansas. Parham believed that the Holy Spirit was going to descend in a special way on the church. He asked his students to read the Book of Acts and to pray that they would receive the Spirit. On 1 January 1901, one of these students, Agnes N. Ozman, is reported to have spoken in tongues and, soon after, many of the students experienced what they believed to be gifts of the Spirit.

The Azuza Street Mission, Los Angeles, California

An itinerant African-American preacher, William James Seymour, also followed Parham's ministry. In 1906, Seymour moved to Los Angeles and led a small prayer group, which rapidly grew as a result of having similar experiences. This group moved to an unused building at 312 Azusa Street and quickly became the largest church in Los Angeles. What was especially striking about this church was that Seymour, as African-American, worked with an interracial congregation of African-Americans, Mexican-Americans and European-Americans.

In the first few decades of the last century, the various churches that focused on these experiences gradually formed denominations including the Assemblies of God, the Foursquare Gospel Church, Elim Pentecostal Church (UK) and the Apostolic Church (Wales). Pentecostal denominations are known for being evangelical in nature. Alistair McGrath notes four qualities of evangelicalism:

1. Scripture is the ultimate authority.
2. The saving death of Jesus on the cross is the only source of redemption.
3. All people need to have a conversion experience.
4. The Christian faith should be shared through evangelism.

However, Pentecostal denominations also manifest the following qualities, which distinguish them from other Evangelical Churches:

- Pentecostal Churches believe that there is a second baptism, that of the Holy Spirit – this takes place after conversion.
- Many Pentecostals believe that speaking in tongues is the confirmation that that person has received this second baptism.
- There is a focus on spontaneous worship and healing, and a belief that these are the 'end times'.
- Pentecostal Churches in the first decades of the twentieth century were anti-ecumenical, rarely having anything to do with 'mainstream' traditional Churches.
- This anti-ecumenical tendency can be seen in Pentecostal attitudes to the Roman Catholic Church, which has been viewed by many Pentecostal Christians as outside of Christianity altogether because of its formalism, hierarchy and worldliness.

The development of the Charismatic Movement post-1960

The *Charismatic Movement* refers to the experience of the gifts of the Spirit in Churches outside of Pentecostal denominations. From the mid-twentieth century onwards, many members of traditional Churches experienced speaking in tongues, healing and other gifts described in the New Testament, but chose to remain in their denominations rather than leave them. They saw their experiences as ways to bring renewal to their denominations. At the same time, the Roman Catholic Church, the Anglican Communion and many other denominations chose to study and observe this phenomenon, rather than to reject it. There were questions about whether this movement was anti-intellectual and could breed an indifference to the classic doctrines of the Christian faith by indulging in emotional experiences.

> **Key quote**
>
> At the heart of Christianity there is and should be an encounter with the Holy Spirit.
>
> **(M Cartledge)**

Specification content
The development of the Charismatic Movement post-1960

At the same time, it was recognised that the Bible advocated spiritual gifts and that the testimony of those in the movement was that it strengthened their faith and their commitment to their Churches.

The Charismatic Movement spread very quickly from the 1960s, finding acceptance in the Roman Catholic Church as well as many Protestant denominations.

> **Key quote**
>
> The heart of charismatic spirituality is the conviction and experience of the present, empowering activity of the Holy Spirit in and through the life of the believer and the Church community.
>
> **(C Cocksworth)**

It can be described as a 'renewal movement' within Churches, and is sometimes referred to as *neo-Pentecostalism* because it shares many traits with Pentecostal denominations. As in Pentecostal Churches, there is the conviction that the gifts of grace Paul describes in 1 Corinthians 12 are just as valid today as they were in the early Church. However, there are some different emphases:

- Speaking in tongues is generally not tied as tightly to someone's first experience of the Holy Spirit as it might be in Pentecostal denominations. There has been a tendency, especially in early Pentecostalism, to see speaking in tongues as the initial proof of Spirit baptism. In the Charismatic Movement, tongues are viewed as a gift to all believers, but not one that necessarily confirms their spiritual experience.
- There is generally fewer references to the baptism of the Holy Spirit as the second part of a two-stage initiation. Churches in the Charismatic Movement prefer to speak of 'being filled by the Spirit' or 'released by the Spirit'. This is to emphasise the biblical teaching that there is only one Baptism and that all Christians have the Spirit of God in their lives, but that Christians can have a fuller experience of the Spirit later in their journey.

T4 Religious practices that shape religious identity (2)

The beginning of the Charismatic Movement

The Charismatic Movement came to world attention in 1960 when an Episcopalian minister in California, Dennis Bennett, had a charismatic experience and introduced it to his congregation. A small group in the church voiced their opposition and, rather than cause a split in the congregation, Bennett resigned. The Bishop of Los Angeles banned speaking in tongues. *Time* and *Newsweek* magazines picked up this story. A bishop in Washington State, more open to these experiences, placed Bennett in a dying church in Seattle. Under Bennett's leadership, this church soon became the largest in the diocese and hosted conferences on the Charismatic Movement for leaders across the country.

However, ministers and lay people in traditional churches were becoming increasingly aware of spiritual gifts apart from Bennett's experience:

- David du Plessis, an Assemblies of God minister, felt called to witness to Pentecostalism in ecumenical circles. He was involved with the World Council of Churches and had audiences with three different popes.
- Oral Roberts, a Methodist minister, brought Pentecostalism to a large audience as a pioneer of televangelism, though his fundraising techniques earned him much criticism.
- The Full Gospel Businessman's Fellowship began in 1953. This was a popular movement that brought together businessmen (women and ministers were excluded) with Pentecostal speakers in informal settings. Many from traditional denominations attended.
- Popular books began to bring Pentecostal themes to wider audiences. One of these was *The Cross and the Switchblade* (1963), the true story of a Pentecostal minister who left his comfortable suburban denomination to work with violent street gangs in New York City.

The first Church of England congregation to declare itself as charismatic was in 1963. Soon after, a national network, the Fountain Trust, was founded to encourage charismatic worship across denominations in the UK.

The popular film adaptation of *The Cross and the Switchblade* (1970)

> ## Key quote
>
> The Charismatic Movement is a form of Christian existentialism.
> (Church of England)

In January 2023, the Center for the Study of Global Christianity at Gordon Conwell Theological Seminary reported: 'There will be over 2.6 billion Christians worldwide by the middle of 2023 and around 3.3 billion by 2050'.

The Charismatic Movement in the Roman Catholic Church

Prior to the rise of the Charismatic Movement in the Catholic Church, Vatican II (1962–65) had focused on the need for renewal. Pope John XXIII began Vatican II with a prayer: 'Divine Spirit, renew your wonders in this our age, as in a new Pentecost'. This openness to renewal is expressed clearly in one of the key documents of Vatican II, *Lumen Gentium* ('Light to the Gentiles'). This document asserts both the authority of the Church and the need to be open to new spiritual expressions.

Scholars often cite February 1967 as the beginning of Charismatic Renewal in the Catholic Church. At Duquesne University, a Catholic university in Pittsburgh, Pennsylvania, two lecturers had been praying for renewal in the Church. They then asked about 20 students to read *The Cross and the*

Switchblade and to gather for a weekend conference. The group then had dramatic experiences of speaking in tongues and other spiritual gifts. The movement spread to the University of Notre Dame, which began to host annual conferences, with thousands of Catholics attending from around the world. Soon, the Charismatic Movement could be found in Catholic Churches on every continent.

> **Key quote**
>
> Some within the Catholic Church consider the Catholic Charismatic Renewal to be introspective and deeply conservative, the antithesis of Liberation Theology
>
> (AH Anderson)

The movement has been recognised in many significant ways by the Roman Catholic Church:

- In 1975, Pope Paul VI welcomed 10,000 charismatic Christians attending a conference on the Charismatic Movement.
- In 1980, Pope John Paul II appointed the charismatic priest Raniero Cantalamessa as a preacher to the Papal household (he remains in this role for Pope Francis).
- In 1993, the Vatican officially recognised the International Charismatic Renewal Services (ICCRS), an organisation that promotes Charismatic Renewal among Catholics across the world.
- In 2017, Pope Francis met a delegation of members of ICCRS and of the Catholic Fraternity and appointed four people to create a new single service for the Catholic Charismatic Renewal in the world.
- In June 2019, Pope Francis spoke at the inauguration of CHARIS (the Catholic Charismatic Renewal International Service).
- In November 2023, Pope Francis met with 4000 members of CHARIS to encourage them 'to appreciate the rich gifts that the Holy Spirit is bestowing in cultural, social and ecclesial contexts very different from their own'.

> **Key quote**
>
> The Catholic charismatics are undoubtedly the strongest and by far the most numerous in the Charismatic Renewal in older churches today.
>
> (AH Anderson)

However, there is still unease among many traditional Roman Catholics, who see the charismatic teaching linked to prosperity Gospel teaching (see page 114), and the emotional worship a dangerous replacement of the liturgy of the Mass. It also promotes an undue familiarity with the Divine, with a lack of silence, which is necessary to hear God's voice. They claim this leads to shallow, stunted spiritual growth and a dependency on feelings, rather than the word of God.

Today, some estimates place the number of Catholics involved in Charismatic Renewal between 10 and 15 per cent of all Catholics worldwide – this could mean that there are as many as 150 million charismatic Catholics. It is difficult to provide accurate numbers because the Charismatic Movement in the Catholic Church does not have a single founder and does not occur in just a single area.

T4 Religious practices that shape religious identity (2)

Toronto Airport Vineyard Church (TAV), renamed Catch the Fire Toronto in 2010, where the 'Toronto Blessing' takes place

Specification content

The Charismatic Movement: main beliefs; implications for Christian practice in the experience of believers and Christian communities; philosophical challenges to charismatic experience (verification and natural explanation)

Other expressions of the Charismatic Movement

In the 1980s and 90s, 'many who had been involved in non-charismatic Evangelical Churches began to join the Charismatic Movement. The fastest-growing Christian movement in Britain in the 1980s was the House Church movement, also known as *Restorationism* for its belief that, through it, God was restoring his Kingdom in the last days. The movement was composed of both Christians who had left established denominations (such as the Brethren, Baptists and those from classical Pentecostal denominations) as well as new Christians. They renounced denominations, had charismatic experiences, met in homes and also formed larger assemblies under those who saw themselves as apostles. There has been a strong eschatological emphasis in the movement, with adherents believing that they were living in the end times when demonic powers would be overcome. Dr Andrew Walker describes the attitudes of those in the Restoration movement: 'The legalism of clericalism, church order, standardised liturgies, denominational certainties and dogmatic doctrines were seen to be swept aside by the coming of the Spirit.'

There have also been a number of movements, festivals and leaders who have been influential in spreading the Charismatic Movement among evangelical Christians. This includes the Toronto Blessing, the Vineyard association of churches founded by John Wimber and the Spring Harvest ministries. Spring Harvest is a non-denominational gathering of Christians of all ages in a festival setting at several locations across the UK. It is known for its charismatic worship and inspiring speakers.

Main beliefs and implications for Christian practice in the experience of believers and Christian communities

Those in the Charismatic Movement believe that Christians outside of their movement should seek a much fuller experience of the Holy Spirit. This can happen in several ways:

1. **Speaking in tongues:** *Glossalia* (*glossa* means 'speaking'; *laleo* means 'language' or 'tongue') is the Greek term used to refer to the miracle of speaking in a language (either human or divine) unknown to the speaker, which the Holy Spirit makes possible. In Acts 2, it appears that the disciples were speaking in human languages that they did not know themselves – but that various members of the international Jewish community who had gathered in Jerusalem recognised. This is known as *xenolalia*: Speaking in a known language that the person has not consciously learned. This seems to be different from the experiences described in 1 Corinthians 12–14, where Paul speaks of a kind of heavenly language that no one can understand without the spiritual gift of interpretation. In 1 Corinthians 14, Paul makes it clear that the language is meant for a divine rather than a human audience; its primary function is in private prayer. It is permissible in public worship if there is someone who can interpret the message. Most theologians believe that these passages are about two different phenomena.

> **Key quote**
>
> God can actually give you a language which enables you to communicate.
>
> (N Gumbel)

> **Key quote**
>
> Many have found that tension, depression, fear and temptations which could not be gotten rid of in any other way are promptly banished when they pray in tongues.
>
> (E O'Connor)

2. **Prophecy:** We normally associate the term *prophecy* with someone foretelling the future. However, in the Bible, a prophet is someone who conveys the word of God in a direct way. Sometimes this has to do with foretelling future events, but more often it has to do with speaking a message that will bring about greater loyalty to God, increased morality or a more worshipful attitude. This is the same in the Charismatic Movement. A *prophecy* is a type of exhortation known for its directness – it claims to come directly from God. In the context of charismatic worship, someone may say, 'I the Lord say unto you …' or 'God wants us to know that …'. The message that follows inspires confidence and obedience among believers. In 1 Corinthians 14:29, Paul says that prophecies need to be tested. For this reason, Churches have criteria to discern true from false prophecy. These criteria usually include that the prophecy does not contradict the teaching of the Bible, is accepted by Church leaders and clearly recognises that Jesus is God.

3. **Healing:** Charismatic Christians believe that the Spirit of God can move to heal believers. They think this can happen through the prayers of elders (James 5:14), but also through those who have the spiritual gift of healing. Prayers for healing often involve the laying on of hands by several people. Sometimes there are healing prayers offered during the administration of the Eucharist. Healing is conceived of, not just in physical terms, but also as having psychological or emotional dimensions – the healing of relationships, buried memories or of conscience.

4. **Inspiration in worship:** Charismatic services are marked by a mood of joyful expectation as to what the Spirit of God might do. Worshippers generally feel free to move their bodies, swaying with the music, raising hands in the air, clapping and dancing. Usually, the style of music is contemporary, with a 'worship band'. Music is also used in informal ways in charismatic churches: times of prayer can be punctuated with spontaneous singing of familiar songs or choruses, there can be gentle singing during the Eucharist and songs can conclude with worshippers transitioning into speaking or singing in tongues.

Philosophical challenges to charismatic experience

One of the appeals of the Charismatic Movement is that it offers an experience of God to Christians who may have possessed only an intellectual relationship with Christianity. In contrast to mere 'knowledge about' God, charismatic believers claim to have direct 'experience of' God's presence, through a variety of experiences. That many people have become believers after observing and experiencing the 'gifts of the Spirit' seems to confirm this belief that God can be known through experience.

> **Key quote**
>
> The sense of knowing is never on its own a sufficient sign of knowledge.
> (P Donovan)

However, Christian Churches do not accept every claim of a charismatic experience as true. Churches have a set of criteria to judge experiences. These vary from denomination to denomination, but usually include whether it conforms to the teaching of the Bible and is accepted by Church leaders.

That Churches have tests for charismatic experiences suggests that, at least sometimes, they see these experiences as not coming from God at all, but perhaps from other spiritual forces or generated by a person's own ego. However, a much wider question can be asked: Is it possible that none of these experiences come from God?

The verification of charismatic experiences

At a surface level, charismatic experiences seem to provide proof. Instead of offering complicated arguments for the existence of God, which can be refuted by complicated counterarguments, the Charismatic Movement seems to point to empirical evidence: Tens of millions of people who have seemingly miraculous experiences with God resulting in healings, speaking in languages previously unknown to believers and offering inspired insights in the context of deeply inspirational worship. To what extent does this count as evidence for the existence of God?

Acts 2 seems to provide such a verifiable experience: The disciples spoke in languages they had not learned (*xenolalia*), and this was interpreted by making sense to those who knew those languages. However, though this is the kind of evidence that could lead to verification, this account comes to us in one ancient religious document without outside confirmation. The Charismatic Movement has sometimes included claims for xenolalia, but this has never been confirmed by any scientific studies.

Furthermore, most current accounts of speaking in tongues are of heavenly languages, known only to God. In this experience, the speaker uses what sounds like nonsense syllables. Often, this form of tongues is not interpreted but, when an interpretation is given, there is absolutely no way to verify a relationship between the interpretation and the language it was supposedly based on. So, though there are physical signs to work with (speech), there is no physical way to prove that these experiences come from God.

Claims for healing present another difficult case to verify. When someone experiences a dramatic improvement in their health after a prayer for healing, some Christians might be tempted to credit the prayer for the healing. However, there are several difficulties with doing so:

- Some diseases, such as multiple sclerosis, are known to have symptoms come and go erratically.
- There are reports of healing that, when followed up, find patients just as ill or worse off.
- Claims for miraculous cures of cancer through prayer have been made when cancer was merely a medical hypothesis rather than proven by biopsy. Thus, the person 'cured' may not have had cancer in the first place.

- Spontaneous remission of disease is rare, but does sometimes happen outside of prayers for healing.
- No scientifically conducted study has yet proven a correlation between prayers for healing and actual healing.

Sometimes those in the Charismatic Movement will make the claim that, if someone isn't physically healed, then there has still been an emotional or psychological kind of healing. In other words, a miracle has taken place whether or not there has been physical healing. The problem is that it sounds like a claim that can never be falsifiable and is therefore meaningless, according to the philosopher **Antony Flew**.

Perhaps the strongest scientific claim that has been made about religious experience is a correlation between religious participation and physical and emotional health. There have been many scientifically conducted studies that can demonstrate benefits to religious belonging. However, these studies aren't limited to charismatic forms of Christianity. Furthermore, their results can be questioned because only people already in fairly good health can attend church, and some religious groups forbid certain behaviours with known negative health effects.

However, even if this claim were to be proven true, this would not entail the existence of God. Thus, it could be true that people are emotionally strengthened after receiving prayers for healing or experiencing tongues or other charismatic gifts, but this fact alone does not verify the existence of God.

Natural explanations for charismatic experiences

Are there alternative explanations for charismatic experiences? One such explanation is to see these experiences as a cultural phenomenon. Cross-cultural studies have shown that traditions other than Christianity have experiences that may be the same or close to the Christian practice of tongues. In cultures where Christianity has been prevalent, speaking in tongues is viewed as a sign of the Holy Spirit, but in other cultures there would be a different understanding of the 'power' behind these experiences. Of course, this does not rule out the existence of a transcendent realm, but it might challenge claims that see the origin of these experiences in a specifically Christian way.

Psychology can also offer naturalistic explanations for charismatic gifts. We live in a world full of anxiety and neediness. This means that some of us may be especially open to experiences that ease our anxiety and meet our emotional needs – no matter how questionable the beliefs associated with those experiences. For example, Sigmund Freud viewed religion as an illusion based on our primal need for a father figure. People have religious experiences because they need to have them regardless of their ultimate truth-value. According to this view, those with charismatic experiences are 'weaker' human beings with more psychological and social needs than the average human being. So, could the absence of relational support in someone's life make them especially prone to a charismatic experience?

> **Key person**
>
> **Antony Flew (1923–2010):** an English philosopher who became a prominent defender of atheism but later declared himself a deist

Antony Flew

Justifying charismatic experiences

A number of arguments could be put forward to defend against the reduction of charismatic experiences to psychological or sociological factors:

1. **These people are not all psychologically deficient.** The sheer numbers of people who have charismatic experiences means that a broad cross-section of society is involved, of differing levels and types of intelligence. Claiming that all people who have these experiences are especially needy or psychologically deficient doesn't fit the diversity in the movement, and certainly has not been proven scientifically.

2. **You can say the brain is involved without saying it originates in the brain.** There is a difference between saying that the brain is providing the experience of God and the brain is 'mediating' an experience of God. Those with charismatic experiences could say that, though the brain plays a role in interpreting the experience, the experience is caused outside of their brain. That these experiences happen in different cultures could be seen as supporting John Hick's view that there is one divine reality that is 'refracted' by different cultures.

3. **These experiences are a part of a cumulative case for God.** While it is true that there is no scientifically proven evidence of the miraculous in the Charismatic Movement, isn't there some weight that tens of millions of people have unusual experiences that bring them joy, happiness, a positive social experience and renewed confidence to live their lives? The philosopher Richard Swinburne says that there is a compelling case for God's existence to be made from the 'cumulative evidence': The sheer numbers of people who believe in God; the sheer number of ways that God's existence can be argued intellectually; and the sheer number of people who have religious experiences. Taken separately, powerful arguments can be made against any one of these areas but, taken together, do they not have evidential force?

Summary

- *Charismatic* means 'gifts of grace'; special qualities listed in 1 Corinthians that Christians believe they receive from the Holy Spirit.
- The *Pentecostal Movement* of the early twentieth century emphasised a 'baptism in the Holy Spirit', and many regarded 'speaking in tongues' as evidence of this experience.
- The *Charismatic Movement* refers to the experience of the gifts of the Spirit in worship in Churches outside Pentecostal denominations.
- The *Renewal Movement* refers to those experiencing the gifts but remaining within their denomination.
- Natural explanations may explain charismatic experiences.
- However, to explain that the brain is providing the experience of God does not rule out the experience originating outside of the brain.
- The experiences could be viewed as part of a cumulative case for God.

AO1 Activity

a Draw a timeline of the key events of the Charismatic Renewal in the Roman Catholic Church from 1967 to the present day.

This helps you prioritise key, relevant material.

b Create a simple dialogue where a charismatic Christian describes an experience; their dialogue partner responds with a specific challenge; then the charismatic Christian defends the authenticity of their experience by directly responding to that challenge. Do this for tongues, prophecy and healing.

This helps you understand the main beliefs and challenges to charismatic experiences and provide relevant examples.

> **This section covers AO2 content and skills**

> **Specification content**
> Whether a natural explanation for charismatic experiences conflicts with the religious value of the experience

Issues for analysis and evaluation

Whether a natural explanation for charismatic experiences conflicts with the religious value of the experience

Possible line of argument	Critical analysis and evaluation
Members of the Charismatic Movement sees the source of their experiences as the Holy Spirit.	There are possible natural explanations to account for their experiences.
Charismatic Christians claim they speak in heavenly language that is unknown to the speaker. Although speaking in tongues occurs in other religions, the source could still be religious (such as Hick's view of one 'Ultimate Reality' that is refracted by different cultures).	There is no way to verify this experience, since the speaker is not aware of the meaning of what they are saying. Charismatic Christians tend to be conservative and evangelical so would reject the source as being some 'Ultimate Reality'.
The 'gift' of prophecy is a supernatural 'gift'. It is referred to as one of the gifts existing in the New Testament Church.	Many of the 'prophecies' are far too vague. Given that the prophecy must not contradict what the Bible already says, this suggests it is derived from what Christians already believe rather than from the supernatural.
The 'gift' of healing is a supernatural gift. Paul refers to it as existing in the New Testament Church.	Some diseases have erratic symptoms so that remission is mistaken for healing. Some 'healings' are claimed where there has been no medical diagnosis. If indeed there were frequent healings, then there would be proof for all to believe – but this is not the case.
The New Testament Church traces its origins to events at Pentecost in Acts 2.	Acts of the Apostles lacks independent attestation from other sources. Its historical reliability has been challenged.
The testimony of charismatic Christians shows that their experiences have religious value: they have found love, joy and peace.	Charismatic experiences can be explained by cultural, sociological and psychological factors.
Studies have shown a correlation between religious participation and high levels of physical and emotional health.	This does not confirm the source of these experiences. However, it may suggest such experiences have value outside of a religious interpretation.

Possible line of argument	Critical analysis and evaluation
Charismatic experiences have natural and religious explanations. God can use culture, society and psychology as avenues through which the Holy Spirit works.	The problem is trying to prove that there is 'something more'.
Charismatic experiences have value because of, not in spite of, their religious interpretation.	Non-believers can see value in charismatic experiences – though not a 'religious' value. If the Charismatic Movement provides this, then it can be affirmed as a source of values.

AO2 Activity

a   Select three lines of argument from the critical analysis and evaluation of whether a natural explanation for charismatic experiences conflicts with the religious value of the experience. Research and select three references from scholars, schools of thought or religious and philosophical texts that would support those arguments.

b   Using the strongest line of argument, try to identify three key quotations that could be used – they could be from scholars, religious texts or schools of thought.

Exam practice

Sample question
Evaluate the strengths and weaknesses of the Charismatic Movement.

Sample answer
The theologian Rudolph Otto warned of European Christianity losing its real power by denying the experiential dimension of the numinous that is found in the Bible. The strength of the Charismatic Movement is that it promotes this experiential dimension. It recognises that each Christian has been given a spiritual gift that can be shared with the 'body of Christ'. It also expects that the Holy Spirit will move in special ways in each and every worship service so that all the congregation members experience these gifts. The Charismatic Movement seems to reflect the New Testament situation of worship that Paul writes about in his letters. Certainly this active engagement of the laity in worship and the lack of formalism has led to dramatic increases in numbers of charismatics worldwide, as well as the growth of individual churches.

Another strength is that the Charismatic Movement focuses on the member of the Trinity that has received the least attention in Christian theology. The focus on this doctrine has mostly been to establish the relationship of Jesus to God. The Charismatic Movement has redressed this imbalance by drawing attention to the

This section covers AO2 content and skills

Specification content
The strengths and weaknesses of the Charismatic Movement

Tennis player / **Detective**

A clear account of a variety of areas of the strengths of the Charismatic Movement. The discussion gives support showing relevant knowledge of the New Testament.

Tennis player / **Detective**

There is identification and discussion of the weaknesses, again showing good relevant knowledge of the New Testament.

Tennis player / **Detective**

There is identification and discussion of well-illustrated further areas of weakness.

Philosopher / **Critical thinker** / **Judge**

Having clearly presented evidence for strengths and also weaknesses, the answer now considers their relative weightings. The opening two sentences identify a key issue for discussion, and the paragraph continues with some good reflective questioning. This is a good paragraph showing thoughtful judgement and a justified conclusion.

---

role the Holy Spirit plays in Christian living. The New Testament describes believers having special experience of 'baptism' in the Holy Spirit and, with it, special empowerment to live and act as Christians. Experiences of miraculous healing and conversions, as well as answers to prayer and inspiration, are seen as part of the Christian life rather than belonging to a past era. Indeed, if they do belong to a past era then we may call into question the genuineness of what is being experienced today. Certainly, many have questioned the authenticity of miraculous healings in the twenty-first century.

Many Christians also argue that there are some serious weaknesses with the Charismatic Movement. They reject the characterisation of non-charismatic church services that imply they are void of spiritual value and life. Surely, traditional worship can provide an active emotional experience. There is clear participation in services and many non-charismatic churches have good music as well as in-depth Bible teaching. If the Charismatic Movement has a judgemental attitude towards other forms of worship then this is a weakness, since the New Testament encourages Church unity.

Doubts are also raised as to whether the forms of expression of the Charismatic Movement are the same as described in the New Testament. In addition, there are a number of 'gifts' listed in the New Testament, such as service, giving, teaching and leadership, that are not so widely referred to in the movement. This suggests that some are more exalted at the expense of other 'gifts', which is what Paul criticised in some of his New Testament letters.

Perhaps one of the most serious weaknesses of the Charismatic Movement is the claim that many charismatics make that those who do not experience the spiritual gifts have not had a full Christian experience. It suggests that non-charismatic Christians are 'second-class' Christians, since those in the movement claim that they now have a spiritual experience that they had not had before.

Clearly, if charismatic experiences are not what they claim then that must surely outweigh any strengths. But if they are the same as the New Testament records, then clearly the Charismatic Movement is an essential part of Christian experience. Indeed, there are many manifestations of love that can be found in charismatic worship services. Also, charismatic experiences do not lead those Christians to leave their churches, but rather to stay and work for them to become stronger. There is much evidence of cross-fertilisation of denominational boundaries, and many denominations in which the Charismatic Movement flourishes are a part of the World Council of Churches. However, in more recent times there are signs that charismatic churches are less connected to the Ecumenical Movement and so it is not clear that the Charismatic Movement is a force that will unite Christians.

Over to you

Your task is to write a response, under timed conditions, to a question requiring an evaluation of naturalistic explanations for charismatic experiences. Do this exercise either as a group or independently.

1. Begin with a list of indicative arguments or lines of reasoning, as you may have done previously. It does not need to be in any particular order at first, although as you practise this you will see more order in your lists, in particular by way of links and connections between arguments.
2. Develop the list by using one or two relevant quotations. Now add some references to scholars and/or religious writings.
3. Then write out your plan, under timed conditions, remembering the principles of explaining with evidence and/or examples. Then ask someone else to read your answer to see whether they can help you improve it in any way.
4. Collaborative marking helps appreciate alternative perspectives and possibly things you may have missed. It also helps highlight the strengths of another answer that you can learn from. With this in mind, it is a good idea to swap and compare answers to improve your own.

When you have completed the task, refer to the band descriptors for A2 (WJEC) or A Level (Eduqas) and, in particular, look at the demands described in the higher band descriptors, which you should be aspiring towards. Ask yourself:

- Is my answer a confident critical analysis and perceptive evaluation of the issue?
- Is my answer a response that successfully identifies and thoroughly addresses the issues the question raises?
- Does my work show an excellent standard of coherence, clarity and organisation?
- Will my work, when developed, contain thorough, sustained and clear views that are supported by extensive, detailed reasoning and/or evidence?
- Have I used the views of scholars/schools of thought extensively, appropriately and in context?
- Does my answer convey a confident and perceptive analysis of the nature of any possible connections with other elements of my course?
- Is specialist language and vocabulary both thorough and accurate?

This section covers AO1 content and skills

Specification content

The basis (political, ethical and religious) of South American liberation theology with reference to Gustavo Gutiérrez and Leonardo Boff

Key person

Gustavo Gutiérrez (b. 1928): a Peruvian philosopher, Catholic theologian and Dominican priest, regarded as one of the founders of South American liberation theology, who viewed Jesus as a liberator from political as well as spiritual oppression

Gustavo Gutiérrez (right)

Key terms

socialism: any economic or political theory that advances collective ownership of production, distribution and exchange of goods

communism: an economic and political system that replaces private property and a free market with public ownership and communal control of goods

capitalism: an economic and political system where private owners control a country's trade and industry for profit

F: Religious identity through responses to poverty and injustice

What is liberation theology?

Liberation theology is a movement that developed in South America in the 1960s. Priest and theologian **Gustavo Gutiérrez** wrote a highly influential book *Teología de la Libercíon* ('A Theology of Liberation', 1971), where he says that theology should start with the fact of human suffering rather than with intellectual and rational reflection. When Christians take seriously the oppression around them, they will be moved to fight for justice.

Gutiérrez contrasts liberation theology with modern European theology. The context of European theology is a world 'come of age' with scientific and technical progress. European theology tries to make a case for God and spirituality in the face of atheism; it tends to be intellectual and rationalistic. The context of liberation theology is that of people dying. Liberation theology springs from the pastoral work of priests, observing suffering in the shadow of technical and scientific progress. It declares that salvation is a 'total gift' that must apply also to this suffering. The Boff brothers, Leonardo (b. 1938) and Clodovis (b. 1944), say that liberation theology is the result of 'faith confronted by oppression'. Gutiérrez says that it is about abolishing the status quo that has led to this suffering, and replacing it with a different set of relationships, which include different relationships to production and the economy.

> **Key quote**
>
> Struggle for liberation alongside the oppressed has provoked persecution and martyrdoms.
>
> **(L Boff and C Boff)**

> **Key quote**
>
> American foreign policy must begin to counterattack (and not just react against) liberation theology.
>
> **(Advisors to US President Ronald Reagan, 1982)**

Thus, liberation theology has a political edge, which has been a target of criticism by some Christians, including some in the Roman Catholic Church, as well as governments opposed to **socialism** and **communism**.

The political basis of South American liberation theology

Liberation theologians say that their theology has grown out of the brutal situation facing many people in South America; they note that South America has faced economic exploitation for 500 years at the hands of colonial powers such as Spain, Portugal and Britain. During this time, the Church was frequently associated with the ruling classes, the elite and the landowners.

In the 1950s, there was hope that economic development would result as South American countries became less dependent on imports and, instead, produced more of their own goods for national use and international export. This was a development model that hoped that by participating in the economies of richer, Western countries, all people would benefit. However, **capitalism** demanded that goods and labour be cheap; the result was that there was no development of a middle class in South America, and poverty continued for most people.

> **Key quote**
>
> Capitalism has a dismal record in Latin America, even the staunchest critics of Liberation Theology do not attempt to defend it.
>
> (A McGovern)

In the wake of the failure of this development model, liberation theologians have seen economic aid packages as simply maintaining the status quo and keeping workers in poverty and passivity. Sometimes the flaws in economic 'development' became obvious, such as the 1954 CIA overthrow of the government of Guatemala, which many see as being motivated only by the United States wanting to protect the US-owned United Fruit Company. All of this played into the socialist and communistic movements of Fidel Castro, Che Guevara and others.

In the 1970s, some priests, inspired by liberation theology, took part in the Sandinista revolution in Nicaragua. This influenced rebellions in Mexico and Colombia, where one of the main guerrilla factions was led by a de-frocked priest. There have been executions and assassinations of bishops, priests and Church workers across South America in this violent context.

Liberation theologians such as Gustavo Gutiérrez have not promoted violence, but have been sympathetic to socialist and communist movements and ideas – especially since capitalist development models have been perceived as helping only the rich. Many bishops in South America have been open to liberation theology, especially in Brazil. In 1968, South American bishops met in Medellín and issued a statement that urged Church action on behalf of people in poverty. They denounced 'institutionalised injustice' and 'institutionalised violence'. These bishops believed that they were acting in accord with the principles of Vatican II, of the Church becoming relevant to contemporary society and making a priority of helping people in poverty.

Capitalist development models have been perceived as helping only the rich

The religious basis of South American liberation theology

Liberation theologians are inspired by many passages in the Bible that reveal, for them, that God desires all people to be liberated from structures that cause oppression:

- In accounts of the Exodus (Exodus chapters 1–14), God hears the cries of his oppressed people and leads them from Egypt on a journey to a 'promised land', where they will be free to establish a society without misery and alienation.
- Many of the prophets harshly criticise social injustice as well as religious adherents who attend worship rituals but avoid the humane treatment of others; see, for example, Micah 6:8.
- Jesus' first sermon in Luke 4:18–19 is an announcement of liberation.

- In Matthew 25:31–46, Jesus announces that the future judgement of humanity will be based on whether those in most need were helped in practical ways.
- Acts 2:45 shows a free and liberating Church community that practises a form of communism: 'They sold property and possessions to give to anyone who had need'.
- 1 John 4:20–21 makes it clear that it is impossible to love God without loving human beings. Liberation theologians say that social justice must not be mechanical – it springs from an experience of loving those who are oppressed.

> **Key quotes**
>
> The Kingdom and social injustice are incompatible.
> (G Gutiérrez)
>
> And what does the Lord require of you? To act justly and to love mercy and to walk humbly with your God.
> (Micah 6:8)
>
> He has sent me to proclaim freedom for the prisoners ... to release the oppressed ...
> (Luke 4:18)

A Christology that liberates

Liberation theologians say that *Christology* (the study of the divine and human aspects of Jesus) has emphasised images of Jesus that place him outside of history and reinforce a passive attitude to human suffering. These images are the impotence of the suffering and dying Christ, the helpless baby Jesus in the arms of Mary and the king Jesus who stands outside of the world. Governments have used these images to support their policies. Contrary to these images, Jesus did not preach about his divine identity or the Church; he presented the Kingdom of God as an inclusive society committed to justice.

In fact, there are three aspects of Jesus' life that stand out:

1. His complex relationships with the zealots, a nationalistic Jewish group committed to violent revolt against the Romans
2. Critical attitudes towards the religious leaders, especially when they burdened people with excessive demands
3. Jesus' death at the hands of political authority.

These aspects reveal that there was a political dimension to Jesus' ministry. We know that there was at least one zealot among the 12 disciples. Though Jesus was not as fiercely nationalistic as the zealots (he accepted the **Samaritans**) and he did not advocate violence, they must have recognised him as having some shared aims, such as the liberation of humans from systems of suffering. Furthermore, Jesus' condemnation of excessive legalism in religion is reminiscent of the social justice of the prophets. Finally, Jesus was perceived as a threat to the Roman authorities – therefore, says Gutiérrez, we should not spiritualise Jesus.

It is true, however, that though Jesus fought for liberation, he did not organise his movement for the long-term application of love and justice in society. The reason for this, says Gutiérrez, is that he was affected by his culture's belief in **apocalypticism** – the sudden and dramatic coming of God to set up a new social order. Since we know that this did not happen,

> **Key terms**
>
> **Samaritans:** a Jewish group not considered orthodox by most Jews of Jesus' time
>
> **apocalypticism:** belief in the sudden and cataclysmic coming of God to rule the world in justice

we should apply Jesus' attitude and teaching to the task of building a less oppressive society. Furthermore, **eschatology** in the Bible is never merely presented as a future reality – it is always viewed as transforming our attitude and actions in the present.

Orthodoxy and orthopraxy

In traditional theology, students start with the Bible or with intellectual thought and seek to determine the truth (**orthodoxy** means 'right teaching') and apply that to life. From the twelfth century, says Gutiérrez, theology considered itself to be a science that presented faith in clear, rational categories. To become more religious, then, meant devotion to study or withdrawing to a monastery to contemplate biblical or theological themes. Both cases start with thought and reflection.

However, we must remember, says Gutiérrez, that for centuries the Church did nothing to help the world; it was involved in creating and reinforcing itself as 'Christendom'. What is needed now is to see the churches, rather than monasteries, academies and cathedrals, as the places where theology happens; it is in pastoral situations that the Church encounters human suffering. This encounter with suffering calls forth a response. Gutiérrez calls this *praxis*; the practice of faith applied to life. **Orthopraxis** must come before orthodoxy.

> **Key terms**
>
> **eschatology:** theological doctrine of the 'last things' including death, judgement, heaven and hell
> **orthodoxy:** authorised theory or doctrine
> **orthopraxis:** literally 'right practice'; correct ethical theory

"Key quotes"

The majority of the Church has covertly or openly been an accomplice of the external and internal dependency of our peoples.

(G Gutiérrez)

Before we can do theology we have to 'do' liberation.

(G Gutiérrez)

The ethical basis of South American liberation theology

The chief concern of liberation theologians is the suffering that poverty and economic exploitation cause. Gustavo Gutiérrez says that it is important to distinguish between three kinds of poverty:

1. **Material poverty:** This kind of poverty is consistently condemned in the Bible as being outside of God's plan for humanity. Poverty contradicts the heart of the message in Genesis that all humans have been created in the likeness of God and given the vocation of taking care of the Earth. It also transgresses the nature of Mosaic religion, which sees God guiding his people to a new and prosperous land.

2. **Spiritual poverty:** This is the inner attitude of being completely ready and available to do God's will. One of the problems in the Church is that sometimes material poverty has been confused with *spiritual*, meaning poor people are thought to be more spiritual than other people (that is, less distracted by material things, and closer to God). However, this interpretation simply serves the interests of the rich minority.

"Key quote"

The cries of the oppressed keep rising to heaven ... God today goes on hearing these cries ... Anyone who does not grasp this has not understood a word of liberation theology.

(G Gutiérrez)

3. **Voluntary poverty:** This is the act of the Church choosing to be poor so as to identify with poorer people. Especially relevant is the example of kenosis, the self-emptying of Christ involved in his incarnation: The second member of the Trinity chose to become 'poor' to relate God's love and justice to the human race. Gutiérrez also notes that something amazing happened to the Church in the Book of Acts when it chose to volunteer its goods to everyone's welfare: Everyone actually had enough (see Acts 4:34–35).

> **Key quote**
>
> There were no needy persons among them.
> (Acts 4:34)

The political, ethical and religious basis of South American liberation theology

Political, ethical and religious dimensions of liberation theology cannot be neatly distinguished from each other, since this theology, as we have seen, is more invested in practical concerns (*praxis*) than it is with establishing a firm rational basis for its expression.

This is clearly seen by the approach of liberation theologians to the subject of poverty, where they view the poverty in their countries as the logical outcome of cheap labour and goods required as a part of the capitalistic enterprise. Only a dramatic change in the system can lead to a better life for poorer people.

Gutiérrez notes how capitalist models of development exploit poorer people in contrast to God's will for society. He observes the creation of two classes in South America: those dominating and those who are dominated. Gutiérrez comes to the conclusion that those who are poor will not discover a better life through capitalism. The experience of capitalism in South America has had disastrous results on the environment, created a class system and generated a humanitarian crisis. Marxism can be valued for criticising capitalism and proposing that a more socialistic society has the potential to be more humane. However, liberation theologians feel that the answer to the poverty they encounter is to be found in some sort of socialism.

In the 1970s, liberation theologians began to use the phrase 'preferential option for the poor'. It does not mean that others are excluded from concern. It means that Christians must make the free choice (*option*) to prioritise the needs and concerns of those who are poor. This teaching represents both an ideal and a challenge to the Church since most people in the world live in poverty-stricken countries.

Base communities

Base ecclesial communities are small groups of about 15 to 20 families who meet together, without a priest, to support one another, read the Bible and apply their insights to their struggles against oppression. According to **Leonardo Boff**, these communities bring together many of the themes important to liberation theology: praxis; the struggle against oppression; and a Christian faith informed by belief in a god who wants justice on Earth.

Gutiérrez concludes poorer people do not benefit from capitalism. Liberation theologians feel the answer to poverty is in some sort of socialism

Key person

Leonardo Boff (b. 1938): a Brazilian theologian, philosopher and former Catholic priest; the Catholic Church saw his support of liberation theology as having 'politicised everything' and reproached his proximity to Marxism – in 1985, he had a year's silence imposed on him, and he was not allowed to teach during this time

> **Key quote**
>
> More important than awareness of the good is doing good.
>
> (L Boff)

Leonardo Boff

Base communities developed in the 1960s as a result of at least two factors:

1. **A movement in populist education across South America, which brought together small communities for literacy and skill-building:** Some governments viewed this with suspicion, as this education enabled poorer people to vote and to take a more active interest in their future.

2. **A shortage of priests, making necessary the lay leadership of Catholic Christian communities:** Pentecostal and Evangelical Churches were spreading across South America and absorbing Roman Catholic Christians, especially in areas where there were no priests.

Boff shares how South American bishops quickly supported the formation of small communities led by lay-leaders. The number of these communities exploded through the 1960s and '70s with 1–2 million people participating by the 1980s in Brazil alone.

Liberation theologians call these communities 'base ecclesial communities'; each word is significant:

- *Base* refers to the nature of these communities as basic 'building blocks' of the Church, a small group of Christians who are exactly the people that the Church says should be prioritised: people in poverty.

- The communities are *ecclesial* in that they have a link to the wider Church. When there is a priest available, they look to the Church for the celebration of the sacraments, such as baptisms, weddings and the Eucharist.

- Finally, they are *communities* because there is sharing, not only of faith, but of all of life; there is mutual support in the quest to build a better life. Sometimes they have functioned as treatment centres for malnutrition and disease.

For the most part, the Vatican has accepted these groups as valid expressions of the Church if they centre on the word of God; avoid a hypercritical attitude towards the larger Church; maintain a link with the wider Church; and remain aware of the benefits of their link to the Church of Rome.

Even though these communities have sprung from the situation of a lack of priests, Boff believes that they actually represent the most important building blocks of the Church. According to Boff, there are two models of the Church:

1. The Church as a grand institution with all its services and resources concentrated in cultural centres in affluent areas of society where it enjoys social power

2. The Church that is centred in the network of basic communities that are composed of the poor masses on the margins of power. In this second model, the institutional Church sees its main task as serving these communities.

Criticism of the Church: religious, ethical and political

Liberation theologians go beyond merely extolling base communities, but see these as highlighting deep problems with the institutional Church. Both Gutiérrez and Boff see the Church as having been relatively open and inclusive until the fourth century, when it became a part of the political establishment under Constantine.

At this point, **ecclesio-centrism** emerged: to be for or against Christ was now interpreted as being for or against the Church. This started a process where the focus of Church life was placed on hierarchy, sacred powers, dogmas, rites, traditions and clericalism. In this institutional Church, Christ was transformed from a suffering servant into an emperor – a priestly power on a throne. The Pope eventually became thought of as God on Earth, as the Church became a conservative force attempting to protect its power, rather than seeking to bring real solutions to human liberation.

> **Key term**
>
> **ecclesio-centrism:** literally 'centred on the Church'

> **Key quotes**
>
> The situation of oppression received the direct or indirect support of the Church's hierarchy, who since colonial times have legitimised the interests of the elites.
>
> (L Rivera-Rodriguez)
>
> The Church has no qualms of conscience in accepting authoritarian and even totalitarian regimes as long as its own rights are not attacked.
>
> (L Boff)

Boff says that the solution to these problems is found by reflecting on the doctrine of the Trinity. The Trinity has three distinct persons, which are in perfect communion with one another. They live in a perfect fellowship (*koinonia*), where each shares in the life of the others, yet retains their uniqueness. Humans, created in the likeness of God, are also mysteries. Therefore, they should also have a koinonia that is marked by both individual uniqueness and perfect sharing.

However, this is not the case: The institutional Church denies participation and equality to a majority of women and men who remain oppressed and permanently marginalised.

> **Specification content**
>
> Roman Catholic Church responses to South American liberation theology

Roman Catholic Church responses to South American liberation theology

Liberation theologians claim that their views are a logical extension of the God revealed in the Bible and in Church traditions, especially those articulated at Vatican II, which urged that theology be made relevant for daily life and that a concern for poorer people be made a priority in the Church.

In South America, two key conferences of bishops strongly supported liberation theology, in Medellín in 1968 and at Puebla in 1979. The bishops at Medellín said, 'Because all liberation is an anticipation of the complete redemption of Christ, the Church in South America is particularly in favour of all educational efforts which tend to free our people … A deafening cry pours from the throats of millions of men, asking their pastors for a liberation that reaches them from nowhere else.'

At the Vatican, liberation theology has had a mixed reception. In 1975, Pope John Paul II wrote a document on the theme of evangelisation (*Evangelii Nuntiandi*). In it, he wrote positively about base communities, but was critical that many opposed and criticised the Catholic Church and became charismatic communities.

However, he was concerned about the potential of liberation theology to reduce evangelism to social justice and to ignore the spiritual and **eschatological** dimensions of salvation. In fact, he warned that, without a spiritual change, new structures can themselves become inhumane.

Furthermore, he condemned the use of violence to bring about social change: 'We exhort you not to place your trust in violence and revolution: that is contrary to the Christian spirit, and it can also delay instead of advancing that social uplifting to which you lawfully aspire.'

Cardinal Joseph Ratzinger, later Pope Benedict XVI, who died in 2022, expanded on this criticism of liberation theology. In the document *Instruction on Liberation Theology* (1984), he recognised the validity of the term *liberation theology* since human freedom from oppression is one aspect of salvation. However, he made several criticisms:

> **Key term**
>
> **eschatological:** concerned with death, judgement and the final destiny of the soul and of humankind

1. **Liberation theology is deluded if it believes that a structural or economic change can bring about salvation.** This is because sin is a larger issue than the challenges economic structures cause. History teaches that those who fight for liberation, in turn, often become oppressors. This is why spiritual solutions are needed.

> **" Key quote**
>
> The management of forces in the soul determine the fate of the community more than the management of economic means
>
> (Cardinal Joseph Ratzinger – later Pope Benedict XVI)

2. **Marxism is not a science, but an atheistic ideology.** Getting involved in Marxism involves a Christian in 'terrible contradictions'. One of these is the loss of theology itself. The Marxist conception of *praxis* says that the truth can be known only by being involved in class struggle against the upper classes. This denies the transcendent nature of truth that is a part of Christian theology.

3. **Marxism makes everyone an enemy who is outside of the fight of the poor and the oppressed.** Furthermore, Marxism encourages violence to bring about change – this is not an ethic that reflects Christian principles.

4. **The Bible is given only a political interpretation.** For example, interpreting the Exodus as only a political liberation misses the importance of Israel's relationship with God. In fact, the Exodus does not end suffering. God provides continuing spiritual liberation and purification. For instance, the Psalms address human suffering from the perspective of spirituality not politics.

In an essay on the subject of eschatology, Ratzinger says that it is delusional to think that a historic golden age can be established by political means. In the Bible, the expectation for a perfect world is outside of history – it is brought about by God after the conclusion of history. One of the main reasons that utopian schemes fail is that they place their trust in a new institution and ignore the need to manage the forces in the human soul.

Pope Francis is the first pope from South America, and he has spoken out strongly about greed, materialism and the evils involved in capitalistic excesses. Interestingly, as a young priest and leader in the Jesuit order in Argentina, he was a harsh critic of liberation theology and sought to prevent

T4 Religious practices that shape religious identity (2)

priests from involvement in political organisations. Instead, he devoted himself to acts of charity and encouraged others to do the same. Later, as Assistant Bishop in Buenos Aires, it is reported that his views on priests involved in social justice softened. Since 2013, he has reconciled with several liberation theologians and celebrated mass with Gutiérrez. Perhaps the most symbolic action has been Pope Francis' use of Leonardo Boff's phrase in his *Laudato Si* encyclical in 2015, demanding we hear 'the cry of the Earth and the cry of the poor'. Though Pope Francis has never proclaimed himself as a liberation theologian, some of his statements appear to be influenced by a similar kind of social awareness.

> **Key quote**
>
> This system, with its relentless logic of profit, is escaping all human control. It is time to slow the locomotive down, an out-of-control locomotive hurtling towards the abyss. There is still time.
>
> (Pope Francis)

Summary

- *Liberation theology* is a Roman Catholic movement that views freedom from social oppression as a key area of Christian concern.
- Gustavo Gutiérrez saw capitalism as widening the gap between rich and poor.
- Liberation theologians argue that right practice (*orthopraxy*) must come before right thinking (*orthodoxy*).
- Leonardo Boff believes that base ecclesial communities are at the heart of the Church, and criticised the Vatican for judging people on the extent to which they support – or don't support – a powerful, centralised Church.
- South American bishops began using the phrase 'preferential option for the poor'. This is the notion that God considers poorer people to have the most urgent moral claim.
- The Roman Catholic Church has been critical of liberation theology, fearing it will embrace violence and atheism. Liberation is brought by God, not by political structures.
- Pope Francis has been a less harsh critic, since becoming Pope.

AO1 Activity

a This unit is full of new terms. To revise, instead of just drawing up a glossary of key terms, change them into a flowchart that links each to understanding of liberation theology.

This helps you develop an ability to present the terms' inter-relatedness, demonstrate extensive depth and/or breadth and ensure that you make accurate use of specialist language and vocabulary in context.

b What key biblical texts would you use if you were writing your own essay on the topic of the religious basis of liberation theology? Choose four to six texts and write a few sentences justifying how each of these texts support liberation theology.

This helps you provide relevant biblical texts and demonstrate extensive depth and/or breadth.

Issues for analysis and evaluation

Whether the political and ethical foundations of liberation theology are more important than any religious foundations

Possible line of argument	Critical analysis and evaluation
Gutiérrez and Boff follow the Marxist distinction between merely philosophising about the world and changing the world. In the face of suffering and oppression, theology should be about taking action to end suffering.	Both Gutiérrez and Boff are concerned that the Church develops religious approaches to oppression and poverty that reflect the attitude of Jesus Christ. Therefore they would argue that religion is more important than politics and ethics.
Many in the Catholic Church see liberation theology as an abdication of religion. The phrase implies an order: liberation first, theology (or religion) second.	The phrase reflects a decision to put the task of rationalising and reflection in second place, since first Christians should be moved by a living faith in the face of suffering.
Liberation theologians speak of orthopraxy preceding orthodoxy, which implies that they serve a political and ethical ideology.	Both Gutiérrez and Boff would argue they are driven by faith rather than politics. Liberation theology is about faith confronted by oppression. Christians should not divorce their faith from the real world.
Although liberation theologians use the Bible, the Roman Catholic Church has accused them of politicising passages such as Exodus.	Liberation theologians use passages from across the entire Bible, including the prophets who fought against social injustice. Jesus' first sermon (Luke 4:16–30) was on the theme of liberation.
The Vatican has been concerned about the Marxist tone of the proposals for liberation. Marxism is associated with atheism.	Liberation theologians argue that socialism holds more promise than capitalism. However, that is not at the expense of the religious dimension.
The Vatican points out that Marxism is a form of utopianism that promises a perfect society in history – which is contrary to biblical teaching. It also involves violence to achieve a just society. Both are outside of God's will.	Liberation theologians challenge this understanding. They distance themselves from violence and do not support the development of Marxism of the form that leads to atheism and loss of human freedom. They simply adopt what is true in Marxism into a broader Christian vision of reality.
Social theories that liberation theologians put forward 'dance' around Marxist ideas.	'Religion' can be defined as 'faith'; a person's heartfelt response to the situation around them. In this sense, liberation theologians seek to apply their Christian faith to the situations they face and so do not put religion in second place.

> **This section covers AO2 content and skills**

> **Specification content**
> Whether the political and ethical foundations of liberation theology are more important than any religious foundations

> **AO2 Activity**
> a Select three lines of argument from the critical analysis and evaluation of whether the political and ethical foundations of liberation theology are more important than any religious foundations. Find three references from scholars, schools of thought or religious and philosophical texts that would support those arguments.
> b Using the strongest line of argument, try to identify three key quotations that could be used – they could be from scholars, religious texts or schools of thought.

This section covers AO2 content and skills

Specification content
The extent to which liberation theology offered a cultural challenge to the Roman Catholic Church

---

Exam practice

Sample question
Evaluate the extent to which liberation theology offered a cultural challenge to the Roman Catholic Church.

Sample answer

Without doubt, liberation theology has influenced the Roman Catholic Church in South America. It has criticised the institutional Church for often placing the institution, rather than the people, at the centre. Similarly, it is accused of regarding the ordained clergy as more important than the laity and of promoting an overly spiritualised theology rather than offering social solutions in the face of suffering. In the late 1960s, the bishops of South America adopted much of the language of 'liberation' theologians, such as the phrase 'preferential option for the poor'. Two key South American conferences of bishops in Medellín (1968) and at Puebla (1979) strongly supported liberation theology. The bishops stated that 'all liberation is an anticipation of the complete redemption of Christ ... the Church in South America is particularly in favour of all educational efforts which tend to free our people'.

[News reporter / Detective] A good introduction setting out the development of liberation theology in South America.

But what about the Roman Catholic Church outside of South America? It seems the Vatican was not so enthusiastic and it received a mixed reception. Pope John Paul II was concerned of the potential of liberation theology to reduce evangelism to social justice and to ignore the spiritual salvation. He argued that the emphasis should be on spiritual change not political change. This view was furthered by Joseph Ratzinger, later Pope Benedict XVI. Again, he argued that structural or economic change could not bring about salvation. Liberation theologians were seen to support Marxism, and Ratzinger saw Marxism as an atheistic ideology. He also thought that Marxism encourages violence to bring about change. The Vatican viewed placing trust in a new institution ignored the need to manage the forces in the human soul. The Vatican silenced Leonardo Boff in 1958 for a year and formally investigated Gustavo Gutiérrez many times. The Church saw the language of liberation theology more as a threat than an opportunity.

[Tennis player / Detective] A good, knowledgeable summary of the reaction of the Vatican to liberation theology, showing how it has opposed it and seen it as a threat. The Vatican has therefore curtailed the influence of liberation theology.

In 2013, Pope Francis became the first pope from South America. As a young Argentinian priest, he was known for discouraging priests from political action and association with liberation theology. Today, he would not want to call himself a liberation theologian, yet he recently approved Gustavo Gutiérrez's visit to the Vatican. Pope Francis has also written critically against the evils of capitalism as it contributes to economic oppression, which is a major theme of liberation theology. It is possible that Pope Francis has brought about a change in the Vatican, which is now more willing to embrace aspects of liberation theology.

[Tennis player / Detective] The answer acknowledges that with Pope Francis the reaction towards liberation theology may be more positive.

One area that is meeting the needs of the Roman Catholic Church is liberation's idea of base ecclesial communities. These gatherings of 15 to 20 families meet without priests to engage with the Bible, singing, prayers and other spiritual activities outside of the sacraments. Boff argues that there is a role for the institutional Church in providing identity and continuity for base communities. However, there is a guarded acceptance of them by the Vatican. On the one hand, the Vatican recognises these communities and affirms them as a valid expression of the Church. However, the Church is also suspicious of such groups as they often appear critical of the institutional Church and have moved from a spiritual focus to an ideology. For the Vatican, evangelism and salvation is about preaching, teaching and administering the sacraments. For liberation theologians, it is about political action for social justice. However, with Pope Francis at the Vatican, it may be that the two positions can co-exist and the Roman Catholic Church moves towards a cultural change offered by liberation theology. At the very least, it seems that liberation theology is far from over.

Critical thinker — **Philosopher** — **Judge**

This final section draws attention to an aspect of liberation theology that shows evidence of some acceptance by the Roman Catholic Church. However, the conclusion is guarded and identifies the key disagreement between the Roman Catholic Church and liberation theology. A good, thoughtful conclusion that is consistent with the arguments given.

Over to you

It is impossible to cover all essays in the time allowed by the course; however, it is a good exercise to develop detailed plans that you can use under timed conditions. As a final exercise:

1. Create some ideal plans by using what we have done so far in the Theme 4 'Over to you' sections.
2. This time, stop at the planning stage and exchange plans with a study partner.
3. Check each other's plans carefully. Talk through any omissions or extras that could be included, not forgetting to challenge any irrelevant material.
4. Remember: Collaborative learning is very important for revision. It not only helps to consolidate understanding of the work and appreciation of the skills involved, but it is also motivational and a means of providing more confidence in your learning. Although you sit the examination alone, revising as a pair or small group is invaluable.

When you have completed the task, refer to the band descriptors for A2 (WJEC) or A Level (Eduqas) and, in particular, look at the demands described in the higher band descriptors, which you should be aspiring towards. Ask yourself:

- Is my answer a confident critical analysis and perceptive evaluation of the issue?
- Is my answer a response that successfully identifies and thoroughly addresses the issues the question raises?
- Does my work show an excellent standard of coherence, clarity and organisation?
- Will my work, when developed, contain thorough, sustained and clear views that are supported by extensive, detailed reasoning and/or evidence?
- Have I used the views of scholars/schools of thought extensively, appropriately and in context?
- Does my answer convey a confident and perceptive analysis of the nature of any possible connections with other elements of my course?
- Is specialist language and vocabulary both thorough and accurate?

Glossary

absolution: declaration by a priest that a person's sins have been forgiven

Advent: a season before Christmas when Christians anticipate both the nativity of Christ and his Second Coming

androcentrism: focused or centred on men

Anglican: the Church of England or any Church in communion with it

apocalypticism: belief in the sudden and cataclysmic coming of God to rule the world in justice

Apocrypha: the extra books in the Catholic Old Testament

apocryphal Gospels: writings about Jesus not accepted by the Church; some exist as complete documents, others as fragments or as quotations in early Christian writings

ascetic: someone who lives a sparse and disciplined lifestyle

asceticism: discipline or training; avoiding various desires to attain a spiritual goal or ideal

Atonement: to make 'at one' or reconcile

base communities: small, self-governing religious groups

Bibliolatry: worship of the Bible instead of God

birth narrative: the accounts of Jesus' birth in the Gospels of Matthew and Luke

capitalism: an economic and political system where private owners control a country's trade and industry for profit

catholicity: having a universal doctrine

charismatic churches: churches that may differ from their denomination by emphasising religious experiences and miracles of healing

Christolatry: worship according to patriarchal categories rather than to a God who is beyond sex and gender

circumcision: the removal of the foreskin from the penis

communism: an economic and political system that replaces private property and a free market with public ownership and communal control of goods

consecrate: set apart as holy; make or declare sacred for religious use

covenant: an agreement between two or more parties based on obedience and involving promises

covenantal nomism: God's election of Jewish people as a chosen nation provided they obeyed his commandments

critical realism: the idea that there are real objects beyond ourselves, but that we know these objects through our own experiences; therefore, we need to be critical about the objectivity of our point of view

cynic: a person who has a bleak outlook about others, always imagining that people are ruled by their worst instincts

demythologise: reinterpreting what are considered to be mythological elements of the Bible

Desert Fathers: early Christian hermits who lived an ascetic life in the Egyptian desert

diaconate: an official body of deacons

ecclesio-centrism: literally 'centred on the Church'

ecofeminist: someone who is interested in both the environment and women's rights

enlightenment: a European intellectual movement emphasising reason as the basis of knowledge over religious revelation and superstition

eschatological: concerned with death, judgement and the final destiny of the soul and of humankind

eschatology: the study of end things, including the soul, death, resurrection, the final judgement, immortality, heaven and hell

Eucharist: one of the names referring to the service commemorating the Last Supper

evangelise: share the Christian message in the hope of conversion

fundamentalism: the movement from the late nineteenth century dedicated to defending key biblical doctrines, later becoming associated with a literal approach to the Bible

Gnosticism: a movement that taught that we are trapped in an evil material world; we must find special knowledge to be redeemed

God hypothesis: Richard Dawkins' phrase to describe the claim that there is an interventionist God in the universe; this should be treated like any other scientific hypothesis

Gospel of Thomas: a book of 114 sayings of Jesus in the fourth century CE, discovered in Egypt in 1945

Gospels: The record of Jesus' life and teaching in the first four books of the New Testament

Great Commission: Jesus' instruction to make disciples worldwide

historicity: historical accuracy

incarnation: God in human form in the person of Jesus

liberalism: in politics, focus on the protection and freedom of the individual

liturgical: the public ritual of formal worship prescribed by a Church body

Magi: Latin for 'wise men', originally the word meant 'an oriental priest, learned in astrology' and probably from Persia (Iran)

Manichaeism: a movement that viewed the world as a conflict between good and evil, with the soul's release found through asceticism

Marxism: the theories of Marx and Engels that developed into communism and aimed for a classless society

Messiah (literally 'anointed one'): a figure who is expected to unite Jewish people and save them from their oppressors, ushering in an era of peace

metaphor: something that represents or is a symbol for something else

Montanism: a movement that believed in asceticism and the imminent end of the world

myth: a story containing divine beings or supernatural themes to explain natural events or social and political concerns

non-overlapping magisteria (NOMA): the view Stephen Jay Gould advocates, that science and religion are two different areas of inquiry

objective: factual, not based on personal belief

orthodoxy: authorised theory or doctrine

orthopraxis: literally 'right practice'; correct ethical theory

Passion: sufferings

Pentecostal denominations: independent churches that emphasise the gifts of the Spirit

polemic: an aggressive verbal or written attack

prosperity Gospel: the teaching that faith and giving to the Church will bring health and wealth

Protestant: a member of the parts of the Christian Church that separated from the Roman Catholic Church during the sixteenth century

Quakers: members of a movement that believes in direct apprehension of God without the need for clergy, creeds or other ecclesiastical forms

realised eschatology: the notion that Christians can experience in the present a quality of life they expect after death

real presence: the actual presence of Christ's body and blood in the Eucharistic elements

redaction criticism: a theory that regards the author of a text as editor of source material that they adapted to suit their own theological interests

Romanticism: an intellectual and artistic movement, critical of the enlightenment; instead focused on emotion and imagination

sacrament: an outward and visible sign of an inward and invisible grace

Samaritans: a Jewish group not considered orthodox by most Jews of Jesus' time

secular: not connected to religion

secularisation thesis: the belief that as societies modernise, religion will decline

secularism: the belief that secularisation is a benefit to society

self-flagellation: striking oneself with a whip, especially as a form of religious discipline

Septuagint: the Greek translation of the Hebrew Bible in the third to second centuries BC; also referred to as the LXX in reference to a legend of 70 Jewish scholars translating the Torah

Shakers: members of an American religious sect dedicated to celibacy and belief in the imminent return of God

socialism: any economic or political theory that advances collective ownership of production, distribution and exchange of goods

Stations of the Cross: pictures or carvings representing 14 key moments in Jesus' trial, crucifixion and burial

Ultimate Reality: John Hick's term to describe the object of religious belief for the world's religions

Vatican II: the council of Roman Catholic leaders that met in 1962–65 to consider the relationship between the Church and the modern world

vernal equinox: the time at which the Sun crosses the plane of the equator, making day and night of equal length

Index

Abelard, Peter 83
Abraham 28
absolution 88
Acts 17, 27, 31, 38, 47–56, 95–6, 112, 165, 181, 222
Adam 19, 28, 81, 130
adoptionism 73
Advent 193–5
Akhazemea, Daniel 123
Amos 113
Anderson, A.H. 219
androcentrism 130
angels 8–9
Anglican Church 197
Anglican–Roman Catholic International Commission (ARCIC) 210–11
anointing of the sick 97
anonymous Christianity 167–8
Anselm 82
anthropic principle 155–6
apocalypse 47, 51
apocalypticism 47–52, 61, 232
Apocrypha 27, 37
apocryphal Gospels 60–1, 64–5
apostles 39, 47, 50, 95
Aquinas, Thomas 130
arianism 73
Arnett, W.M. 51
Arweck, Elisabeth 149
asceticism 61, 113–14, 118–19
Ash Wednesday 197
Ashers Baking Company 146
Athanasius Creed 73
atheism 143, 157, 160, 163–4
Athenagorus 40
Atonement theories 81–7
Augustine 28, 40, 82, 178–80, 196
Aulen, Gustaf 81
Babylon 29
baptism 90, 97, 178–84, 197
Baptist Church 97
Barclay, W. 194

Barnett, P. 115
Barth, Karl 41, 76–7, 181–2
base communities 133, 234–5
Bauckham, R. 38
Beckford, James A. 149
Bennett, Dennis 218
bereavement 31
Bible 27–9
    canon 36–9
    and mythology 51–2
    New Testament 27–8, 29, 37–8, 47–51, 57–60, 74, 104, 165
    Old Testament 10, 21, 27–9, 31, 36–9, 68, 74, 103
    as source of authority 36
    teachings 29–33
    as word of God 40–4
Bibliolatry 134
birth narratives 8–14
Black Majority Churches (BMCs) 123
Blomberg, Craig L. 110, 115
body of Christ 97
Boff, Leonardo 230, 234–6
Bonhoeffer, Dietrich 159
breaking of bread 95–6
British Humanist Association (BHA) 145
Buddha 171
Bullivant, S. 73
Bultmann, Rudolf 14, 20, 50–3
Caesar Augustus 8–9
Calvin, John 42–3
canon 36–9
capitalism 230, 234
Cartledge, M. 217
Catechism of the Catholic Church 40, 90
catholicity 136
census England and Wales 124, 142–4
Chalcedonian creed 172
charismatic movement 114, 122–3, 215–28
Christingle 194
Christmas 193–5, 201–2

Christolatry 134
Christus Victor theory 81, 83, 85
Church
    as community of believers 97–8
    contemporary 100
    decline of 142–4
    role of 97–8, 101–2
    see also denominations by name
circumcision 178–9
Cocksworth, C. 217
Codex Vaticanus 39
Collins, R.F. 37
Colossians 49, 74, 81, 178–9
communism 230
confirmation 97
Congregationalists 97
conscience 105
consubstantiation 187–8
Copernican revolution 168–9
Copson, A. 143
Corinthians 19–20, 21, 23, 32, 41, 74, 90, 105, 113, 115, 186, 203, 215
Cornerstone Fostering Service 147
Council of Carthage 39, 178
Council of Chalcedon 12
Council of Hippo 39
Council of Nicea 73, 74–5
Council of Trent 89–90, 187
covenant 36, 57
covenantal nomism 90
Craig, William 84
critical realism 57–63
Crossan, John Dominic 59–62
Crosskeys Full Gospel Mission 123
crucifixion 20–1, 29, 68–9
Cynicism 62
Dalai Lama 144
Daly, Mary 130, 133–5
Daniel 21
David 28
Davie, G. 144
Dawkins, Richard 154–61

degree Christology 172
demythologising 20, 51
Desert Fathers 114
design arguments 155, 159–60
Deuteronomy 73, 74, 103, 113, 165
diaconate 136
Diogenes of Sinope 112
diversity, religious 165–75
Dodd, C.H. 47–8, 50, 95, 98
Donovan, P 222
Easter 196–202
Eastern Orthodox Church 75–6, 97, 195, 197–9, 200
Ecclesiastes 30, 38
ecclesio-centrism 236
Ecklund, Elaine 157
ecofeminism 67
Ecumenical Movement 203–12
Edinburgh Missionary Conference 204–5
Einstein, Albert 157
Elijah 29
Enlightenment 41, 57, 76
enlightenment worldview 57–8
Ephesians 88, 105
epicycles 168–9
Equality and Human Rights Commission (EHRC) 146
eschatology 49–51, 58, 233, 237
Eucharist 97, 186–91, 194, 198
evangelism 114, 124–5, 220
Eve 28, 81, 130
evil 28–30, 70, 81, 112, 114, 131, 160
exclusivism 165–75
exile 29
Exodus (Book of) 29, 104
exodus (Israelites) 28, 237
Ezekiel 21
faith 30, 88–94
Faith and Order Movement 205
faith schools 144–5
Fall, the 28, 130
fasting 194, 197–8
fellowship 97
feminist theology 130–41
    ecofeminism 67
filioque controversy 74–6
First Council of Nicea 11

Flew, Antony 157, 223
Floyd, George 123
forgiveness 106
Franklin, Benjamin 103
fundamentalism 41
Galatians 82, 88
gender identity 146
Genesis 17, 28, 42–3, 74, 113, 178–9
genocide 134
Gentiles 11, 29, 96
Gnosticism 52, 131
God
    as designer 155
    as Father 66–7, 73–4
    impassibility/immutability 68–70
    judgement 29
    loving 104
    as Mother 67, 71–2
    omniscience 12
    revelation 28, 36, 41, 104
    transcendence 42
God hypothesis 155–6
Good Friday 197
Good Samaritan 30, 103–4, 121
good works 89–90, 92, 97–8
Gospel of Thomas 60–1
Gospels 27, 37–8, 39, 41, 58, 121, 198
    apocryphal 60, 64–5
    John 11, 17–19, 30, 66, 74–5, 90, 104, 165, 173, 203
    Luke 8–14, 20, 30, 38, 47–9, 112, 179, 232
    Mark 12, 29, 50, 74, 83, 110–11, 113, 178
    Matthew 8–14, 22, 29, 30–1, 50, 61, 74, 81, 98, 106, 111, 113, 166, 179
Gould, Stephen Jay 158
Great Commission 179
Great Schism 75–6
Gumbel, N. 221
Gutiérrez, Gustavo 231–3
Harmon, S. 205, 206
healing 61, 221–3
Hebrews (Book of) 82
Hegarty, John 146
Herod 8–10
Hick, John 168–72
Holbein, Hans 43

Hollenweger, W. 123
Holy Communion *see* Eucharist
Holy Spirit 8, 17, 29, 30, 40, 48, 66, 74–7, 96, 220
Holy Week 198
Homer 22
homosexuality 147
House Church movement 220
humanism 143, 145
humanitarian crises 121
Huxley, T. 32
hypostatic union 12
idolatry 110, 130
immigration 121–3
immutability 68
impassibility 68–70
incarnation 11–14, 81
inclusivism 165–75
indulgences 89
inspiration 40–6, 221
International Charismatic Renewal Services (ICCRS) 219
International Missionary Conference 205
Irenaeus 82
Isaiah 10, 21, 66, 74, 82, 113
Israel 28
Israelites 28, 105, 121
James 50, 89
Jeremiah 36
Jerusalem 28
Jesus Christ
    birth narratives 8–14
    crucifixion 20–1, 29, 68–9
    healing 61
    incarnation 11–14, 81
    as Messiah 17, 21–2, 29, 58–9
    as peasant 59–60
    as prophet 58
    resurrection 17–26, 29
    as Saviour 29
    as substitute 82–5
John the Baptist 8, 29, 113, 178, 181
John's Gospel 11, 17–19, 30, 66, 74–5, 90, 104, 165, 173, 203
Joseph 8–11
Josephus 9, 38
Joshua 165

Index

243

Judah 28–9
Judaism 27, 29, 36
   apocalypticism 47
   beliefs about resurrection 21–2
   Hebrew Bible (Tanakh) 36–7, 38
Judas the Galilean 59
justification 88–94
kenosis 12
kenotic theology 12–13
kerygma 47–54
Kethuvim 36, 38
Kilby, K. 167
Kings (Book of) 111
Last Supper 36, 186
Lazarus 20
Lent 196–7
Leviticus 103, 113, 121
Lewis, C.S. 66, 104
liberalism 132
liberation theology 230–41
Life and Work Movement 205
Liturgy of St Basil the Great 195
Lord's Prayer 146
Lord's Supper 95
Luke 8–14, 20, 30, 38, 47–9, 112, 179, 232
Luther, Martin 39, 88–90, 188
Maccabees 111
magi 8
Magina, J. 207
Malachi 29
Manichaeism 114
Marcion 39
marginalisation 131
Mark 12, 29, 50, 74, 83, 110–11, 113, 178
marriage 97, 146–7
Marxism 132, 237
Mary
   birth narratives 8–11
   virgin birth 10, 14, 130
Mary Magdalene 17, 24, 136
Mass *see* Eucharist
Matins 195
Matthew 8–14, 22, 29, 30–1, 50, 61, 74, 81, 98, 106, 111, 113, 166, 179
Maundy Thursday 197
McFague, Sallie 67–8

McGovern, A. 231
McGrath, Alister 89, 154, 157–61, 216
McGrath, Joanna Collicutt 154, 157–61
meaning 29–30
Medawar, Peter 158
memes 156
memorialism 188
Messiah 17, 21–2, 29, 36, 58–9
metaphor 67
Micah 232
migration 121–3, 127–8
mission 97
missionaries 124–6, 204–5
Moltmann, Jürgen 68–9
Montanism 114, 131
moral principles 103–8
moral-example theory 83, 85
Mosaic Law 31, 90
Moses 28, 29, 42
Mothering Sunday 197
multiverse theory 156
Muratorian Canon 39
myths 20, 24, 50–3
nativity 194
natural selection 155
neighbour, love of 103–4, 107
neo-Pentecostalism 217
Nevi'im 36
New Testament 27–8, 29, 37–8, 47–51, 57–60, 74, 104, 165
   see also Books by name; Gospels
Nicene Creed 73
non-overlapping magisteria (NOMA) 158
O'Connor, E. 221
Ofsted 147
Old Testament 10, 21, 27–9, 31, 36–9, 68, 74, 103
   see also Books by name
omniscience 12
ordination 97
   of women 135–7
Origen 81, 113
original sin 28
Orthodox Patriarch of Constantinople 205
outreach 97
Ozman, Agnes N. 216

Paley, William 154
Palm Sunday 197
Parham, Charles Fox 216
Paschal candle 197
Passion of Christ 197
Paul 12, 19–20, 23, 29, 31, 38–40, 49, 74, 90–1, 113, 136, 186, 203
penance 97
Pentecost 17, 29, 96
Pentecostal denominations 114, 122–3, 216
Pentecostalism 216
Peter 18, 40, 106
Pharisees 21–2, 31
Philemon 49
Philippians 12
Plato 22
Plessis, David 218
pluralism 165, 170–7
Pope Benedict VIII 75
Pope Benedict XVI 209, 237
Pope Francis 76, 136–7, 144, 147, 194, 196, 219, 237–8
Pope John Paul II 219, 236–7
Pope John XXIII 209
Pope Paul VI 187, 219
Pope Pius XI 209
poverty 31, 233–4
prayer 96
Presbyterians 97
Promised Land 28
prophecy 221
prophetic tradition 131–2
prosperity Gospel 114–15
Protestantism 27, 37, 82, 89–90, 97
Proverbs 38, 113
Psalms 21, 28, 30–1, 34, 38, 113
Ptolemy 168–9
purpose 30
'Q' 60–1
Quakers 131
Quirinius 9
racism 123
Rahner, Karl 166–8, 187
rape 134
Ratzinger, Joseph 237
realised eschatology 50
redaction criticism 10–11, 15–16

Redeemed Christian Church of God 123
Reformation 42, 89
Regan, Ronald 29
Reimarus, Herman Samuel 47
religious experience 171, 222–4
religious pluralism 165, 170–7
Rembrant 121
Restorationism 220
resurrection 17–26, 29
   as myth 20–1, 24
revelation 28, 36, 41, 104
Revelation (Book of) 27, 32, 38, 82
reverse mission 124–6
Rivera-Rodriguez, L. 236
Roberts, M. 8
Roberts, Oral 114, 218
Roman Catholic Church 75–6, 97
Romans (Book of) 31, 66, 88, 90, 110
romanticism 132
Rousseau, Jean-Jacques 105
Ruether, Rosemary Radford 130–3
Rumi, Jalaluldin 170
Russian–Ukrainian war (2022–) 121
sabellianism 73
sacraments 97, 178, 180, 197
Sadducees 21–2, 29
Samaritans 232
same-sex marriage 146–7
Samuel 105
Sanders, E.P. 90–1
Satan 81
Saul 28
Schillebeeckx, Edward 187
schools 144–5
Schweitzer, Albert 50
science, and religion 154–62

scientism 161
Sea of Galilee 18
secularisation 125, 142–52
secularism 124–5, 148
self-flagellation 114
Septuagint 11, 37
Sermon on the Mount 31, 106, 111
Seymour, William James 216
Shakers 131
sick, anointing 97
Simeon ben Kosiba 59
sin 28, 31, 81, 88, 130
Sirach 111
sisterhood 135
Smalley, S. 11
socialism 230
sola fide 88
Solomon 28, 111
Song of Solomon 38
soul 22–3
South America, liberation theology 230–8
speaking in tongues 220
Spurgeon, C. 181
St Peter's Basilica 166
Stations of the Cross 196–7
stewardship 112–13
Stott, John 83
Street Pastor movement 148–9
substitution theory 82–5
suffering 32, 82
   of God 68–70
supernatural events
   birth narratives 9–10
   as myths 20
Swinburne, Richard 160
Tanakh 36–7, 38

temptation 31
Ten Commandments 28, 31, 111
Tertullian 73
Tetzel, Johann 89
Thomas, Gospel of 60–1
Timothy 40, 42, 49, 81, 112, 165
tithing 97
Torah 36, 38
transcendence 42
transfinalisation 187
transubstantiation 186–7
Trinity 73–80, 236
Tyndale, William 81
Ultimate Reality 169, 172
unification 203
universalism 173
Vallely, P. 210
Vatican II 166, 209
vernal equinox 196
Vespers 195, 198
virgin birth 10, 14
Walker, Andrew 220
wealth 110–15
Wesley, John 95, 113
Williams, R.D. 40
Wimber, John 220
women
   feminist theology 130–41
   ordination 135–7
Woodhead, L. 142, 148
Word-Faith movement 114
World Council of Churches 205–14
World Missionary Conference 203
worship 97
Wright, Nicholas T. 21–2, 57–8, 84
Yancey, P. 98
Zwingli, Huldrych 180

Photo credits

Photos reproduced by permission of: **p.9** © Lemélangedesgenres/stock.adobe.com; **p.18** Google Arts & Culture using dezoomify-rs; **p.20** © GRANGER - Historical Picture Archive/Alamy Stock Photo; **p.21** © Trinity Mirror/Mirrorpix/Alamy Stock Photo; **p.27** © Radekprocyk/stock.adobe.com; **p.29** © Swellphotography/stock.adobe.com; **p.31** © Gift of H. F. Ahmanson and Company, in memory of Howard F. Ahmanson; **p.36** © Ungvar/stock.adobe.com; **p.39** © Zev Radovan/BibleLandPictures/Alamy Stock Photo; **p.43** © The Picture Art Collection/Alamy Stock Photo; **p.47** © Popperfoto/Getty Images; **p.59** © Lynceus/Flickr; **p.60** © Art Collection 2/Alamy Stock Photo; **p.67** Vanderbilt University; p.69 © Leonardo Cendamo/Getty Images; **p.75** © Album/Alamy Stock Photo; **p.76** © GRANGER - Historical Picture Archive/Alamy Stock Photo; **p.82** © Renáta Sedmáková/stock.adobe.com; **p.88** © FineArt/Alamy Stock Photo; **p.96** © David L/peopleimages.com/stock.adobe.com; **p.103** © Renáta Sedmáková/stock.adobe.com; **p.115** © 4kclips/stock.adobe.com; **p.120** © Niday Picture Library/Alamy Stock Photo; **p.121** © Fitz/stock.adobe.com; **p.131** © Janet Knott/The Boston Globe/Getty Images; **p.140** Office for National Statistics; **p.141** © Michele/stock.adobe.com; **p.142** © World Religions Photo Library/Alamy Stock Photo; **p.145** r © JOHNNY ARMSTEAD/Shakeyjon/Alamy Stock Photo, br © RealyEasyStar/Fotografia Felici/Alamy Stock Photo; **p.147** © Colin McPherson/Alamy Stock Photo; **p.152** l © Al Teich/Shutterstock.com, r © David Levenson/Getty Images, bl © Art Collection 2/Alamy Stock Photo; **p.164** l © Bettmann/Getty Images, c © Album/Alamy Stock Photo; **p.166** © Peter Hermes Furian/stock.adobe.com; **p.169** © Leremy/stock.adobe.com; **p.178** t © New Africa/stock.adobe.com, l © Nickolae/stock.adobe.com; **p.179** © Marco Averion/Shutterstock.com; **p.186** © GiorgioMorara/stock.adobe.com; **p.191** © Allan/stock.adobe.com; **p.192** c © Leila Cutler/Alamy Stock Photo, bl © Neuroshock/stock.adobe.com; **p.193** © O1559kip/stock.adobe.com; **p.194** © Renáta Sedmáková/stock.adobe.com; **p.195** © Matthew Mirabelli/Alamy Stock Photo; **p.196** © Massimo Pizzocaro/Alamy Stock Photo; **p.197** © Emily M Wilson/Danita Delimont/Alamy Stock Photo; **p.202** 1910 World Missionary Conference; **p.204** © Sue Edmondson/stock.adobe.com; **p.206** © GFC Collection/Alamy Stock Photo; **p.207** © Album/Alamy Stock Photo; **p.209** © Vatican Media/Catholic Press/Independent Photo Agency Srl/Alamy Stock Photo; **p.213** © Tom Carter/Alamy Stock Photo; **p.214** The AFM on Azusa Street in 1907; **p.216** © Everett Collection, Inc./Alamy Stock Photo; **p.218** © Catch the Fire Toronto, Former Toronto Airport Christian Fellowship logo; **p.221** © John Lawrence/Shutterstock; **p.228** © Douglas Healey/Associated Press/Alamy Stock Photo; **p.229** © Nuvolanevicata/stock.adobe.com; **p.232** © GoodIdeas/stock.adobe.com; **p.233** © Celso Pupo/Shutterstock.com.